"In *What Kind of Christianity*, William Yoo
tory of self-interested and self-justifying whit
wealth, intellect, and even Scripture itself to ᴅᴇʟᴇɴᴅ slavery and define
Black persons as racially inferior. Yoo's focus is on the long run up to
emancipation, and for every brave abolitionist in his story, there are
tens of slavery apologists and enthusiasts. Still, this retelling of history
is liberating in its clear-eyed view of the truth of the past, with out-
standing attention to its subjects' words, motivations, and institutional
contexts placed within a fluid grasp of the best of contemporary scholarship on race and slavery."

—James Hudnut-Beumler, Anne Potter Wilson
Distinguished Professor of American Religious History,
Vanderbilt Divinity School, and Professor of History,
College of Arts and Science, Vanderbilt University

"This is a compelling read. William Yoo deftly and powerfully reveals
the active participation and complicity in Black enslavement and anti-
Black racism of the Presbyterian Church (U.S.A.). Although some
Presbyterians were brave, Yoo also shows how a minority of Black and
white Presbyterians proved incapable of achieving abolition and dis-
lodging anti-Blackness; and ultimately, the PCUSA succumbed to sectionalism on the eve of the Civil War. By debunking persisting myths,
What Kind of Christianity offers the necessary balm for institutional
reconciliation and repair in the present."

—Hilary N. Green, Professor of Africana Studies,
Davidson College

"Yoo's book is a powerful, well-written, and carefully researched narrative of a tragic chapter in the history of American Christianity. Beyond
that, it shows that the events of that time were so deeply connected
with the capitulation of the church to American interests and values
that contradict the very core of Christianity, making it not enough just
to feel shame and remorse for what happened in the past. In the end,
Yoo's book is nothing less than a call for the reformation of all American Christianity."

—Justo L. González, author of *The Story of Christianity*
and *A History of Early Christian Literature*

What Kind of Christianity

What Kind of Christianity

A History of Slavery and Anti-Black Racism
in the Presbyterian Church

WILLIAM YOO

WESTMINSTER
JOHN KNOX PRESS
LOUISVILLE • KENTUCKY

First edition
Published by Westminster John Knox Press
Louisville, Kentucky

22 23 24 25 26 27 28 29 30 31—10 9 8 7 6 5 4 3 2 1

Book design by Drew Stevens
Cover design by Mary Ann Smith
Cover photos: (top) Unseen Histories / Unsplash.com; (bottom) Kristina Blokhin / Alamy Stock Photo

Library of Congress Cataloging-in-Publication Data

Names: Yoo, William, author.
Title: What kind of Christianity : a history of slavery and anti-Black racism in the Presbyterian church / William Yoo.
Description: First edition. | Louisville, Kentucky : Westminster John Knox Press, [2022] | Includes bibliographical references and index. | Summary: "Presbyterian historian William Yoo reviews the PC(USA)'s complicated history with race and racial equality movements in America to convey the difficult story of how Presbyterians are reckoning with their white supremacist past to move toward an anti-racist future"-- Provided by publisher.
Identifiers: LCCN 2022010537 (print) | LCCN 2022010538 (ebook) | ISBN 9780664264673 (paperback) | ISBN 9781646982509 (ebook)
Subjects: LCSH: Presbyterian Church (U.S.A.)--History. | Slavery--Religious aspects--Presbyterians--History. | Racism--Religious aspects--Presbyterians--History.
Classification: LCC BX8969.2 .Y66 2022 (print) | LCC BX8969.2 (ebook) | DDC 285/.137--dc23/eng/20220315
LC record available at https://lccn.loc.gov/2022010537
LC ebook record available at https://lccn.loc.gov/2022010538

Most Westminster John Knox Press books are available at special quantity discounts when purchased in bulk by corporations, organizations, and special-interest groups. For more information, please e-mail SpecialSales@wjkbooks.com.

*For my spouse, Sarah, and our children, Maddy and Caleb,
with unending gratitude and love*

Contents

List of Images

1

"What Kind of Christianity?"

Katie Geneva Cannon, a womanist theologian and the first Black American woman to be ordained as a minister in the United Presbyterian Church in the U.S.A. (in 1974), once asked, "Where was the Church and the Christian believers when Black women and Black men, Black boys and Black girls, were being raped, sexually abused, lynched, assassinated, castrated and physically oppressed? What kind of Christianity allowed white Christians to deny basic human rights and simple dignity to Blacks, these same rights which had been given to others without question?"[1]

In 1836, approximately 250 commissioners from across the northern and southern states gathered in Pittsburgh for the annual meeting of the General Assembly of the Presbyterian Church in the United States of America (PCUSA), the largest Presbyterian denomination in the nation with over 2,800 congregations and nearly 220,000 members. One of the matters these Presbyterians would grapple with was their church's position on the enslavement of more than two million Black persons. It would neither be the first nor the last time Presbyterians at a General Assembly meeting would engage slavery, but this particular occasion presented one of the clearest opportunities for the denomination to answer important questions about where the PCUSA stood on slavery and what kind of Christianity it would profess and practice.

On May 19, the meeting began at 11:00 in the morning with a worship service. William W. Phillips, a white pastor of First Presbyterian

Church in New York City and moderator of the previous year's General Assembly, preached from Romans 1:16–17, a text emphasizing that Christians must not be ashamed of the gospel of Christ and imploring the just to live by faith.[2] Yet some Presbyterians were in fact deeply ashamed of their denomination's reluctance to participate in movements for the emancipation of enslaved Black persons. In 1835, the Chillicothe Presbytery in Ohio sent a letter to other presbyteries beseeching them to adopt its resolutions on slavery. The members of the Chillicothe Presbytery were aware that some of their fellow Presbyterians, even in northern states that had abolished slavery, either demurred on or outright declined to address slavery because they understood it as a political matter outside the spiritual jurisdiction of their church. In response, the Chillicothe Presbytery found Black enslavement to be a "heinous sin and scandal" demanding action from all Presbyterians because their church's "purity and prosperity" was at stake.[3] One of the presbytery's most controversial recommendations was more stringent disciplinary measures against slave-owning members, such as suspension from the Lord's Supper, a significant sacrament within the Presbyterian tradition. Although the General Assembly in 1818 declared "the voluntary enslaving of one part of the human race by another" was a "gross violation" of human rights and "totally irreconcilable with the spirit and principles of the gospel of Christ," the exhortation to "forbear harsh censures" toward enslavers in the same resolution resulted in no concrete actions toward Black liberation and produced the kind of Christianity that the Chillicothe Presbytery could no longer tolerate.[4]

The General Assembly commissioners in Pittsburgh knew that they would have to engage slavery. In the previous year, "a memorial on the subject of slavery, signed by 198 persons" was presented to the General Assembly and referred to a committee of five white ministers, with Samuel Miller, a professor from Princeton Theological Seminary, serving as the chairperson.[5] This committee's report was first presented on May 23 and stated that the PCUSA had no proper means to interfere with Black enslavement because it was "inseparably connected with and regulated by the laws of many of the states in this Union" and a complex subject with a "great diversity of opinion and intensity of feeling" within the denomination. Because any action, either to support emancipation or defend enslavement, would surely distract and divide their membership and fail to assist the plight of enslaved persons—identified in the report with the oddly passive language as "those whose welfare is immediately contemplated in the memorials in question"—the majority of the committee recommended "that it is not expedient for the Assembly to take any further order in relation to this subject." One of the five members dissented and offered a minority report several times lengthier than the 211 words in the brief majority report. James H. Dickey, who had pastored several congregations within the Chillicothe Presbytery, appealed to the history of religious and social reform movements in the Presbyterian tradition, noting how their descendants in England and Scotland were "uncompromising opposers of tyranny," and he observed that the "slavery of the Africans and their descendants" was becoming "more deeply rooted" and "intimately incorporated" in both their country and their church. Dickey's minority report recommended that the PCUSA "take a more firm and decided stand on this subject" in order to embody and enact the kind of Christianity that would "bring about the emancipation of the slaves in these United States and throughout the world."[6] The commissioners agreed to vote on the majority and minority reports one week later, on May 30.

But the vote on May 30 was postponed because another matter, an appeal from Albert Barnes, a white pastor of First Presbyterian Church in Philadelphia, regarding church discipline for what the Synod of Philadelphia deemed as doctrinal error in Barnes's preaching and writing on original sin, had yet to be resolved. Eight days later, on the morning of June 7, the commissioners voted to rescind the synod's decision to suspend Barnes from his pastoral ministry by a vote of 145 in favor, 78 in opposition, and 11 abstentions. Immediately after Barnes had won his appeal, the commissioners returned to the reports on slavery. Both reports were read aloud, but a motion was made to again postpone a vote and consider a new recommendation that had just been presented. Whereas the majority report did not mention biblical support for Black enslavement, this recommendation contained stronger language regarding slavery as sanctioned in both the Old and New Testaments as "an existing relation" and "not condemned by the authority of God."[7] The commissioners agreed to table their decision on slavery until the afternoon, which would grant them more time to contemplate this new recommendation alongside the two reports.

When the commissioners resumed meeting in the afternoon, another motion was introduced, which recommended "this whole subject be indefinitely postponed" for three reasons: (1) an interpretation of the constitution of the PCUSA that prevented the construction of ecclesial laws binding the individual conscience; (2) the "urgency" of other remaining "business"; (3) the "shortness of the time" permitting to "deliberate and decide judiciously on the subject of slavery."[8] Where was the Presbyterian Church when over two million enslaved Black persons were being abused, raped, and oppressed? In 1836, the PCUSA General Assembly was focused on examining the doctrinal intricacies and implications of one of its clergypersons. The commissioners devoted several days and multiple sessions to Barnes's appeal. By comparison, the "subject of slavery" was introduced at one session with a majority report comprising a mere 211 words, postponed in two other sessions, and then indefinitely postponed by a vote of 154 in favor, 87 in opposition, and 4 abstentions.[9] Two weeks after his sermon exhorting fellow Presbyterians to practice their faith as unashamed ambassadors of the gospel, William W. Phillips voted in favor of an indefinite postponement on any discussion and decision regarding slavery.

One of the commissioners from the Chillicothe Presbytery, John Rankin, voted in opposition to the indefinite postponement. Rankin was a white pastor of a Presbyterian congregation in Ripley, Ohio, and two months after his vote he accepted a position to serve as an agent of the American Anti-Slavery Society (AASS), an abolitionist organization founded in 1833 that advocated for the immediate emancipation of enslaved persons. One of its founders, William Lloyd Garrison, observed in 1832 that white Christians in the United States were guilty of racial prejudice against Black persons in their discriminatory attitudes and actions toward free Black Americans and their participation in Black enslavement. Garrison believed white congregations and denominations like the PCUSA required a purification "as by fire" because of their resistance to the cause of immediate abolition and their reluctance to censure and cast out enslavers within their ecclesial bodies. Garrison castigated white Christians, including Presbyterians, for willfully employing the "sanctity of religion" as a mantle to obscure the "horrid system" of slavery.[10]

In 1824 and 1825, Rankin published a series of twenty-one letters in a local newspaper against Black enslavement. Rankin's immediate audience was his brother, Thomas Rankin, who had purchased enslaved persons in Virginia, but Rankin desired to publish his letters in a broader effort to present his arguments against both slavery and anti-Black racism. Rankin asked his brother, and all white Americans, to confront the dehumanizing and oppressive evils of slavery. Rankin's understanding of Christianity entailed a God who created all human beings as equal such that persons of African descent were not naturally or providentially inferior to persons of European descent, as some white

Presbyterians and other Christians believed, and called for an honest accounting of the physical abuse, sexual violence, spiritual oppression, and family separation that enslaved persons experienced. Rankin also addressed how Black enslavement was destroying the moral integrity of white persons for the ways it permitted, if not promoted, the depravity of enslavers in their cruel treatment of enslaved persons. One of the many criticisms Rankin detailed was the sinful reality that "every slave-holder has power to strip his female slaves" and "thousands of them are base enough to put such power into exercise."[11]

A commissioner from the Hopewell Presbytery in Georgia, Eugenius A. Nisbet, also voted in opposition, but for different reasons from Rankin's. Although Nisbet likely agreed with Rankin that the indefinite postponement of any action on slavery lacked clarity and courage, Nisbet desired for their denomination to adopt a stronger position with an unequivocal defense of Black enslavement and a firm rebuke of the abolitionists within and beyond the PCUSA. Two months before the General Assembly meeting, Nisbet's presbytery gathered to prepare for the forthcoming deliberations on slavery in Pittsburgh. The presbytery designated its own committee to construct a report with "instructions to commissioners to General Assembly." The members of the Hopewell Presbytery maintained that "no instance can be produced of an otherwise orderly Christian, being *reproved*, much less *excommunicated* from the Church, for the single act of holding domestic slaves, from the days of Abraham down to the date of the modern Abolitionists." The presbytery also resolved that the General Assembly lacked the ecclesial authority to interfere with the political institution of slavery and that any such interference, including changes to church polity, would be interpreted as "tyrannical and odious." As a commissioner, Nisbet was encouraged to "use all Christian means to prevent the discussion of domestic slavery in the Assembly" and "protest in our name against all acts that involve or approve abolition."[12]

Nisbet was a white ruling elder with significant influence in his state's legislature and jurisprudence as a politician, lawyer, and judge. In 1836, Nisbet's career was on the rise as a state senator who was elected to the U.S. House of Representatives three years later and the Supreme Court of Georgia in 1845. Nisbet's ardent defense of slavery is most evident in his role as the delegate to the Georgia Convention in 1861 who introduced the resolution to immediately secede from the United States in response to the presidential election of Abraham Lincoln. Nisbet was also highly regarded for his Christian faith. One

contemporary biographer described Nisbet in 1854 as deeply committed and connected to the Presbyterian Church such that religion had
given to his life "a beautiful symmetry and form."[13] As a commissioner
to the PCUSA General Assembly in 1836, Nisbet urged his denomination to be unwavering in its disapproval of the AASS and all other
abolitionist movements.

Confronting the Kinds of White Christianity
That Participated in Black Enslavement

In returning to one of Cannon's searing questions asking what kind of
Christianity allowed white Christians to deny basic human rights and
simple dignity to Black persons, the most obvious answer is "the wrong
kind of Christianity." In 1845, Frederick Douglass, a formerly enslaved
Black man who escaped his enslaver in Maryland, differentiated
between genuine Christianity and the "corrupt, slaveholding, women-
whipping, cradle-plundering, partial and hypocritical Christianity of
this land" in his autobiographical narrative. In the years following his
autobiography, Douglass emerged as one of the most prominent abolitionists, intellectuals, and social reformers of the nineteenth century.
Like Douglass, we too are "filled with unutterable loathing" when we
confront the history of slavery, anti-Black racism, and Presbyterianism
in the United States. Douglass's criticism of Christianity in the United
States as comprising "men-stealers for ministers, women-whippers for
missionaries, and cradle-plunderers for church members" is certainly
true of Presbyterianism.[14]

Nearly twenty years after Rankin published his letters on the immoralities of Black enslavement and anti-Black racism, Douglass wrote
that the "horrible inconsistences" among white Christians continued.
Some white congregations included in their membership enslavers who
physically abused and sexually violated enslaved persons. White Christians upholding marriage and family as divine blessings denied millions
of enslaved persons these basic human rights with the absence of laws
protecting enslaved marriages and families from separation in auctions,
sales, and transfers: "The warm defender of the sacredness of the family
relation is the same that scatters whole families—sundering husbands
and wives, parents and children, sisters and brothers,—leaving the hut
vacant, and the hearth desolate."[15] In the same year of Douglass's autobiography, a journal published by the Associate Reformed Synod of

the West lambasted Columbia Theological Seminary, a Presbyterian institution in South Carolina, for benefiting from a public auction of enslaved persons. The journal found it tragic to see human beings— "the following negro slaves, to wit: Charles, Peggy, Antonett, Davy, September, Maria, Jenny, and Isaac"—listed as property akin to animals, lands, and other capital in a local Savannah newspaper. But it was especially infuriated to behold a Presbyterian seminary in the listing as the recipient of the funds derived from the sale. The journal criticized the lack of shame or remorse from the seminary as "scandalous."[16]

While "the wrong kind of Christianity" is the most obvious answer to Cannon's question, this book maintains that a more historically precise and honest answer is "the Presbyterian kind of Christianity." White Presbyterians actively participated in the enslavement of Black persons and the perpetuation of anti-Black racism. Individual members and congregations owned enslaved persons. All these Presbyterians unjustly profited off the uncompensated labor of enslaved persons. Some of these Presbyterians, including ministers, are guilty of committing acts of physical, psychological, sexual, and spiritual abuse against enslaved persons. Elizabeth Keckley, a formerly enslaved Black woman with a successful career as an artisan, including a stint working in the White House as a seamstress for First Lady Mary Todd Lincoln, recounted the cruel oppression she experienced from a family of Presbyterian enslavers. Keckley received her first beating at the age of four, and it was a lashing so severe that she never forgot the incident.

Even more painful was when Keckley's father was separated from her and her mother to migrate westward with another enslaver: "I can remember the scene as if it were but yesterday;—how my father cried out against the cruel separation; his last kiss; his wild straining of my mother to his bosom; the solemn prayer to Heaven; the tears and sobs—the fearful anguish of broken hearts."[17] At the age of fourteen, Keckley was separated from her mother to live with her enslaver's son, a white Presbyterian minister named Robert Burwell, in Virginia. Four years later, in approximately 1835, Keckley moved with Burwell to Hillsborough, North Carolina, and experienced physical abuse at the hands of both Burwell and a white school principal who was a member of Burwell's congregation. At the behest of Burwell's wife, who sought to subdue what she regarded as Keckley's haughty spirit, Burwell and the school principal whipped Keckley on multiple occasions. The school principal also forcibly stripped Keckley naked. Shortly thereafter, Keckley was raped by another white man, Alexander Kirkland, resulting in her pregnancy and the birth of a child. Robert Burwell is listed in the minutes of the PCUSA General Assembly of 1836 as the minister of a Presbyterian congregation of forty-nine members in Hillsborough and a member of the Orange Presbytery.[18]

Estimates on the exact number of Presbyterian enslavers are elusive but not indiscernible. In 1853, James W. C. Pennington, a Black Presbyterian pastor, surmised in his sermon to the Third Presbytery in New York City that white Presbyterians owned approximately 80,000 enslaved persons.[19] Two years earlier, the annual report of the American and Foreign Anti-Slavery Society published an estimate that Presbyterians, with 333,458 members in its two largest denominations, owned 77,000 enslaved persons.[20] In 1852, one white Presbyterian minister, John Robinson, thought it was "probable that about one-third of the ministers, and one-half of the members of the Church" in the southern states owned enslaved persons, and he suggested that "perhaps from one hundred to one hundred and fifty thousand of her members" in total were enslavers from the colonial period to the time of his writing.[21] In 1780, before the abolition of slavery in Pennsylvania, Presbyterians in Philadelphia and Chester County accounted for approximately 30 percent of enslavers who self-identified as belonging to a religious group. In Philadelphia, the three largest groups of enslavers were Episcopalian (132), Presbyterian (81), and Lutheran (28). In Chester County, the three largest groups of enslavers were Presbyterian (43), Episcopalian (41), and Baptist (7). Of 307 South Carolina Lowcountry planters who owned more than 100 enslaved persons on a single plantation in 1860, nearly all self-identified as Christian, with approximately 67 percent as Episcopalian, 14 percent as Presbyterian, 10 percent as Methodist, and 8 percent as Baptist.[22]

In a response to the Chillicothe Presbytery, James Smylie, a white minister in Mississippi belonging to the Amite Presbytery, estimated in 1836 that three-fourths of all Baptists, Episcopalians, Methodists, and Presbyterians in the southern states owned enslaved persons. Smylie argued that if slavery was as heinous a sin as the Chillicothe Presbytery understood it to be, then the overwhelming majority of white Presbyterians from the southern states were in fact "of the devil" and would ultimately call into question "whether God, is, or is not, a true witness."[23] One historian, James O. Farmer, estimates that there were roughly 100,000 Presbyterians across several denominations from the southern states in 1860.[24] In my investigation of the General Assembly minutes in 1860 from the largest Presbyterian denomination, the Presbyterian

Church in the United States of America (Old School), I estimate that approximately 90,000 of the 292,927 members came from the southern states.[25] Therefore, I support Farmer's estimate as plausible. After combining this estimate of 100,000 Presbyterians from the southern states with Robinson's approximation (50 percent) and Smylie's approximation (75 percent) on the number of Presbyterian enslavers, the result is a range of 50,000 to 75,000 Presbyterian enslavers in 1860.

Constructing a More Accurate and Faithful Accounting of the Presbyterian Past

In *Lies My Teacher Told Me: Everything Your American History Textbook Got Wrong*, James W. Loewen finds several problems with how slavery is taught in high schools across the United States. Loewen observes that white Americans remain perpetually startled at slavery. Even many years after high school, white adults are aghast when confronted with the horror and pervasiveness of slavery in the American past. It seems they did not learn, or have quickly forgotten, that George Washington and Thomas Jefferson were among the multitudes of white Americans who owned enslaved Black Americans as their human property. Loewen surmises that the ignorance of white Americans on slavery can be traced back to high school classrooms. History textbooks incorrectly present slavery as an "uncaused" tragedy and "minimize white complicity" in the enslavement of Black Americans. Students are meant to feel sadness for the plight of four million enslaved persons in 1860, but not anger toward the approximately 390,000 enslavers, because these enslavers, and their unjust actions, do not appear in the pages of the textbooks. Loewen explains that the miseducation on slavery is one part of a larger pattern that attributes "anything bad in American history" to anonymous actors.[26]

When moving from high school classrooms to seminary and Sunday school classrooms, the miseducation on slavery is no less a problem. In fact, there are likely more problems in our teaching and learning about slavery in white Christian contexts. One problem is the glaring omission of any education on white Christian involvement in slavery and anti-Black racism. The ignorance of some white congregations regarding basic historical facts about slavery is alarming. A pernicious myth I encounter is the notion that most white Christians in the antebellum period were abolitionists pushing for the immediate emancipation of enslaved persons. This is simply not true. Very few white Christians held this position, and there was little support for immediate emancipation in the Baptist, Episcopalian, Methodist, and Presbyterian denominations. Many white Christians defended slavery so vigorously that some Black and white abolitionists identified white churches as the most impenetrable strongholds against their cause. Benjamin Morgan Palmer, a white pastor and professor at Columbia Seminary, emerged as one of the most vociferous advocates for Black enslavement. After serving as a pastor of Presbyterian congregations in Georgia and South Carolina from 1841 to 1855, Palmer taught at Columbia Seminary for roughly two years and returned to congregational ministry as the pastor of First Presbyterian Church in New Orleans in 1856. Palmer proclaimed in a sermon four years later that slavery was a providential trust that white Christians must preserve and perpetuate because the natural condition of Black Americans was servitude.[27] Palmer was neither reviled nor rebuked for his white supremacist views. Instead, he received acclaim from white southern politicians for his religious defenses of both slavery and secession. Palmer's white ecclesial colleagues also held him in the highest esteem. Several months following his virulently racist sermon, Palmer was elected to serve as the first moderator of the newly formed Presbyterian Church in the Confederate States of America in 1861.

James W. C. Pennington, Theodore S. Wright, and other Black Presbyterians emphasized the eradication of anti-Black racism as an essential component in their abolitionism. But too many white Christian abolitionists in the northern states fell woefully short in their advocacy against anti-Black racism. Archibald Alexander, a white pastor and the first professor of Princeton Seminary, who taught there for nearly four decades in the first half of the nineteenth century, supported the colonization movement to send free Black Americans to Liberia, because he felt the discriminatory contempt white Christians held against Black Americans was too insurmountable to overcome. In 1846, Alexander wrote that anti-Black racism was wrong and unreasonable, but he did not commit to working toward racial equality. Instead of teaching white Christians to repent of their sins of racial prejudice, Alexander preferred that Black Americans, once emancipated, leave the country and find another home on the African continent where their skin color would not be so despised.[28]

This book therefore aims to provide a more accurate and faithful accounting of the causes of Black enslavement. In addition to correcting a legacy of treating the history of slavery and anti-Black racism as an uncaused tragedy, there is the need to address three existing interpretations that misdirect our attention and minimize white Christian complicity. The first incorrect interpretation is that white Americans living in the age of Black enslavement did not know all its evils, immoralities, and injustices. This spurious rationale suggests that if they had known, then surely white Americans, and especially white Christians, would have done more for the sake of abolition. Yet the inverse is true in terms of comprehension regarding slavery. White Americans understood the atrocities within Black enslavement far better and exceedingly more than we do today. As a young child in Charleston, South Carolina, the white abolitionist writer Angelina Emily Grimké was horrified at school one day when she saw the raw and bloody wounds on the back and legs of an enslaved child when he was opening the classroom windows. As the Black child reached for the windows, Grimké witnessed his face grimacing in severe pain. Grimké fainted once the enslaved child limped out of the room. The incident left an indelible mark in Grimké's mind and was the initial catalyst for her lifelong abolitionist activism.[29] In the same city, a white Baptist pastor also encountered the wickedness of Black enslavement up close. While ministering at the First Baptist Church of Charleston, Basil Manly's work involved preaching, teaching, and counseling in a congregation with both white and enslaved Black members. In his private journal, Manly detailed how one member, an enslaved woman, confided to him that "her master *compels* her to live in constant adultery with him" and that she would no longer receive Communion in fear of God's punishment for the sin. Manly advised the enslaved woman to resist her enslaver's sexual advances, but her enslaver continued to rape her for four more years. Manly never confronted the enslaver and instead purchased the enslaved woman himself in what he recounted as one of the most challenging moral dilemmas of his life and ministry.[30]

The second faulty interpretation lies in what I find is the primary focus of the teaching and learning about slavery in seminary and Sunday school classrooms—the centering of biblical interpretation. Rather than fully grappling with the histories and legacies of economic exploitation, sexual violence, and virulent anti-Black racism perpetrated by white Christians, seminary students and church members today are left with a neatly packaged lesson on slavery emphasizing the dangers of deficient biblical interpretation and proof-texting the Scriptures. Such instruction misses a crucial point that Black and white abolitionists themselves made, which is the need to identify and confront the sinfulness of white Christians in their active participation and intentional complicity in Black enslavement. The attention devoted to biblical interpretation also implies that if white Christians then had access to the exegetical tools and hermeneutical sophistication we have now, they would have made different choices and acted more justly. But this fallacious line of thinking is no less dangerous than the perils of scriptural misuse for the ways it deflects blame and distorts truth. In addition to misdirecting our anger from actual individuals and institutions to more anonymous ways of reading the Bible, this interpretation is false. Black and white abolitionists appealed to the Bible to construct scriptural arguments to examine how Black enslavement was a sin against God, expose anti-Black racism as a betrayal of Christ's teachings, and endorse immediate emancipation as the only acceptable pathway for faithful believers. In 1851, John Gregg Fee, a white Presbyterian minister from Kentucky who helped to found Berea College, the first interracial and coeducational college in the state, gravely warned that white Presbyterians deploying scriptural arguments to defend slavery were ruining Christian witness by turning the Bible into a "cunningly devised fable" and a "fiction" in the eyes of those persons with clear moral vision regarding both the evils of slavery and the failings of too many white churches.[31]

Alongside this overemphasis on biblical interpretation one can find the third erroneous interpretation, which is a gross miscalculation on the stakes and consequences of slavery. In subtle yet perverse forms, white Presbyterians have expressed that the most tragic result from the age of Black enslavement is the division of their church. When the PCUSA General Assembly met in 1795, the commissioners responded to the Transylvania Presbytery in Kentucky, in which there were serious disagreements over abolition and slavery, with instructions to heed the call of Jesus to be peacemakers and not allow disputes on slavery to divide the presbytery. It was paramount that the presbytery "keep the unity of the Spirit in the bond of peace" and for its members to engage one another with a spirit of forbearance.[32] In the age of Black enslavement, white Presbyterians, including and sometimes especially Presbyterians from the northern states, grieved that "the subject of slavery," as they so often described the oppression of millions of enslaved persons, was causing divisions within congregations, presbyteries, and the General Assembly. They wept not for the abuse that enslaved women like Elizabeth Keckley endured. Rather, they shed tears of anguish over their worries about ecclesial schism. Presbyterians were able to ward off regional divisions longer than Methodists and Baptists, who split into northern and southern denominations in 1844 and 1845, respectively. The second largest Presbyterian denomination, the Presbyterian Church in the United States of America (New School), ruptured in 1857. The largest denomination, the Presbyterian Church in the United States of America (Old School), remained united until May 1861, one month after Confederate soldiers fired the first shots of the Civil War at Fort Sumter.

Presbyterians remained in regional denominations until 1983. Yet this malicious misdirection on the tragedy of slavery has persisted such that the greatest, or at least most discussed, sorrow when looking back at the age of Black enslavement entails the broken bonds of fellowship and denominational divisions. In Presbyterian congregations, conversations, and history books, one encounters tremendous sadness over ecclesial divisions that lasted over one hundred years. Yet one struggles to find the requisite anger over the pain and torture that millions of enslaved persons suffered from white Presbyterian enslavers, supporters of Black enslavement, and guilty bystanders who chose to be complicit through inaction and indecision. In one Presbyterian history book, the "sad consequences" of the schisms over abolition and slavery do not center on enslaved persons or free Black Presbyterians. Instead, the historian writes wistfully of the painful separations that prominent white Presbyterian clergy experienced with melancholy vignettes of John Leighton Wilson, a pastor and missionary from South Carolina serving as a secretary of the Board of Foreign Missions in a New York City denominational office, bidding farewell to his ministerial colleagues to return to his southern home, and William Anderson Scott, a pastor from Tennessee ministering at Calvary Presbyterian Church in San Francisco, receiving scorn and ultimately a dismissal from his congregation after publicly praying for two presidents, Abraham Lincoln of the United States of America and Jefferson Davis of the Confederate States of America.[33]

Another Presbyterian history book concludes that the regional separations of Presbyterians in 1857 and 1861 were "unfortunate and a detriment to each church's witness" and notes how some Presbyterians today "lament any barrier that prevents Christ's followers from being one, especially when they bear the same denominational name" in a section entitled, "The Withering of Presbyterianism."[34] I find it deeply troubling that the withering of Presbyterianism is attributed to these

ecclesial schisms and not the active participation of white Presbyterians
in slavery. It is also infuriating that Black enslavement is presented as
a barrier to church unity rather than a tragedy. When historical interpretations accentuate or isolate the regional ruptures within Presbyterianism, what goes missing is a crucial, if not central, point: the abject
moral failings of white Presbyterians living in the age of Black enslavement. And the terrible result is that some white Presbyterians today feel
more remorse for church disunity than the oppressive abuse and rep-
rehensible violence that their Presbyterian predecessors inflicted upon
enslaved persons.

In addition to an overemphasis on the ecclesial schisms within Presbyterianism, there exists an inaccurate legacy that presents Presbyterian
history in the age of Black enslavement as a church divided and gives
the impression that every white Presbyterian from the northern states
was an abolitionist. Yet the largest Presbyterian denomination, the
PCUSA (Old School), with three-fourths of its membership from the
northern states, remained steadfast in its commitment to fully include
enslavers and supporters of slavery as fellow members. Year after year,
General Assembly commissioners elected and appointed white members from the southern states to preach, participate on committees, and
serve as moderators and hold other important denominational positions. In the years following the divisions of the largest Methodist and
Baptist denominations, white Presbyterians intentionally and strategi-
cally elected leaders from the southern states. In 1847, James Henley
Thornwell, a white slave-owning theologian and one of the most pro-
lific defenders of slavery, was elected moderator. Six years later, when
the General Assembly gathered in Philadelphia, Benjamin Morgan
Palmer, another unabashed and well-known proponent of slavery, was
elected as the temporary clerk. The election in 1853 of John C. Young,
a white pastor from Kentucky advocating for the gradual emancipation
of enslaved persons, as moderator with 126 of 251 votes (50.2 percent)
and then of Palmer as temporary clerk, with 130 of 222 votes (58.6
percent), reflect the denomination's commitment to the continuation
of both ecclesial unity and Black enslavement.[35] After Young's election,
which eased the consciences of some commissioners, a greater majority
quickly voted for Palmer to make clear the denomination maintained
its position that slave ownership was not subject to any church discipline. The elections and appointments of Thornwell, Palmer, and other
enslavers from the southern states were only made possible because of
significant support from white members in the northern states.

The Fallacy of Presbyterianism as a Divided
Church over Abolition and Slavery

It is therefore inaccurate to summarize Presbyterianism in the age of Black enslavement as a "divided church, divided nation," as one historian does in a recent history of Presbyterians and American culture.[36] Were white Presbyterians really divided on abolition and slavery? Some individuals were internally conflicted. John C. Young detested slavery, but he also owned enslaved persons. Young eventually emancipated some of his enslaved persons, but he supported a gradual approach to ending slavery that drew the ire of Black and white abolitionists as a position lacking moral clarity and Christian conviction. I believe it is incorrect to present the larger "Presbyterian Church"—by which I mean the congregations, presbyteries, synods, General Assemblies, colleges, seminaries, and other institutions of the various denominations that existed in the North American colonies and antebellum United States—as divided such that we imagine in our minds today a grand drama with righteous abolitionists successfully persuading enslavers and enablers of slavery to join their cause in hallowed Presbyterian church buildings across the nation. A more accurate representation is what Angelina Emily Grimké experienced in her short time as a Presbyterian in Charleston. After leaving her family's Episcopal church in protest of its religious teachings, Grimké joined a local Presbyterian congregation. She initially relished the church's ministry, experiencing growth in her faith and spirituality, but with this growth came stronger convictions that slavery was irreconcilable with Christianity. Grimké shared these concerns first with the pastor, who told her that he agreed with her but that the most faithful response was to "pray and wait." Dissatisfied with the pastor's counsel, Grimké approached the church's session. These ruling elders, all of whom were enslavers, noted Grimké's young age and also encouraged her to wait. But the session also disagreed with Grimké and told her that she would learn to see the wisdom of Black enslavement as she matured out of her childish naiveté into adulthood. Grimké soon thereafter decided to leave the Presbyterian congregation. The pastor and other church members tried to convince Grimké to remain, in no small part because her family was wealthy and among the elite in Charleston, but Grimké simply refused to remain in a proslavery church.[37]

John Rankin also concluded that the mainstream Presbyterian denominations were untrustworthy because of their proslavery positions and practices. In the fall of 1836, Rankin wrote a letter to fellow Presbyterians in a local Cincinnati newspaper imploring them to remain united. Although the General Assembly four months prior voted to indefinitely postpone discussion of slavery, an action that Rankin himself voted against, Rankin urged Presbyterians to avoid schism because ecclesial disunity was "sinful" and in opposition to the "example and doctrines of Christ and the apostles." He feared a division of the Presbyterian Church would result in "great evil" and "self-destruction."[38] Over the next eleven years, Rankin realized that there were greater evils than church disunity. Rankin could no longer tolerate how white Presbyterians in the two largest denominations, the PCUSA (Old School) and PCUSA (New School), continued to falter on Black liberation, and he gathered some of his colleagues in Ohio to form a new denomination, the Free Presbyterian Church, in 1847. At the inaugural meeting in Cincinnati, Rankin and the other members of this fledgling denomination included in their organizing documents—alongside the Westminster Confession of Faith (WCF) and the same form of government utilized in the PCUSA (New School)—a *Declaration of Human Rights*, which unequivocally stated that Black enslavement was "destructive to all the ends for which man was created" and "one of the greatest evils that can be inflicted upon human nature." The *Declaration* also refused church membership to any "person holding slaves" or "advocating the rightfulness of slaveholding" and denied fellowship with any Christian groups comprising enslavers or supporters of slavery.[39] Rankin and his wife, Jean Lowry Rankin, included participation in the Underground Railroad as a component of their ministry. Together they assisted the journeys of approximately 2,000 formerly enslaved persons to freedom, with the deployment of their house as one of the covert stations on a route of the Underground Railroad.

The examples of Jean Lowry Rankin and John Rankin are sometimes employed to advance the notion that Presbyterianism in the age of Black enslavement is best understood as divided between abolitionists on one side and enslavers on the other side. Although the abolitionist side, with faithful Presbyterians like John Gregg Fee and James W. C. Pennington, is certainly worthy of our attention today, I believe the heavy imbalance in how we remember the past leaves us with the wrong impression. These Black and white Presbyterian abolitionists were deeply unpopular and received scant support in the larger church. They were not elected to positions of ecclesial authority, and their voices carried little weight among other white Presbyterians.

If we highlight the Free Presbyterian Church as a shining beacon of the best of the Presbyterian tradition, we should also include how the denomination struggled to gain members, acquire resources, and exert influence. Six years after its founding, the Free Presbyterian Church in 1853 had approximately 1,000 members, in comparison to over 300,000 members across the two largest Presbyterian denominations.[40] Rankin's denomination never grew beyond 2,000 members and consisted of mostly small congregations that were stretched financially in trying, and often failing, to meet the costs of building maintenance, pastoral compensation, and abolitionist witness in their church budgets. Despite, or more likely because of, their unwavering commitments to eradicate Black enslavement and anti-Black racism, the Free Presbyterian Church did not make inroads in changing the trajectory of the wider Presbyterian tradition.

The minuscule influence of the Free Presbyterian Church therefore more clearly illustrates the worst, rather than the best, of the Presbyterian tradition. There were Presbyterian abolitionists, but what does it mean that the most outspoken activists for abolition and racial justice either renounced their connections to Presbyterianism or were marginalized within Presbyterianism? In addition to John Rankin, four other Presbyterian ministers are among the twenty-five inductees in the National Abolition Hall of Fame and Museum: John Gregg Fee, Beriah Green, Elijah Lovejoy, and James W. C. Pennington. Like Rankin, Fee and Green left the mainstream Presbyterian denominations on moral and religious grounds. In 1837, Lovejoy was killed in a gruesome and violent act while defending the printing press he used to publish his abolitionist newspaper from a rabid white proslavery mob in Alton, Illinois. Pennington escaped his enslaver in Maryland and became the first Black student at Yale Divinity School. Pennington attended lectures there for two years, but he was not permitted to officially enroll as a student or speak in class. He later served as the pastor of the largest Black Presbyterian congregation in New York City, Shiloh Presbyterian Church, and received an honorary doctorate from the University of Heidelberg in Germany. But Pennington, like the other esteemed abolitionist inductees, was more influential outside of Presbyterianism. During his years as a Presbyterian minister, Pennington grew frustrated with his denomination, the PCUSA (New School), for its reluctance to act more decisively to end slavery, and he experienced racial prejudice from white members of his presbytery. Angelina Emily Grimké is also in the National Abolition Hall of Fame and Museum, in part because she protested as a young woman against a white Presbyterian pastor's counsel to "pray and wait" for a solution to slavery with the words, "No, we must pray and work!"[41]

Yet most white Presbyterians living in the age of Black enslavement regarded abolitionists and racial justice activists like Angelina Emily Grimké, James W. C. Pennington, Jean Lowry Rankin, and John Rankin as troublesome nuisances and unrealistic radicals. Pennington appealed to white members in his presbytery to confront the enslavers and defenders of slavery in their denomination. He acknowledged that "some leading Presbyterian theologians among us have, in their zeal, undertaken to justify slavery from the Bible," but Pennington identified an accompanying problem—the silence and complicity of other white Presbyterians that allowed this immoral and racist proslavery theology to define their faith and witness. In this sermon from 1853, Pennington advanced a modest proposal for "a fair and open discussion" with the hope that some would speak out against existing proslavery positions and practices as contrary to what it meant to be Presbyterian.[42] But there was little discussion and no division among the faculty and boards of seminaries such as Princeton and Columbia and among the clergy and ruling elders of the largest and wealthiest congregations in the northern and southern states. Instead, there was a shared commitment to perpetuate Black enslavement.

The refusal among most white Presbyterians to heed Pennington's call was intentional. At one level, white Presbyterians were like other white Americans living in the age of Black enslavement. Less than 2 percent of the 27 million white Americans in 1860 were enslavers, but the sinful institution of slavery was so ingrained in the civic, economic, religious, and social systems of the United States that many non-enslaving white Americans did not want to disrupt the foundational order of their lives. In 1846, Albert Barnes lamented that slavery was a central feature of life across the United States. All the "great questions of industry, literature, agriculture, commerce, and morals" involved slavery such that there was not a town, school, or church throughout the northern and southern states untouched by this unjust institution.[43] But at another level, these white Presbyterians also self-identified as Christians. They professed to have a higher calling as a people redeemed by the grace of God through the death and resurrection of Jesus Christ to act justly so that all may flourish. At their first meeting as the General Assembly of the PCUSA in 1789, the commissioners published a letter to George Washington. One month after Washington took his oath of office as the new nation's first president, Presbyterians committed to work toward a "pure and virtuous patriotism" as citizens endeavoring to "add the wholesome instructions of religion" in service to God and country.[44] Yet white Presbyterians chose to practice the kind of Christianity that upheld and propagated, rather than dismantled and opposed, Black enslavement.

My decision to present white Presbyterians as choosing to perpetuate slavery and anti-Black racism is meant to serve as an important corrective to the notion that Presbyterians could not solve the dilemmas of Black enslavement. One of the most problematic legacies that has been passed down for generations is a myth about the relationship between Black enslavement and Presbyterianism. We are led to believe that the evils of slavery ensnared Presbyterianism and left white Presbyterians powerless and rudderless. The truth is that white Presbyterians consistently leveraged their power to make a myriad of calculated decisions and deliberate actions that harmed Black Americans. The idea that white Presbyterians were passive agents who found themselves stuck in an irrepressible conflict over abolition and slavery is not only false, but this fallacy also generates feelings of undeserved sympathy for the white Presbyterians who oppressed and supported the oppression of millions of enslaved persons. Even John Robinson, in his lengthy defense of the PCUSA (Old School) in 1852 against abolitionist criticisms of the denomination as immoral and anti-Christian, recognized that no one could "rationally claim" that white Presbyterians were blameless: "It is freely admitted, nay, held, that there is guilt, great guilt, on the part of members of the Presbyterian Church, growing out of slave-holding."[45] But Robinson stopped short of full confession and attributed "the guilt of slavery" to civil realities more than ecclesial relations. Whereas Barnes argued that the centrality of slavery to American life was grounds for immediate abolition, Robinson cautioned that Black enslavement was "so completely woven into the structure of society" that it could not be eradicated at once, or even in a generation.[46]

Robinson described Presbyterians as "moderate" and "wise" in their decisions to postpone open discussion of slavery and refuse motions to censure and excommunicate slave-owning members. Although Robinson personally abhorred slavery, he believed the prayers of white Presbyterians on behalf of enslaved persons comprised the most faithful pathway.[47] Abolitionists within and outside Presbyterianism expressed outrage in tearing apart the implications and ramifications of Robinson's proposal. They questioned the compositions of these prayers and surmised that some intercessions were for the kinder treatment of enslaved persons rather than their emancipation and that other petitions beseeched the Almighty God for a solution to Black enslavement that neither damaged economic profits nor disrupted existing social mores segregating the superior white race from the inferior Black race. In 1831, William Lloyd Garrison, in the inaugural issue of *The Liberator*, explained that the aim of his abolitionist newspaper was to "strenuously contend for the immediate enfranchisement of our slave population," adding that he would not apologize for his use of abrasive and accusatory language, which some white Christians, including Presbyterians like Robinson, found inflammatory and un-Christlike. Garrison deemed it necessary to "be as harsh as truth" and lambasted the kind of Christianity that appealed to gradual abolition, African colonization, and other moderate compromises: "Tell a man whose house is on fire, to give a moderate alarm; tell him to moderately rescue his wife from the hand of the ravisher; tell the mother to gradually extricate her babe from the fire into which it has fallen;—but urge me not to use moderation in a cause like the present."[48] But Robinson and other white Presbyterians would not relent in prioritizing ecclesial unity over Black liberation. However, Garrison's vivid metaphors were not completely irrelevant to them. In their hearts and minds, they connected the images of a burning house and an imperiled wife to the crisis of church disunity instead of the calamity of Black enslavement.

"My Master Taught Theology to Him": Presbyterian History as a Tragedy, an Indictment, and a Reckoning

For over thirty years *The Liberator* roused and provoked white Christians to action for the righteous cause of Black liberation. On several occasions, the weekly newspaper published and reprinted articles about Presbyterians. In 1838, one issue reprinted two articles. One article criticized the Charleston Union Presbytery for advancing a motion seeking a repeal of a denominational declaration that identified slavery as a "gross violation" of human rights and "totally irreconcilable" with Christianity. The presbytery in South Carolina viewed the earlier resolution from the General Assembly in 1818 as hostile and "injurious to the Christian character" of all white Presbyterians in the southern states. This article rebuked the presbytery for its assault on both Christian abolitionists and the Christian God, emphasizing the blasphemy entailed when falsely claiming divine approval for its enslaving sins. Another article on the same page reprinted a statement from Samuel Eli Cornish—a Black pastor who organized the first Black Presbyterian congregation in New York City—critical of white Christians for their rampant discrimination against the free Black population in the city.[49] In the fall of 1861, several months into the carnage of the Civil War, the newspaper published its own article denouncing Presbyterianism as the most proslavery of all the religious groups: "In no church have the ministers and church-members been more determined in the maintenance of slavery; in none have greater hardness of heart and blindness of mind been manifested, both in the systematic allowance of the worst features of the system, and in the manufacture of arguments by which to maintain its necessity and propriety." The author added that Presbyterians had significant influence as the third largest religious group in the nation in terms of "relative numbers and weight of membership," behind Methodists and Baptists, and therefore bore their share of responsibility for the immense evils of Black enslavement.[50]

This book supports *The Liberator*'s assessment that Presbyterians in the United States were among the most proslavery of all religious groups and consequently among the most responsible for centuries of oppression against millions of Black Americans. This history is therefore also a tragedy, an indictment, and a reckoning. Joseph S. Moore, a historian of transatlantic Presbyterianism and slavery, concludes that "Presbyterians changed the actual situation of slavery very little" but suggests that slavery did in fact change Presbyterianism. Moore proposes that the disagreements over abolition and slavery created another Presbyterian "orthodoxy" alongside other doctrinal controversies, such as the debate over subscription to the WCF.[51] Just as where one stood on the doctrine of adopting every article in the WCF determined the kind of Presbyterianism one inhabited, so too did a Presbyterian's position on abolition and slavery. But the notion of treating abolition and slavery as two different orthodoxies, akin to holding a strict or a loose view of subscription to the WCF, does not adequately capture the gravity and magnitude of white Presbyterian participation in Black enslavement. The historical reality that some Presbyterians were ardently proslavery ought not be described in dispassionate language or couched in arcane theological terms as a debate between two contrasting ways to interpret the Bible. Instead, we must confront the real consequences of what *The Liberator* rightly ascertained was the "active complicity" of white Presbyterians in perpetuating slavery.[52]

The first part of the book therefore focuses on the tragedy of Black enslavement from the colonial period to the middle of the nineteenth century. Some history books emphasize how white Presbyterians were defending a literalist approach to scriptural interpretation and practicing an evangelistic form of Christianity that prioritized spiritual salvation over legal emancipation. At first glance, these two emphases are not at all surprising, since they are the very points white Presbyterian enslavers and supporters of slavery underscored themselves. But we must look deeper to comprehend what everyone living in the age of Black enslavement knew more closely and intimately than we will ever know. All white Presbyterians understood that slavery featured the painful separation of enslaved Black families, the rape and sexual assault of enslaved Black women, the physical torture of enslaved Black children, and the withholding of free access to literacy and Christian instruction. Theodore S. Wright, the first Black graduate of Princeton Seminary and a Presbyterian pastor in New York City, charged that these cruel, dehumanizing, and racist elements of slavery wounded both Black bodies and souls in a speech before the New York State Anti-Slavery Society in 1837. In his address before the U.S. Congress in 1865, Henry Highland Garnet, the pastor of Fifteenth Street Presbyterian Church in Washington, D.C., and the first Black American to speak in the Capitol Building, defined slavery as "snatching man from the high place to which he was lifted by the hand of God, and dragging him down to the level of the brute creation," with the deleterious effect of obliterating the *imago Dei* within the enslaved person.[53]

The second part of the book follows as an indictment that delineates the various offenses of white Presbyterians in relation to Black enslavement and anti-Black racism. Several historians have identified the first half of the nineteenth century as a period of tremendous flourishing for Presbyterians in the United States. Presbyterians increased their membership, founded new congregations, established seminaries, accumulated wealth, and exerted influence in the halls of power across rural towns and urban cities throughout the nation. For example, the PCUSA comprised 17,871 members in 1807. Seven years later, membership had more than doubled to 37,767 members. By 1817, membership had almost tripled in one decade to 47,568 members. In 1836, the PCUSA grew to 219,126 members—more than twelve times the membership from 1807.[54] But what some historians have missed or minimized in their interpretations is that this period of growth, which one history book characterizes as "the flowering of American

Presbyterianism," concurred with the rise of Black enslavement.[55] The enslaved population grew from approximately 700,000 persons in 1790 to over 3,200,000 persons in 1850. Though some white Presbyterians professed a strict division between ecclesial and civil affairs, the actual boundaries between Christianity and politics were porous and ambiguous. Proslavery Presbyterians maintained that slavery was a political institution outside the realm of ecclesial authority, but they also charged that it was right for churches to protest any political action endeavoring to limit Black enslavement. In his racist sermon from 1860 defending the enslavement of Black Americans as a "divine trust" that God did not desire to be broken, Palmer explicitly weighed in on the politics of the day from his pulpit.[56]

The third part of the book then constitutes a reckoning that investigates the ramifications of these foundational sins. An accounting of how white Presbyterians participated in Black enslavement and perpetuated anti-Black racism is one part of a larger history. Another part of this history comprises how proslavery Presbyterians changed, influenced, and transformed Presbyterianism in the United States during and after the age of Black enslavement. Although slavery is no longer with us— the arrival of federal soldiers in Galveston, Texas, on June 19, 1865, finally ending Black enslavement—some of the practices and theologies defending slavery remain in Presbyterianism today. Moreover, the growth of Presbyterianism in the first half of the nineteenth century did not merely manifest alongside the expansion of Black enslavement as two separate and unrelated movements. William Wells Brown, a formerly enslaved Black man and one of the most accomplished authors in the nineteenth century, recalled his encounters with the white pastor of his enslaver's Presbyterian congregation. Brown found that the "whole aim" of the pastor's ministry was to "please the slaveholders" in the church: "When they wanted singing, he sung; when they wanted praying, he prayed; when they wanted a story told, he told a story." Brown concluded this pastor did not teach any Christian theology to the slave-owning church members, but instead "my master taught theology to him."[57] Presbyterianism may not have changed the actual situation of American slavery, but American slavery certainly corrupted Presbyterianism. It is not difficult to make this determination about the tarnishing of Presbyterianism. Rather, the only difficulty lies in discerning the depths of the corrosion.

In Google's early years as a start-up company, some of its engineers adopted a mantra that became their guiding ethic: "Don't be evil."

After an initial meeting with the *Washington Post*, these engineers were concerned that a partnership with the newspaper might betray their commitment to producing search results without external interference or economic influence. One engineer therefore wrote on a whiteboard, "Don't be evil," to frame their pursuit of revenue with a moral reminder about their values. These three words became the first line in the company's code of conduct, but over time Google wrestled with how to abide by this principle as it grew into a technological behemoth and one of the most powerful entities in the world.[58] For Christians, the standard of "Don't be evil" is likely too low a bar for individuals and ministries professing the grace of Jesus Christ, the love of God, and the communion of the Holy Spirit. And yet Presbyterianism in the age of Black enslavement failed to meet this bar. In 1851, John Gregg Fee warned white Presbyterians that their ongoing participation in slavery would result in the demise and ruin of Presbyterianism: "A church that can sanction and fellowship one of the greatest outrages upon humanity, they feel to be worse than no church, a delusion, a den of wolves, where the lambs of the flock are in danger of being devoured."[59] Unfortunately, too few white Presbyterians then shared Fee's outrage and heeded his counsel. And all Presbyterians today continue to live with the consequences.

PART I

The Tragedy

2

"Can Christian Americans Deny These Barbarous Cruelties?"

In 1829, David Walker, a free Black man born to an enslaved Black father and a free Black mother in Wilmington, North Carolina, published his first book in Boston. It contained a summary of his abolitionist activism from previous speeches and newspaper articles, along with new arguments about Black enslavement and white Christianity. The title of the book emphasized that it was an "appeal" to "the coloured citizens of the world," especially Black persons, free and enslaved, in the United States. Walker's book encouraged Black Americans to see themselves as God's beloved creation with divine appointments to be free, equal, virtuous, and victorious participants in a nation that belonged to them no less than to white persons. Although Black Americans were "the most degraded, wretched, and abject set of beings that ever lived since the world began," their oppression was not of their own making. Rather, the perpetrators responsible for their enslavement and the racial discrimination holding them down were "the white Christians of America." Walker referred to these white Christians by their more proper identification as "pretenders to Christianity" for their sinful acts of abuse and torture, which included restrictions against education and Christian worship, brandings with hot irons, beatings, whippings, mutilations, and murders within a wicked system in which all enslaved persons were economically exploited and stripped, both literally and psychologically, of their dignity. The "devouring hands of the white Christians" were also responsible for the horrors of the transatlantic slave trade. In the face of these unjust realities and the divine wrath surely awaiting enslavers and enablers of Black enslavement, Walker asked, "Can Christian Americans deny these barbarous cruelties?"[1]

White Presbyterians did not deny the barbarous cruelties of Black enslavement, but they disagreed on the ubiquity of such abuses and the solution to the human rights violations connected to slavery. In 1857, the white Presbyterian pastor George D. Armstrong differentiated between incidental and essential sins in his defense of Black enslavement. Armstrong was a native of New Jersey serving as a pastor of a Presbyterian congregation in Norfolk, Virginia, when he published his "Christian doctrine of slavery." In his refutation of abolitionists, especially the scriptural arguments of Albert Barnes, Armstrong charged that they conflated the unjust features of slavery with the institution of slavery itself. Armstrong acknowledged some of the abuses, though far more gently and obliquely than abolitionists like Walker did, but he interpreted these cruelties as incidental and infrequent sins that did not result in negative judgment of the essential nature of slavery. In the same ways that incidents of spousal and parental abuse did not disprove the divine purposes of marriage and family as blessed institutions, Armstrong argued that he and his fellow white Presbyterians prohibited enslavers from violating their enslaved persons, just as they admonished malicious husbands and vicious parents in their congregations.[2] A wicked husband did not mean marriage was an evil institution. And an abusive enslaver was not grounds to dismantle slavery.

Other Black and white Presbyterians differed with Armstrong's assessment. In 1792, David Rice, a white Presbyterian pastor in Kentucky, argued that the unjust abuses within Black enslavement were not simply corrupt features of an inherently good system in need of small reforms, but rather that these abuses were central to slavery and made it utterly "inconsistent with justice and good policy." Rice defined an enslaved person in the United States as "a human creature made by law the property of another human creature" deprived of "every privilege of humanity" such that the separation of families, the rape of enslaved women, and other widespread cruelties were what constituted the essential nature of slavery in the United States.[3] James W. C. Pennington, in his autobiography recounting his oppression in enslavement, observed that the sin of slavery was found in its essence and not its incidents. He endeavored to correct "professing Christians," especially white clergypersons like Armstrong, who proclaimed falsities and perversions regarding the example of "Christian masters" as righteous enslavers. The physical torture, starvation, and nakedness of enslaved persons were three of the many inescapable human rights violations and "inevitable consequences" of slavery.[4]

There was less disagreement among white Presbyterians about the immoralities of the transatlantic slave trade. Even some proslavery Presbyterians agreed with Rice's understanding of the slave trade as an abhorrent tragedy that could not be considered "without a bleeding heart and weeping eyes."[5] In 1815, the PCUSA General Assembly commissioners affirmed an earlier resolution from twenty years prior that Black enslavement was a complicated matter requiring a charitable spirit of peace because of the great diversity of viewpoints within their denomination, but they added to their resolution a note stating that the "buying and selling of slaves by way of traffic" was "inconsistent with the spirit of the gospel."[6] Howell Cobb belonged to a prominent Georgia family with deep Presbyterian roots and was a powerful politician who served as Speaker of the U.S. House of Representatives from 1849 to 1851 and the state's governor from 1851 to 1853. In his scriptural defense of Black enslavement in 1856, Cobb conceded that the transatlantic slave trade was one of the greatest tragedies in world history and constituted "an unmitigated horror" deserving opprobrium and severe censure. But Cobb only held the European nations responsible for the transportation of enslaved Africans to North America, South America, and the Caribbean. Cobb's ire was especially directed toward England for introducing Black enslavement to the North American colonies. Despite the cruel origins of Black enslavement in the United States, Cobb argued that the practices of white American Christian enslavers had demonstrated how slavery was the "Providentially-arranged means" for enslaved persons of African descent to receive Christian instruction and gain access to a more civilized culture compared to the degradations of African society. In Cobb's telling, white American Christians, upon winning their freedom from the tyranny of British colonial rule, began the earnest work of reforming and perfecting an institution they had inherited with evil defects due to "England principally" as well as France, Portugal, Spain, and the Netherlands.[7]

A "Virgin Soil Pandemic" and the Emergence
of the Transatlantic Slave Trade

In 1441, Portuguese slave traders captured and transported the first sub-Saharan African person to Europe. The woman was seized in Senegambia.[8] Although little else is known of this woman, accounts of other kidnapping raids and slave auctions illustrate the barbarous cruelties at the core of Black enslavement. Gomes Eanes de Zurara, a fifteenth-century writer working in the Portuguese royal court as head archivist and chronicler, detailed the origin and expansion of Portuguese involvement in the transatlantic slave trade. In one account, Zurara described a multiday raid in which Portuguese slave traders journeying along the coast of Senegambia attacked a village. On the first day, the traders departed their ship to assail some of the men, killing one whom they believed was a respected leader in the village. The next day, the traders returned and seized some of the women fishing in a creek. One woman was with her young son and she bravely fought off the assailants. Zurara recounted how the Portuguese traders marveled at the woman's strength, as she skillfully resisted three of them at once. Failing to subdue the woman, the traders took her son to their boat and "love of the child compelled the mother to follow" without any more resistance.[9] In another account, Zurara narrated the first slave auction in Lagos from 1444 with a perverse blending of national pride and human empathy. Zurara celebrated the moment as signifying the growing power of Portuguese colonialism, but the royal chronicler conceded the pangs of a guilty conscience and "piteous feeling" when considering that the enslaved Africans, some weeping loudly and others holding defiant gazes, were also "the sons of Adam" created in the image of God. Though the Portuguese could not understand what the enslaved Africans were saying, it became clear that most agonizing of all was the painful division of families during the sales as parents were separated from their children and spouses from one another.[10]

In the fifteenth century, the Portuguese expanded their enslaving efforts in the regions of Mauritania, Senegambia, and the Gold Coast. In 1482, they erected an enormous fortress, Castelo de São Jorge da Mina, in their slave trading post in Elmina, Ghana. Portuguese slave trading grew from approximately 800 enslaved Africans annually in the 1450s and 1460s to over 2,000 enslaved Africans annually in the 1480s and 1490s and surpassed over 3,000 enslaved Africans annually by the 1510s.[11] Other European nations also began to participate in the transatlantic slave trade. Bartolomé de las Casas, a Catholic priest from Spain and missionary belonging to the Dominican Order, recommended the use of enslaved African laborers in the Americas. He also criticized Spanish colonial oppression of Indigenous persons in his widely reprinted book, *A Short Account of the Destruction of the Indies*, which was written in 1542 and first published ten years later. In 1562, John Hawkins augmented British participation in the slave trade, with Hawkins's first transport culminating in the violent seizing and selling of approximately 300 captives from Sierra Leone to planters in the Dominican Republic in 1563. Though las Casas came to regret his endorsement of African enslavement in the Americas, the transatlantic slave trade continued to grow long after his death in 1566. Between the years of 1514 and 1866, there were 10,642,683 enslaved Africans transported on 34,443 voyages.[12]

The increasing demand for enslaved Africans was closely tied to labor shortages in the Americas. Las Casas castigated Spanish colonists for their mistreatment of the Indigenous persons they had enslaved with coercive agricultural labor practices that he described as the most inhumane "torments neither seen nor heard of before."[13] In addition to the oppressive conditions of enslavement, the Indigenous populations in the Americas also suffered from imported diseases—including influenza, malaria, smallpox, and yellow fever—at a tragic and heavy rate of mortality that is referred to as a "virgin soil pandemic" because of the disastrous ways that diseases from abroad annihilated Indigenous populations in the previously isolated Western Hemisphere. One historian, David Brion Davis, argues that this systematic extermination of Indigenous persons—with some estimates of a 90 percent decrease of the Indigenous population in central Mexico over seventy-five years and even greater rates of Indigenous mortality in the Caribbean—was the "greatest known population loss in human history."[14] In 1542, las Casas surmised that the Indigenous population of Hispaniola (present-day Haiti and the Dominican Republic), which included the Taínos, had declined from approximately three million persons to "scarce three hundred persons," a staggering loss of over 99.9 percent of the population.[15] In response to the "virgin soil pandemic," as well as their abusive practices, European enslavers looked to Africa for replacement workers.

As more enslaved Africans were transported to the Americas, European colonists were pleased with the results. Enslaved Africans, like Europeans, proved less susceptible than Indigenous communities to the imported pathogens, and enslaved Africans possessed prodigious knowledge and skill for large-scale agriculture. Some enslaved Africans also made iron and steel tools more adroitly than either Indigenous or European persons in the Americas. European enslavers therefore came to a consensus that "the labor of one black was worth that of several Indians."[16] In 1785, Thomas Clarkson, a son of an Anglican clergyman in England, won an essay contest at Cambridge University with the prompt "Is it right to make slaves of others against their will?" Clarkson was a bright student, but he had given little thought to the international slave trade and Black enslavement. After conducting his research, he concluded it was wrong to enslave, buy, sell, and transport Africans. Clarkson made use of available resources, giving special credit to Anthony Benezet, a French Quaker abolitionist in Philadelphia, for his historical account of the slave trade in 1771, to meticulously detail the horrors of the slave trade and rebut European arguments defending it. In the essay, which Clarkson published in 1786, he refuted the false notion that European slave traders were primarily appeasing African, not European, desires when transporting an overabundance of African prisoners of war to the Americas. Rather, the demand for more laborers in the Americas drove European slave traders to "entice the Africans to war" and instigate the violent seizure of innocent Africans by European and African traders.[17]

Clarkson also denounced the erroneous claim that most enslaved Africans were prisoners of war. One way European and white American Christians defended Black enslavement was to employ scriptural permissions for enslaving prisoners of war in the Old Testament. In 1779, Alexander Hewat, a native of Scotland who pastored a Presbyterian congregation in Charleston, South Carolina, from 1763 until he migrated to England after the first battles of the American Revolution, observed that "many of the most civilized nations in the world" followed "the custom and practice of ancient nations" in the Bible regarding the divine sanction to enslave prisoners of war.[18] Clarkson excoriated the merits of this scriptural defense for Black enslavement as absurd, but he also estimated that prisoners of war amounted to only a small portion of the enslaved population. Clarkson argued that the highest number among the enslaved were kidnapped victims (more than 50 percent). The second highest number comprised prisoners, but they were captured in violent skirmishes across Africa motivated wholly by the transatlantic slave trade, not existing African wars.[19]

"But Is Not the Slave Trade Entirely a War with the Heart of Man?": The Horrors of First Passage, Middle Passage, Auctions, and Scrambles

Two autobiographies from formerly enslaved Africans, Ottobah Cugoano and Olaudah Equiano, demonstrate the veracity of Clarkson's indictment of the transatlantic slave trade. Cugoano published his book, *Thoughts and Sentiments on the Evil and Wicked Traffic of the Slavery and Commerce of the Human Species*, in England one year after Clarkson's work. Cugoano began with a recounting of the terrors he experienced as a teenager from his initial abduction to his voyage on a slave ship. Cugoano was a native of Ajumako in southern Ghana born to an elite family, with a father serving as a "companion to the chief" of their village.[20] During a visit to an uncle in a distant village, Cugoano was kidnapped while playing with other children. The African traders then transported him from the inland to the coast to exchange him for goods from European traders. Clarkson observed that some captured Africans traveled up to 1,200 miles from the inland to the slave markets along the coast, in what was referred to as a "First Passage" marked by chains and punishments over days and weeks on foot and by boat.[21] Upon arriving at the coast, captured Africans would endure the "Middle Passage" in oppressive and overcrowded slave ships from the West African coast to the Americas. The average length of the Middle Passage was 60.4 days, and the mortality rate ranged from 8.2 percent to 29.8 percent on Dutch, English, French, Portuguese, and Spanish slave ships between the years of 1590 and 1867.[22]

Cugoano described the transition from the First Passage to the Middle Passage as "a most horrible scene," with "nothing to be heard but rattling of chains, smacking of whips, and the groans and cries of our fellow-men."[23] On the slave ship, Cugoano was among the enslaved men in chains below deck, but he observed that some of the enslaved women were not in chains for ease of access when some of the crew on the ship raped them. Cugoano remembered that "it was common for the dirty filthy sailors to take the African women and lie upon their bodies."[24] Though Cugoano expressed the sorrow and trauma he felt led him to think "death was more preferable than life," he and several other captives did not endure their humiliations without resistance. They, like enslaved Africans on numerous slave ships, endeavored to assail the crew and gain control of the ship, such as the successful mutiny of the *Amistad*, which landed with fifty-three Africans at New

York's Long Island in 1839. But the insurrection attempt of Cugoano and his coconspirators was thwarted when an enslaved woman "who slept with some of the head men of the ship" divulged their intent to the crew.[25]

Like Cugoano, Equiano and his sister were also abducted as children from their village in southeastern Nigeria. In his book, *The Interesting Narrative of the Life of Olaudah Equiano*, published in England in 1789, Equiano explained how his father was an Ibo tribal elder of the "highest distinction" and that he too expected be an elder in adulthood because of the hereditary form of government in the village.[26] But when Equiano was eleven, he and his sister were kidnapped from their home while their parents were laboring in the fields. During their First Passage, Equiano and his sister were bound at their hands and forced to eat when resisting food. Equiano fell into deep despair when the captors sold his sister to another trader and took her on a different route from his. Upon reaching the coast, Equiano was thrust on a slave ship below deck and remembered the initial shock of encountering the "intolerably loathsome" stench and experiencing the horrors of close confinement, unbearable heat, physical illness, and psychological trauma. All enslaved men on slave ships were chained and sometimes bound together in pairs with fetters around their necks, arms, or legs. As a child, Equiano was spared from chains, but he felt suffocated by the lack of ventilation and overcrowding such that "each had scarcely room to turn."[27] In 1789, the Society for Effecting the Abolition of the Slave Trade (SEAST) in England published a diagram of the Liverpool slave ship *Brooks* (also spelled *Brookes*) with its dimensions and capacities to transport human cargo to illustrate the inhumane realities of the slave trade. Though the diagram was not drawn to scale, its estimate on the slave decks measuring 3,349 square feet and holding 470 captives was not an exaggeration. British vessels in the eighteenth century carried approximately 267 captives, but the *Brooks* was a larger ship that could hold more than double the average of other slave ships. And a British naval captain's report in 1788 calculated the "median degree of crowding on 251 voyages before 1789 was 6 feet, 4 inches, square," which is actually less, not greater, than the *Brooks* diagram from SEAST, which had an average of 7 feet, 2 inches, square.[28]

Equiano was one of hundreds of thousands, if not millions, of enslaved children forced to endure the Middle Passage. Of the 34,443 voyages from 1514 to 1866, 4,208 recorded the numbers of adults and children. Children accounted for 21.5 percent of the captives on these voyages, which Equiano recounted were "absolutely pestilential," with the nauseating odor of sweat and feces and "a scene of horror almost inconceivable" that drove two captives, chained together, to escape and jump overboard to their deaths.[29] Clarkson found that suicide was one form of resistance and revolt was another. He argued it was not surprising that enslaved Africans made violent attempts for freedom and revenge on the slave ships, and he observed that captives from the Windward Coast (stretching across present-day Ivory Coast and Liberia) frequently rebelled to "punish their enslavers at the hazard of their own lives" because many were trained hunters and warriors. In the decade prior to Clarkson's essay (1771 to 1780), 65,186 of 755,667 captives embarking from Africa were from the Windward Coast. The fear of insurrections drove many slave ships and trading companies to purchase insurance covering potential losses from mutiny.[30]

Equiano's voyage ended in the port city of Bridgetown in Barbados. In addition to Bridgetown, three other major port cities of the international slave trade were Kingston, Jamaica; Charleston, South Carolina; and New York City. As Equiano's ship approached land, the crew expressed joyful shouts with anticipation of rest and profit. After the ship docked, European merchants and planters entered the ship to inspect the human cargo. In Equiano's telling, these enslavers performed invasive examinations in which the captives were forced to jump, among other physical activities.[31] The dehumanizing inspections upon arrival were a dreadfully familiar experience by this point of the cruel journeys for enslaved Africans. Slave traders thoroughly examined captives before embarking from Africa. On the coast, the captives were often stripped of their clothing, made to jump up and down, and forced to endure foreign fingers and hands being placed in their mouths and genital areas. Some were branded with hot irons no different than cattle. Once aboard the ships, many of the captives remained naked but for their shackles.[32] Although Equiano does not explicitly mention his nudity, there are implicit but clear references to the indignities of nakedness in his descriptions of the clothing he and other Ibo villagers wore, made of "calico or muslin," and of Ibo women as "uncommonly graceful, alert, and modest to a degree of bashfulness."[33] Nudity was not customary for Equiano, as some European travel writers incorrectly propagated was true of all Africans, but rather his forced nakedness was a ferocious assault on his human dignity. In his autobiography, Pennington highlighted nudity alongside physical torture and starvation as three significant cruelties of Black enslavement. The shame of nakedness for enslaved persons was not intrinsically about their bodies, but it was grounded in the coercive and dehumanizing nature of their nudity on public display in contexts where persons with power, or simply persons who were not Black or enslaved, were fully dressed.

After their examinations, enslaved Africans disembarked from the ships and were sold as human merchandise. Clarkson outlined three common methods of sale. The first method was called *agency*, by which intermediary brokers purchased enslaved Africans on behalf of various planters. These brokers understood the needs and wants of their planter clientele and bought directly from the ship captains. The second method was known as *vendue*, which entailed a public auction with competitive bidding for the enslaved. In many auctions, enslaved Africans were groomed for display with thorough cleanings and glistening of oils, some adorned in fine clothing and others remaining with little to no clothing. Some bidders would also conduct their own examinations of enslaved Africans in whom they had interest, fondling various body parts, including genitals, of the enslaved up for auction. Some enslaved women, including young teenagers, endured cruel and crude inspections of their vaginas and breasts from prospective bidders seeking to discern their childbearing and childrearing capacities. The third method, termed *scramble*, was designed to be more economically equitable for middle-class purchasers. As with auctions, preparations included the examining, washing, and oiling of enslaved Africans. But the method of sale diverged at this point. Rather than bidding on individual enslaved Africans, purchasers held ropes in their hands and ran at a group of enslaved Africans, once the signal was given, to seize as many enslaved men, women, and children as they could in an abhorrent scene of roughshod competition between purchasers and chaotic terror among the enslaved. Clarkson lambasted this method as exceedingly nefarious for two reasons. In addition to the horrors the scrambles inflicted upon enslaved Africans, the "scrambling for human flesh and blood" revealed the depths of how low European enslavers had sunk in their moral degradation. Yet scrambles became commonplace throughout the Caribbean and in South Carolina by the late seventeenth century precisely because this method leveled the playing field for less wealthy purchasers.[34]

The works of Clarkson, Cugoano, and Equiano, published in 1786, 1787, and 1789, respectively, differentiate between Christianity as a religion and the Christians guilty of active participation in the slave trade. As the slave trade developed, a few early European ship captains and

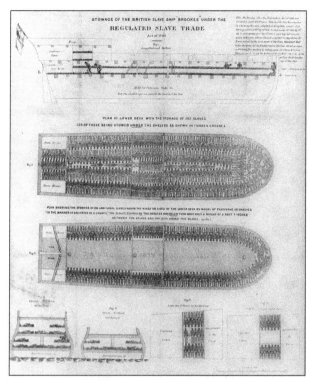

Stowage of the British slave ship Brookes *under the Regulated Slave Trade Act of 1788*

slave traders questioned the morality of their actions. In 1594, André Álvares de Almada, a Luso-African captain from Cabo Verde, reported that Christians traversing the Gambia River had an understanding that they should not trade for Africans who were clearly kidnap victims.[35] But many European traders abducted innocent Africans themselves, and nearly all created the conditions for rampant kidnapping with their escalating and insatiable demands for enslaved Africans. Cugoano criticized the palpable injustices of transactions in which European goods, such as rum and guns, were exchanged for African persons and questioned how a person with any moral compass, "whether he be a Christian or an heathen," could justify the seizing, trading, and enslaving of fellow humans as anything but abject evil.[36] Equiano asked, "But is not the slave trade entirely a war with the heart of man?" He then surmised that the growth of the slave trade led its participants down a destructive path that dulled their ethical sensibilities and ruined their spiritual souls.[37] Clarkson agreed with Equiano's assessment and emphasized

To be sold, on board the ship Bance Island,
at Ashley Ferry, South Carolina

how European Christians were directly responsible for the slave trade and Black enslavement.[38] Cugoano believed that European slave traders and enslavers—evildoers who "call themselves Christians"—were not in fact Christians because Christianity espoused a "system of benignity and love" and the values of honesty and justice.[39]

However, most European Christians up until the late eighteenth century did not challenge the systems of the international slave trade and Black enslavement. Although a few Christian slave traders had qualms about transporting African abductees, the promise of more revenue in a lucrative European economy increasingly shaped by the slave trade overruled any pangs of remorse and guilt they experienced. The British geographer and writer Richard Hakluyt, when recounting Hawkins's first slave transport, described Senegambians as "merchandise" to signify the connection between African persons and commercial trade. Jennifer L. Morgan, a historian of the transatlantic slave trade, finds that several influential sixteenth-century English writers, including Hakluyt, "evoked the Black body as one of many possible trade goods from the continent and imbued it with meaning in the context of early modern England's relationship to Africa and, of course, to settlement in the Atlantic."[40] In 1784, James Ramsay, an Anglican minister with roughly twenty years of experience residing in the Caribbean, asked the Church of England in his native country to consider the human costs and moral ramifications of the cocoa, coffee, rum, sugar, tobacco, and other imported goods that bolstered the British marketplace. Ramsay witnessed the brutalities of Black enslavement firsthand and concluded that the commodification of enslaved Africans as "mere machines or instruments of our profit, of our luxury, [and] of our caprice" went against the essential principles of Christianity.[41] The complicity of European and white American Christians did not derive from a lack of knowledge. The problem was not that they did not know about the barbarous cruelties of overcrowded slave ships transporting African captives to a lifetime of forced labor an ocean away in the Americas. Rather, they did not want to know and actively chose to remain ignorant and uninformed. Even Clarkson, an accomplished intellectual with an Anglican cleric as his father, opted to ignore the unjust systems that brought great wealth and commerce to his country until he entered an essay contest in his mid-twenties.

"The Child Follows the Mother" and the Laws That Followed Black Enslavement

In 1834, George Bourne, a white abolitionist with experience serving as a pastor of Presbyterian congregations in Virginia, looked back at the introduction of Black enslavement in the United States and wondered what would have happened in 1619 if the British colonists refused to buy "the first cargoes of the Africans" who had arrived on a slave ship at Point Comfort (present-day Fort Monroe in Hampton, Virginia). Even though the approximately twenty enslaved Africans were purchased, Bourne believed that if the clergy in the North American colonies then had preached against Black enslavement in its infancy, with international slave traders still unsure of their "risks and expenditures" north of the Caribbean, slavery may have met an early demise in the North American colonies.[42] But there was little resistance among seventeenth-century white colonists, including clergypersons, to the incipient expansion of the transatlantic slave trade to North America. Black enslavement did not become a formal system immediately in

1619. The laws did not initially regulate slavery and determine the rights of Black persons. Instead, white enslavers and legislators drafted and enacted laws throughout the seventeenth century in response to the multifarious tensions and opportunities that arose in their enslaving practices and interracial communities.

The first legal distinctions between Black and white persons in the North American colonies emerged in the 1660s. In 1655, Elizabeth Keye, the daughter of a white British man and an enslaved African woman in Virginia, petitioned the court for her emancipation after the death of her father. Until her father's death, Keye navigated an uneasy life as a biracial child whose father, Thomas Keye, held power as a member of the Virginia House of Burgesses. Elizabeth Keye was placed in indenture as a child, a category of labor and identity with more rights than her mother's enslavement. Keye resided in a community that knew of her paternal lineage and a larger colonial society observing the English common law of *partus sequitur patrem* that granted children the same legal status as their father's. But questions about whether Keye was an enslaved, indentured, or free person always lingered in the background. Keye fell in love with a white man, and they had a child together. Because the questions about Keye's status were thrust into the foreground after her father's death, and endangered both her and her child, Keye sought more formal legal protection. Her case went through multiple layers in a complicated judicial and legislative process in which Keye initially won her freedom before a higher court overturned the lower court's decision. The General Assembly in Virginia ultimately decreed that Keye was a free person, responding to a petition from the white man with whom she had a child, and they wed afterward.[43] But in 1662, interracial persons like Keye were denied the same rights as white persons. Legislators changed the law in Virginia to meet the economic and racial demands from a white populace seeking more certainty and stability in their favor. Children of an African woman and a white man would possess the status of the mother, not the father.

Other colonies also adopted this legal change, which departed from a bedrock statute of English common law. For centuries, English common law had established patrilineal and patriarchal systems regarding hereditary and inheritance rights. One translation of *partus sequitur patrem* is "The child follows the father." But white legislators wrote a new law under a different principle, *partus sequitur ventrem*, translated as "The child follows the mother" or "The child follows the womb," to ensure that the children of free or enslaved Black mothers, regardless of the race or status of their fathers, would not have access to the legal rights of their fathers. This law, which continued in every slaveholding state after U.S. independence, proved useful in regulating one of the growing tensions in Black enslavement: the sexual assault of enslaved Black women by white slave-owning men. Not every biracial child was the result of rape, but in many cases these children were visible evidence of sexual violence perpetrated by white men, often married to white women, in slave-owning families that desired for these children to remain as enslaved laborers lacking the legal rights of their fathers.

In addition to this matrilineal law, two other major legal developments in response to Black enslavement concerned property rights and Christian baptism. The two primary systems of labor in the North American colonies were wage labor, in which employers and employees agreed upon monetary compensation for specific tasks or hours of labor, and indentured servitude, a contractual system in which one person agreed to labor for another person for a specific amount of time, such as four to seven years, to repay a loan, which was often the cost of the person's transatlantic passage, housing, and food. The wealthier person paying for these expenses owned the contract, or indenture, and it could be sold or transferred to another person. Colonial policies were careful to note that the indenture gave the holder rights to a servant's labor contract and not the personhood of the servant. Black enslavement in the immediate years following 1619 sometimes resembled indentured servitude, and some seventeenth-century Africans labored as indentured servants, with a specified length of contract, and not as uncompensated enslaved laborers in perpetuity.[44] But several colonies constructed new laws to clarify the distinctions between Black enslavement and white indentured servitude. In 1827, George M. Stroud traced the legal history that ensured enslavers completely owned an enslaved person like other property not remotely akin to an indenture. He cited state laws like one in Maryland from 1798 stating that personal property includes "slaves, working beasts, animals of any kind, stock, furniture, plate, books, and so forth" to illustrate that "the cardinal principle of slavery" was that an enslaved person was regarded "as a thing" and "a chattel personal" sans any protection of the enslaved person's human rights.[45]

White colonists also endeavored to clarify an English legal ambiguity regarding the emancipation of enslaved persons baptized as Christians. In England and other European nations, one of the scriptural justifications for the international slave trade was the right of Christians to enslave persons who were not Christian, sometimes referred to as "heathens" or "infidels," based on a selective interpretation of Old Testament passages in which the Israelites enslaved people belonging to other nations. However, this malicious rationale granting biblical sanction for Black enslavement raised a corollary question concerning the legal status of enslaved Africans who converted to Christianity. If Christians did not have divine permission to enslave fellow Christians, what should become of enslaved African Christians? Some European nations, such as France, made clear that the conversion of enslaved Africans to Christianity was not grounds for emancipation. In 1685, the French Code Noir encouraged planters in the Americas to baptize and instruct their enslaved Africans in the Christian faith. But in England, the legality of enslaving Africans who were baptized as Christians was challenged in the courts, which motivated English enslavers in the North American colonies to seek a definitive resolution. Between 1664 and 1706, at least six colonies passed laws stating that the baptism of enslaved persons did not result in their freedom, with some of these laws more explicitly noting the dangers if enslaved persons learned of the legal ambiguities in England and pretended to be Christians to make their own emancipatory claims.[46]

The three legal developments of maternal lineage, property rights, and Christian baptism illustrate the malleability of colonial, state, and federal laws relating to enslaved persons. These laws provided foundational order to a society that grew increasingly reliant on Black enslavement, but the process was not impartial. The evolving conditions of Black enslavement dictated the legislative process. Stroud observed that the change from patrilineal to matrilineal status across the colonies was such a radical break from English common law doctrine, with scant legal precedent, that the only reason it occurred was the presence of biracial children born of enslaved Black women and white men.[47] In other words, if not for these children, the matrilineal law may not have ever appeared. White enslavers were not simply obeying the laws; they were making and remaking the laws. The impermanent nature of lawmaking, as white legislators passed acts and statutes to clarify and fortify Black enslavement, had devastating, tragic, and permanent consequences for the enslaved.

In 1845, George Lewis recounted his travel experiences from Scotland to the United States. Lewis was a Presbyterian minister in the Free Church of Scotland visiting Presbyterian congregations throughout the United States, from New York to Louisiana, on a fundraising tour to support his fledgling denomination, which was born out of an ecclesial conflict with the established Church of Scotland. Upon arriving in Alexandria, Virginia, he was astonished because the majority of enslaved persons there looked biracial to him: "The greater number of the coloured population in Alexandria are not negroes but mulattoes."[48] One historian of anti-Black racism in the United States, Winthrop D. Jordan, finds that the word *mulatto*, taken from the Spanish, was "in English usage from about 1600 and was probably first used in Virginia records in 1666" to identify persons with both African and white European ancestry.[49] Colonial and state laws began adding "mulattoes" to their laws on slavery and revised the definition of *mulatto* over time to confirm multigenerational white ownership of the children, grandchildren, and great-grandchildren of an enslaved Black woman. For example, North Carolina changed the definition of *mulatto* from one-eighth to one-sixteenth African ancestry.[50] From 1619 to 1865, enslaved Black women in the United States endured the constant and unrelenting threat of rape by white men. The "mulatto" laws only protected white rapists, not enslaved Black women. In some cases, these laws enabled slave-owning men to increase their economic capital. When they violently impregnated the enslaved women they owned, they subsequently also owned (and could sell) the children they fathered.

In 1861, Harriet Jacobs, a formerly enslaved Black woman, recounted her traumatic experiences under the ownership of a white Episcopal family in North Carolina. As a child, Jacobs did not know she was enslaved until she was six years old. The historian Daina Ramey Berry analyzes the "childhood realization of enslavement" as a "moment of shock when children first learn they are chattel."[51] Until that moment, enslaved children played with other children, including white children from slave-owning families, and were often cared for by elderly enslaved persons while their parents labored all day in the fields. Jacobs describes the time before her realization of enslavement as "six years of happy childhood."[52] But from six years of age, Jacobs began to witness more of the horrors of Black enslavement, such as observing the whippings of older enslaved persons on the plantation and the weeping of an enslaved mother as her children were sold at an auction, and to experience the fear and oppression of Black enslavement herself. Like other enslaved women, Jacobs's abuse and torment escalated at puberty. At fifteen years of age, Jacobs became an alluring sexual object in the eyes of her enslaver, James Norcom, a churchgoing physician with a good reputation in his local white community. Norcom whispered lascivious threats in Jacobs's ear and commanded her to have sex with him. Jacobs recalled, "He told me I was his property; that I must be subject to his will in all things. My soul revolted against the mean tyranny."[53] Jacobs resisted Norcom's advances for several years and ultimately risked her life to escape because she saw no other way to be free from the incessant and debilitating fear of sexual violence.

In Adrienne D. Davis's scholarship on slavery, Davis[54] argues that "the economy of American slavery systematically expropriated black women's sexuality and reproductive capacity for white pleasure and profit." Davis also cites the work of Toni Morrison to engage the challenges we face in attempting to retell the history of Black enslavement because of "the paucity of language to describe the horror of American slavery" and "the void of slavery in the nation's memory."[55] Jacobs provides poignant language in her autobiography to illustrate the tragedy of Black enslavement through her life experiences. She describes puberty as "a sad epoch in the life of a slave girl" and details the cruel realizations that ensued: "She will become prematurely knowing in evil things. Soon she will learn to tremble when she hears her master's footfall. She will be compelled to realize that she is no longer a child. If God has bestowed beauty upon her, it will prove her greatest curse."[56] The laws of matrilineal status and enslaved Black persons as "chattel personal" enabled white men like James Norcom to sexually abuse Harriet Jacobs and millions of other enslaved Black girls and women without hesitation or concern of any repercussions.

In addition to Norcom's coercive sexual advances, Jacobs also encountered the mounting rage of Norcom's wife. Norcom's wife, like many other married slave-owning women, knew her husband was sexually abusing Jacobs, but she did not confront him. Instead, Norcom's wife unleashed her frustration and anger upon Jacobs. Countless narratives of enslaved Black persons explain this transfer of retribution as white slave-owning women punished enslaved Black women for the wicked crimes of their husbands with harsh words and vicious whippings. In his abolitionist work, Bourne observed that white slave-owning women chose to "connive at the grossest sensuality in their husbands, sons, fathers, and brothers" rather than publicly acknowledge and confront the widespread sexual violence in Black enslavement.[57] The white slave-owning author Mary Boykin Chesnut believed that slave-owning women were "abolitionists in their hearts and hot ones too" because they resented their husbands' marital infidelities and sexual violations.[58] But the overwhelming impulse among slave-owning women was to suppress these painful and sinful realities, as exemplified in Chesnut's observation: "Every lady tells you who is the father of all the mulatto children in everybody's household, but those in her own she seems to think drop from the clouds."[59]

Enslaved families were fraught because enslaved spouses, parents, and children could be separated via auctions, sales, debt collections, and inheritances, but the sexual violence of white men caused especially immense pain and deep trauma. In 1849, Henry Bibb, a formerly enslaved Black man, expressed the humiliation and shame he had experienced when he could not protect his wife, Malinda, from the physical and sexual abuse their enslaver had inflicted upon her.[60] In Angela Davis's analysis of the history and legacy of Black enslavement, Davis contends that "the rape of the black woman was not exclusively an attack upon her" but also an assault on the entire enslaved community by disrupting marital relations and perhaps more importantly signifying the absolute power of the enslaver over the enslaved.[61] Some enslaved men were demoralized by their helplessness and despaired at their inability to prevent the attacks. Others, like Bibb, were ashamed but became further motivated to resist and escape. After Bibb's wife gave birth to their daughter, he resolved to escape with his family because the thought of his daughter enduring the cruelties of Black enslavement that violated "female virtue" was "too much to bear."[62] Enslaved women also resisted their enslavers. Jacobs hid in a crawl space in one of the enslaved quarters on Norcom's plantation for seven years before escaping to the northern states. Other enslaved women committed suicide to be free from the sexual abuse. Some enslaved men violently confronted the white men raping their wives, sisters, and daughters, with the full recognition that even if they were successful in killing the rapists, the most likely outcome was their subsequent death at the hands of other white men in the community.

The hypersexualization and commodification of enslaved persons were sometimes intertwined. Sojourner Truth, a formerly enslaved Black woman, criticized the breeding practices of enslavers in her autobiography from 1850. Truth described the insidious ways in which enslavers urged their enslaved persons to marry and have sex for the sake of biological reproduction to increase their holdings in human capital. She noted that conversations about breeding occurred in private and that some enslavers vehemently denied engaging in such immoral practices, but the reality was that breeding practices were "silently

tolerated." Truth called upon white Americans to publicly acknowledge "the present state of licentiousness their own wicked laws have
created."[63] In addition to encouraging marriages among their enslaved
persons, which Truth observed were in fact a sham because the unions
of enslaved persons were not recognized by civil law, some enslavers
utilized overcrowded lodging conditions as a means to encourage sexual
activity and biological reproduction. Thomas S. Clay, a white Presbyterian planter from Georgia, shared a report in 1833 focused on "improving the moral condition of our negroes" with his presbytery. Among
his observations were the "evils obviously arising from the mode of
lodging" when enslavers forced their enslaved persons of all genders to
reside in tightly confined spaces together.[64] Implied in Clay's report is
the notion of an aggressive and insatiable Black sexuality commonplace
in white transatlantic societies in the nineteenth century. Beginning
in the fifteenth century, European geographers and writers presented
Africans as hypersexual beings, emphasizing what they viewed as their
promiscuity and anatomical prowess. They disseminated the idea that
African men had large penises. English accounts of West Africa in the
seventeenth century highlighted the "extraordinary greatness" of the
penises there.[65] Some enslavers therefore treated their enslaved persons
like animals, with the expectation that cultivating the right kind of
habitats would result in more human stock. Thomas Jefferson was not
an advocate of breeding, but he was an enslaver who owned more than
140 enslaved persons and therefore acknowledged the obvious financial
benefits of reproduction: "I consider a woman who brings a child every
two years as more profitable than the best man on the farm. What she
produces is an addition to capital, while his labors disappear in mere
consumption."[66] Jefferson, like all enslavers, monitored the pregnan-
cies and births among the enslaved persons on his plantation.

The Trauma of Black Enslavement
and the Dehumanization of "Chattel Personal"

James W. C. Pennington also sharply lambasted the sexual violence of
Black enslavement. He employed the logic of white Christians defending slavery and then used that logic against them. In the homes and
on the plantations of "Christian masters" practicing "the mildest form
of slavery," Pennington observed the exploitation of enslaved young
women, especially light-skinned Black women. When enslaved in

Maryland, Pennington recalled the sale of an enslaved woman named Rachel because one of the white sons in the slave-owning family was enamored with her and they were engaging in sexual relations. It is not clear from Pennington's account whether Rachel reciprocated romantic affection for the white man, but the reason the family sold Rachel against her will is not in doubt. The white man's mother and sisters were displeased with his sexual activity and decided the easiest way to stop it was to sell Rachel, which would mean callously separating her from her parents. On the day of the sale, Rachel's enslaved father sought in vain to find a local purchaser, but the enslaving family insisted Rachel be sold to a slave trader executing sales for long-distance buyers in the lower southern states. Pennington also criticized the problem of forced prostitution. Some enslaved women were purchased for sexual labor. Though the sexual labor often went unmentioned at the point of sale, Pennington observed that the higher prices, sometimes two to three times more than the average amount, clarified intentions and expectations.[67] In 1843, a white Methodist pastor from Ohio raised funds to purchase a light-skinned enslaved woman from an auction in Kentucky because she was in danger of being sold for sexual labor. At the public auction, the seller unbuttoned the enslaved woman's dress to reveal "her superb neck and breast" and then raised her skirt to display "bare her beautiful, symmetrical body, from her feet to her waist," in an effort to generate higher bids.[68] White persons in attendance, both buyers and bystanders, expressed their disgust at the seller for his brazen avarice, but it is difficult to discern whether they were genuinely opposed to the lurid and coercive implications of the seller's wanton actions or simply displeased with the seller's foolish recklessness in being more obvious than was necessary.

Like the narratives of Cugoano and Equiano from the late eighteenth century, Pennington's narrative from 1849 emphasized the shame of enslaved Black nudity. The former two narratives center on the experiences of native Africans enduring the transatlantic slave trade. Cugoano connected the "nakedness of slavery" with the "merchandizing of men" to illustrate the inhumane treatment of stripping enslaved Africans in the Caribbean of both their clothing and their dignity to debase them to the levels of cattle and chattel.[69] More than six decades later, Pennington's account of Black enslavement in the United States maintained that the absence of adequate attire comprised a significant element in the dehumanization of enslaved persons. Many states had laws to regulate clothing provisions for enslaved persons, but the mandates were slight and often ignored because enforcement was rare. Stroud cited and criticized the law in Louisiana, in which an enslaver was required to supply "*one* linen shirt and pantaloons (*une chemise et une culotte de toile*) for the summer, and a linen shirt and woollen great-coat and pantaloons for the winter."[70] Two seasonal ensembles, one given in the summer and the other given in the winter, for an enslaved person laboring in harsh conditions were woefully insufficient. What were enslaved persons supposed to wear when washing their one summer or winter outfit? Some made extra clothing for themselves or bartered for additional attire in informal plantation markets. Others were often nude or semi-nude. Bourne lamented that "coloured boys and girls grow up together in nakedness, until they arrive at almost mature age; and in the most exposed condition, wait upon visitors."[71] Jordan's history of anti-Black racism illustrates the ubiquity of enslaved Black nudity from the perspective of white northern persons visiting their friends and family members in the southern states. These "visitors commented upon the casualness with which this exposure was taken by their hosts, male and female; and probably this casualness was entirely genuine, for whenever nudity is customary it soon ceases to shock."[72] But Pennington, Bourne, and other Black and white abolitionists insisted that the nakedness of Black enslavement was appalling because it created a visible and inescapable distinction between white and Black, free and enslaved. Enslaved persons were reminded daily of their demeaning status as "chattel personal," especially in the presence of white and free persons, when looking down at what they wore (or did not have to wear) and looking ahead at the variety of apparel adorning their white enslavers and other free persons.

Clay's plan for "improving the moral condition of our negroes" recommended a sufficient supply of clothing and food, but he disagreed with Stroud on what constituted adequate provisions. Clay found the practice of providing enslaved persons with "two suits of clothes annually," one in April or May for the heat and the other in November for the cold, was appropriate. But Clay conceded that this provision was "often neglected" and a "very great" number of enslaved persons suffered in the winter months. He emphasized to his fellow white Presbyterians that this sartorial neglect was especially injurious because it sometimes prevented enslaved persons from going to church with their enslavers: "However well a negro may endure the cold when at work, or sitting by his fire-side, the want of warm clothing would be considered a good reason for not attending church."[73] Clay also supported the legal mandate of giving one peck (one-fourth of a bushel) of corn per week to enslaved persons. In Louisiana, the law stated that rice, beans, or other grain could substitute for corn and included a monthly allotment of one pint of salt alongside the corn or equivalent grain.[74] But Horace Moulton, a white Methodist pastor in Massachusetts, criticized the food rations of Black enslavement as utterly inadequate and cruel for the ways it left enslaved persons in near starvation. In 1839, Moulton recalled his previous residence in Savannah, Georgia, and compared the weekly provisions for enslaved persons with his own dietary habits. Moulton estimated that he consumed the same amount of food as forty-six enslaved persons.[75] Though Clay insisted the one-peck allotment of corn was fair, he also offered the caveat that some enslavers met the mandate in terms of quantity but with low-quality corn. He reported that the poor quality of corn caused enslaved persons to go hungry and seek other food on the plantations.[76]

Clay was displeased when enslaved persons stole from their enslavers to fill their starving bellies with other grains and poultry beyond their allotments, but he gently acknowledged that negligent enslavers were responsible for creating the conditions that led enslaved persons to thievery. But enslaved persons also demonstrated their resourcefulness in acquiring food for themselves, such as hunting for opossums, rabbits, and squirrels, and making delicacies from the rough meat of these animals (which was undesirable to their enslavers) with the spices available to them. Anthony Dawson, a formerly enslaved Black man from South Carolina, explained, "I love 'possum and sweet 'taters, but de coon meat more delicate, and de hair don't stink up de meat."[77] Although white enslavers did not dine on opossum, they praised the culinary acumen of Black Americans, and many assigned their enslaved persons with the task of preparing the cuisine for their daily meals and special occasions when entertaining guests. Robert Quarterman Mallard, a white Presbyterian minister from Georgia, believed the "African female intellect" possessed a "natural genius" for cooking.[78] But as with the sparse clothing provisions for enslaved persons, the stark inequities between their diets and those of their enslavers demonstrated the degrading and dehumanizing sins of Black enslavement. Frederick Douglass remembered eating "coarse corn meal boiled," referred to as mush, throughout his enslaved childhood. Douglass and the other enslaved children ate from a trough on the ground like animals: "The children were then called, like so many pigs, and like so many pigs they would come and devour the mush; some with oyster-shells, others with pieces of shingle, some with naked hands, and none with spoons."[79] On their hands and knees, enslaved children suffering from starvation were reduced to jostling with one another for access to food in a trough. Many other autobiographies from formerly enslaved persons divulge similar accounts of trauma from food deprivation.[80]

In his enslaved adulthood, before escaping to freedom, Douglass experienced the adverse psychological and spiritual effects of Black enslavement. After enduring several months of brutal treatment from a white farmer with a "very high reputation for breaking young slaves," Douglass described "being broken in body, soul, and spirit" and losing all sense of his humanity: "My natural elasticity was crushed, my intellect languished, the disposition to read departed, the cheerful spark that lingered about my eye died; the dark night of slavery closed in upon me; and behold a man transformed into a brute!"[81] In abject despair, Douglass mindlessly performed his labor, the drudgery leaving him in such a debilitated state that he contemplated suicide. Pennington also experienced the deadening effects of Black enslavement upon his mind and soul and believed this psychological and spiritual trauma captured "the extent of the mischief" that slavery had wrought. He argued that Black enslavement had completely taken away the first twenty-one years of his life, which could never be returned to him.[82] Joseph Ide, a white Baptist lawyer in Vermont, wrote a letter to his pastor, William Scales, after witnessing firsthand the horrors of Black enslavement during a visit to the southern states. The corporal punishments and inadequate provisions troubled Ide, but he also highlighted an indelible moment that illustrated to him the dehumanizing tragedy of Black enslavement: "I have seen from forty to sixty, male and female, at work in a field, many of both sexes with their bodies entirely naked—who did not exhibit signs of shame more than cattle."[83] Ide was shaken at the sight of a group of humans who looked to him no different from a herd of cattle. This dreadful scene was a bizarre aberration to Ide, but it was also a commonplace reality of Black enslavement.

In 1830, David Walker died one year after publishing the first edition of his *Appeal*, but he knew that the book had reached the southern states and caused a stir. Copies of the *Appeal* were smuggled on ships from Boston to southern ports and ultimately found their way into the hands of both enslaved persons and their enslavers. Enslavers opted to ban the *Appeal* rather than address Walker's question to white Christians about their culpability for the "barbarous cruelties" of Black enslavement. White legislators, planters, and pastors in the southern states denounced the book as an instrument fomenting insurrection and insubordination among enslaved persons. One police report in 1830 from Wilmington, North Carolina, the city of Walker's birth, attributed the insurrection plots of enslaved persons partly to an underground circulation of the *Appeal*.[84]

In returning to Walker's question about culpability, one irrefutable answer is that white Christian enslavers were responsible for the tragedy of Black enslavement. The autobiographies of formerly enslaved persons, such as Henry Bibb, Ottobah Cugoano, Frederick Douglass, Olaudah Equiano, Harriet Jacobs, Sojourner Truth, and James W. C. Pennington, make clear that white Christians were liable for the individual sins and systematic abuses of Black enslavement. For example, Cugoano identified the worst perpetrators in the Caribbean: "Protestants, as they are called, are the most barbarous slave-holders, and there are none can equal the Scotch floggers and negroe-drivers, and the barbarous Dutch cruelties."[85] Jacobs also found that most white slave-owning Christians in the United States were cruel.[86] The earliest laws regarding Christian baptism sought to discourage enslaved persons from pretending to be Christian in legal efforts to win their freedom, but many enslaved persons believed their enslavers were the ones pretending to be Christian. Some believed these enslavers betrayed the faith and were no longer worthy to bear the name of Christ. Others did not make this distinction and ultimately determined that Christianity was an utterly unworthy religion. The consequent lack of Christian conversions among the enslaved Black population emerged as the primary focus of white Presbyterians in their ministry and mission. In prioritizing the evangelization of enslaved persons, white Presbyterians thought they were addressing the greatest tragedy of Black enslavement. But their efforts largely failed and revealed how much Black enslavement had corrupted their communities, their congregations, and their consciences.

3

"Was There Anything Very Bad in All This?"

Eleven months before the end of the Civil War, the General Assembly of the Presbyterian Church in the Confederate States of America (PCCSA) met in Charlotte, North Carolina, on May 5, 1864. The moderator from the previous year's General Assembly, James A. Lyon, a white pastor in Mississippi, preached at the opening worship from 1 Thessalonians 2:4. This scriptural passage instructs Christians to place their trust in the gospel and remember that their primary aim is to please God, not other people, because God is the ultimate judge who tests the human heart. The General Assembly published a "Narrative of the State of Religion" that included a summary of reports from all the presbyteries on the "spiritual welfare" of enslaved persons. The commissioners found that the reports revealed "a deeper conviction of the divine appointment of domestic servitude" and a "clearer comprehension of the duties we owe to the African race." White Presbyterians in the southern states were convinced that God approved of Black enslavement and that their mission, despite the divisions in both their church and nation, was "to conserve the institution of slavery, and to make it a blessing both to master and slave."[1] In March 1866, one of the commissioners from the General Assembly in 1864, John B. Adger, reflected on the meeting. Although Black enslavement had since been abolished, Adger maintained that the General Assembly then was right to defend slavery because it was an institution that God had entrusted to white Christians as the means to evangelize enslaved persons. Adger belonged to one of the wealthiest white families in Charleston, South Carolina, and worked as a missionary in Turkey and a pastor in Charleston before he joined the faculty of Columbia Theological Seminary in 1857. Adger's life, except during his years abroad, had revolved around Black enslavement. It shaped his home, his church, and all the economic, political, and social systems that Adger inhabited. Eleven months after the end of the Civil War, Adger looked back at how white Presbyterians participated in and perpetuated Black enslavement and asked, "Was there anything very bad in all this?"[2]

In 1856, Benjamin Drew published a collection of narratives from 114 Black persons residing in Canada. Almost all of them had escaped from slavery in the United States through the Underground Railroad or other methods. A few were free Black Americans who migrated to Canada because of the ferocity of anti-Black racism in northern states such as Indiana, New York, Ohio, and Pennsylvania and the persistent threat of illegal kidnapping, which escalated after the Fugitive Slave Act was passed in 1850. Drew, a white abolitionist from Massachusetts, compiled a diversity of perspectives in his endeavor to share the unfiltered stories of Black persons and "their experiences of the actual workings of slavery."[3] Many accounts revealed the horrors of Black enslavement, with details of physical abuse and sexual violence. Other formerly enslaved persons noted more tolerable physical treatment from their enslavers, but they too detailed the immense psychological and spiritual cruelties of Black enslavement. David West, a formerly enslaved Black man from Virginia, was "treated well" by an enslaver who was "as good a man as there is in the whole South," but West did not believe Black enslavement could be justified with any rationale, especially from the Bible.[4] Though West's enslaver professed to be a Christian, West did not think it was possible for him to be in heaven on account of his sinful participation in Black enslavement. Harriet Tubman's account in Drew's collection condemned slavery as "the next thing to hell."[5] Two of Tubman's sisters were sold to a slave trader and chained in a *coffle* with other enslaved persons in a harrowing journey from the upper southern states to the lower southern states. *Coffle* was an African term derived from the Arabic word *cafila*, used to describe a "chained slave caravan."[6] Tubman described her enslavement as existing in a perpetual state of fear and remembered shuddering every time she saw a white man. She surmised, "If a person would send another into bondage, he would, it appears to me, be bad enough to send him into hell, if he could."[7] Unlike Adger, Tubman was certain that everything about Black enslavement was very bad.

In 1850, Harriet Beecher Stowe began writing a story about Black enslavement. Stowe's father, Lyman Beecher, was a pastor of Presbyterian and Congregational congregations in New York and Connecticut before moving with his family to Cincinnati, Ohio, to serve as president of Lane Theological Seminary, a Presbyterian institution, in 1832. As a young adult, Stowe attended a series of debates on abolition, colonization, and slavery at the seminary in February 1834. The debates stirred the fires of abolitionism among many of the students, which agitated the board of trustees, and her father sought a compromise between the students seeking to be bolder and more strategic in their activism and the trustees urging the school to focus on theological subjects and training future clergy for church ministry. In December of the same year, fifty-one students published a statement protesting the institutional leadership of both the trustees and Beecher and explaining why they were withdrawing from the seminary. The students vehemently disagreed with institutional attempts to censor and regulate their mobilizing efforts on campus for abolition and accused the school's leaders of cowardice and betraying the call of Jesus Christ: "Are our theological seminaries to be awed into silence upon the great questions of human duty? Are they to be bribed over to the interests of an unholy public sentiment, by promises of patronage or threats of its withdrawal?"[8] Stowe's literary career began to flourish around the same time as she published many essays and stories in periodicals, but she returned to the topics discussed at Lane Seminary for her most famous and influential work, *Uncle Tom's Cabin*, which was first published in serial form in the *National Era*, an abolitionist newspaper, in 1851, and then in book form the following year.

Stowe's novel about the arduous journeys of two enslaved persons, Tom and Eliza, engaged the atrocities of Black enslavement, the sinfulness of enslavers, and the resiliency of enslaved persons in their resistance, forbearance, courage, and Christian witness. In 1853, Stowe published a book entitled *The Key to "Uncle Tom's Cabin"* to delineate the sources for her novel and demonstrate to some critics that she was not exaggerating the horrors of Black enslavement. If anything, Stowe demurred, her book did not fully capture the actual evils of slavery in the United States. Like Tubman and contra Adger, Stowe concluded that "there is no bright side to slavery."[9] Enslavers and enablers of Black enslavement often referred to it as a "peculiar institution" to illustrate its virtues and characterize its injustices as necessary contradictions. Adger's denomination, the PCCSA, described its active participation in Black enslavement as the "peculiar mission of the Southern Church."[10] But Stowe believed "what is peculiar to slavery" was "evil, and only evil, and that continually."[11] With *Uncle Tom's Cabin*, Stowe endeavored to take readers into the depths of slavery's evils. In *The Key to "Uncle Tom's Cabin,"* Stowe proved these evils were endemic and dismantled Adger's position that white Christians could make slavery a blessing unto enslaved persons.

"No Other Inducement to Work but the Lash": The Centrality of Physical Abuse in the Management of Enslaved Black Labor

One disparaging reviewer of *Uncle Tom's Cabin* complained that Stowe devised her story "to present slavery in three dark aspects: first, the *cruel treatment* of the slaves; second, the *separation of families*; and, third, their *want of religious instruction*."[12] Though it was not the critic's intention, Stowe found that the tripartite summary served as a useful thesis to express her book's main argument in a "clear, concise, and intelligible form."[13] In addition to published book reviews, Stowe received private correspondence from white readers in the southern states. One reader from Richmond, Virginia, criticized Stowe for failing to mention the existence of "formalised laws of the Southern States" prohibiting excessive physical abuse in disciplining enslaved persons and provided as an example a law in Louisiana: "The slave is entirely subject to the will of his master, who may correct and chastise him, though not with unusual rigour, nor so as to maim or mutilate him, or to expose him to the danger of loss of life, or to cause his death."[14] Christa Dierksheide, a historian of slavery on plantations in the Americas, identifies the construction of laws setting ground rules for the corporal punishment of enslaved persons as one part of a larger effort among elite planters to gradually improve the conditions of slavery, which they called "amelioration." Enslavers embraced the concept of amelioration because it reinforced their economic and social control by endorsing slavery as beneficial for enslavers and the enslaved. The amelioration campaign rallied around the idea that Black enslavement could be transformed from a barbaric system, in which enslavers were viewed as wicked oppressors, to a "model plantation household" with a representation of white planters as wise patriarchs and matriarchs. But Dierksheide argues "the real goal of amelioration" among elite planters was "the expansion of plantation empires" to maximize their profits and stabilize their society.[15]

Stowe rightly argued that the frequency and ubiquity of corporal punishment against enslaved persons constituted cruel treatment and demonstrated that "slavery in itself" was an essentially abusive system that could not be satisfactorily ameliorated and made humane or ethical.[16] Even enslavers conceded that slavery was not possible without corporal punishment. Charles C. Jones, a white slave-owning Presbyterian pastor in Georgia, acknowledged the moral and religious contradictions inherent in Black enslavement. Jones understood that an oppressive system in which enslaved persons received no compensation for their labor and belonged to their enslavers as "chattel personal" required the constant threat of punishment. But he employed the passive voice and an oblique writing style to concede that while "the fear of punishment" was necessary, many enslavers inflicted corporal punishment against enslaved persons too often and too harshly: "The government to which they are subjected is too much physical in its nature. . . . While the necessity is admitted, yet the appeal should be made as seldom as possible and in the mildest form consistent with the due support of authority and the reformation of the transgressor."[17] Jones urged that corporal punishment be utilized judiciously and as a last resort, but he also divulged that his recommendation was not the reality on most plantations.

Frederick Law Olmsted, a prominent white travel writer and landscape architect born in Hartford, Connecticut, published several books in the 1850s and early 1860s documenting his two trips throughout the southern states. Olmsted wrote with more vivid and direct prose than Jones and limned his conversations and encounters with white planters, Black and white overseers, and enslaved Black persons to encapsulate the inner workings of southern plantations. In *A Journey in the Back Country*, Olmsted pointed to the centrality of whipping in the management of enslaved labor. When observing the coercive conditions on cotton plantations, Olmsted found that the "whip was evidently in constant use" and was told it was "necessary to the maintenance of adequate discipline on every large plantation" to ensure that enslaved persons performed their labor efficiently and fully. Therefore, the daily rhythms on a plantation included the sounds of a whip lashing on human flesh and the admonishing threats of an overseer shouting, "If you don't work faster," or "If you don't work better," or "If you don't recollect what I tell you, I will have you flogged." On one of his visits, Olmsted followed a white overseer on a routine day and witnessed him inflicting punishment on an enslaved teenage woman whom he accused of lying about her whereabouts to avoid her regular assignment of picking cotton. The overseer commanded the teenager to get on her knees, and he "struck her thirty or forty blows across the shoulders with his tough, flexible, 'raw-hide' whip." The woman winced but would not admit of any wrongdoing during the punishment. The overseer then forced her to remove all her clothes and lie on the ground before proceeding "to flog her with the rawhide, across her naked loins and thigh, with as much strength as before." The woman shrieked and pleaded, "Oh, don't sir! Oh, please stop, master!" Olmsted recalled that it was the first time he had ever seen the whipping of an enslaved woman, and the two phenomena he remembered most clearly were the severity of the whipping and the "perfectly passionless but rather grim business-like face of the overseer." The overseer explained to Olmsted that the severity of the punishment was necessary for two reasons. The first was to quell the enslaved teenager's desires to evade her manual labor. The second was that by inflicting the punishment in full view, the overseer believed he was dissuading the other enslaved laborers from shirking their field work.[18]

The laws designed to protect enslaved persons from undue physical violence were rarely enforced because the testimony of enslaved or free Black persons against white persons was inadmissible in court. George M. Stroud argued that the disciplinary laws were therefore "illusory" and in practice a "dead letter" because of the improbability of white persons admitting guilt or testifying against other white persons.[19] And large plantations, such as the one where Olmsted witnessed the brutal flogging of the enslaved young woman, were often sprawled out in isolated areas and so lacking white neighbors to witness cruel punishments. A large plantation was like a self-contained community in which every person who was not a family member of the white enslaver was either an enslaved Black person or a white person working on the payroll of the enslaver. The disciplinary laws themselves illustrated the prevalence of excessive physical abuse against enslaved persons. In 1740, a law in South Carolina enacted a financial penalty (but no prison sentence) for persons who "cut out the tongue, put out the eye, castrate, or cruelly scald, burn, or deprive any slave of any limb or member." The law added that it was forbidden to inflict punishment apart from "whipping or beating with a horsewhip, cowskin, switch, or small stick, or by putting irons on, or confining or imprisoning such slave."[20] The detailed infractions reveal the actual conditions of Black enslavement, in which enslavers and overseers were known to cut out tongues, remove eyes and genitals, and burn enslaved persons. The precise regulations also illustrate the instruments of torture that enslavers and overseers wielded in their routine management of enslaved labor.

Henry Gowens was a formerly enslaved Black man who experienced the physical violence of slavery in Alabama, Mississippi, North Carolina, Tennessee, and Virginia before escaping north to Canada. Even when he labored under the discipline of the "kindest overseers," he and other enslaved persons were whipped regularly. But ruthless overseers opted to punish incessantly: "It was whip, whip, continually, old and young; nobody got too old to be clear of the lash." On one plantation in Alabama, the planter was Presbyterian, and the overseer was exceedingly harsh and sadistic in his punishments. At the height of cotton season, the overseer stripped enslaved women naked and whipped them if they did not pick cotton at the pace he desired. If any of the enslaved women lifted their heads to look at him, the overseer punished them more severely, "cutting their flesh terribly, till the blood ran to their heels." He also stripped and bound enslaved men to a log, tying their hands together and their feet together, to whip them while they were face down. In some instances, the overseer forced enslaved spouses to assist in the punishments of their partners. The slave-owning man, as the patriarch of his plantation household, heard rumblings of discontent among his enslaved persons, but he did nothing and told them that they were forbidden to speak about the overseer with him or his wife. After several months, an elderly enslaved woman, against the planter's instructions, told the planter's wife about the overseer's abusive crimes, which included raping enslaved women, and she urged her husband to action. He instructed the overseer to moderate his punishment of the enslaved women, but he did not terminate the overseer's employment. Gowens therefore advanced a different question than Adger. Whereas Adger asked whether there was anything very bad in proslavery Presbyterianism, Gowens charged, "Who will tell of the good of slavery?"[21] White pastors like Adger and Jones preached about the responsibilities of enslavers to make slavery "a blessing to the slave," but their lofty and spiritual visions of Black enslavement only existed on Sunday mornings in their churches and dissipated after congregants received the benediction and returned to their farms and plantations.

William T. Allan was a white Presbyterian pastor in Chatham, Illinois, born in Huntsville, Alabama, in a slave-owning family with a father who was a Presbyterian pastor in the city. His experiences with Black enslavement were primarily with white slave-owning Christians, and Allan found that the rhetoric of amelioration differed from the reality on white Christian plantations. Allan witnessed overseers cruelly whipping and torturing enslaved persons. In the town square, Allan saw enslaved persons in tears and anguish at slave auctions. From their school, his brother viewed an enslaver punish an enslaved man for taking a break from the task of laying bricks without permission: "When his master got him back, he tied him by his hands so that his feet could just touch the ground—stripped off his clothes, took a paddle, bored full of holes, and paddled him leisurely all day long." Allan also learned of the killings and tortures of enslaved persons escaping from their enslavers. Some enslaved persons, called "fugitives" or "runaways," were killed while white slave patrols pursued them. Others were tortured by their enslavers when caught and returned. One enslaver's "usual punishment for running away" entailed the following deliberate process: "[He would] lay his slaves on a large log, which he kept for the purpose, strip them, tie them with the face downward, then have a kettle of hot water brought—take the paddle, made of hard wood, and perforated with holes, dip it into the hot water and strike." One slave-owning woman from Courtland, Alabama, shared with Allan that she often plugged her ears, and sometimes left her home, because she could not bear the sounds of the whip and the screams of enslaved persons.[22]

Other slave-owning women were less squeamish about the corporal punishment inflicted upon enslaved persons. They also inflicted the punishment themselves. In some cases, the punishment was an immediate and furious response to an error in domestic tasks. When enslaved persons did not set their dining table properly or accidentally pricked them or their children with a needle while tailoring their dresses, slave-owning women struck them with a stick, paddle, or another blunt instrument within arm's reach. Charles Peyton Lucas, a formerly enslaved Black man, was beaten over the head with "a dairy key about as big as a child's fist" by his enslaver, the white wife of a Baptist pastor in Leesburg, Virginia.[23] In 1858, Lucilla McCorkle, the white wife of a Presbyterian pastor in Alabama, wrote in her diary about punishing an enslaved person before going to church on a Sunday morning: "O what a precious quiet sabbath! but it dawned rather unpropitiously. The severest whipping I ever gave my darling G_____ I gave this morning before breakfast." McCorkle explained that she was angry because the enslaved person was tardy, and she wondered several hours later whether the punishment was too harsh. But McCorkle justified her actions by remembering that she felt the whipping was "necessary and right" at the time.[24]

The impulsive nature of McCorkle's actions reflects a common phenomenon in slave-owning families. In Drew's compilation of narratives from formerly enslaved persons, one woman shared with Drew that an inch-long scar on her head was the result of a stab wound from her enslaver when he erupted in fury upon discovering she had forgotten to place his fork at the table before a meal.[25] These capricious punishments illumine the absence of trust and the devaluing of labor in plantation households and economies. Philemon Bliss, a white Presbyterian lawyer in Ohio with experience living on plantations in Florida, lamented that enslaved persons had "no other inducement to work but the lash."[26] He observed that all human beings required motivation, such as monetary compensation, to labor. Enslavers like McCorkle meted out severe penalties for minor mistakes because the system of Black enslavement fostered duplicity, mischief, secrecy, and subtlety. In an oppressive system in which enslaved persons were deprived of basic human rights and motivation to work, some resisted in covert and shrewd ways, such as intentionally adopting a slow pace or performing a task poorly. Olmsted observed this resistance and called it "sogering," explaining the guile involved on the part of enslaved persons: "Not that they often directly refuse to obey an order, but when they are directed to do anything for which they have a disclination, they undertake it in such a way that the desired result is sure not to be accomplished."[27] The travel writer argued that sogering was an unavoidable consequence of the unjust system of Black enslavement. Enslavers were more keenly aware of sogering than Olmsted, since they experienced it daily, and it enraged them. They interpreted slight slipups, like a missing fork on a dining room table or a tardy morning arrival, as blatantly disrespectful. McCorkle, like so many other enslavers, responded with physical violence. Some enslavers believed corporal punishment could eradicate, or at least reduce, sogering. Others simply assaulted enslaved persons as a means of release, to make them feel better in the moment, with no other disciplinary purposes in mind.

"Family Ties Are Often Disregarded in This Traffic":
The Tyranny of Black Enslavement and the Second Middle Passage

Benjamin Drew highlighted a method of cruel punishment that he learned about in his interviews with formerly enslaved persons, which was referred to as being staked down, or the punishment of four stakes. While lying face down with each hand and foot tied to a stake and arms and legs spread wide, an enslaved person received a whipping. Drew found especially revolting the practice of digging a deep hole to provide the extra space required for a pregnant woman before she was staked down. He explained that the rationale was "to avoid the pecuniary loss which sometimes ensued" when pregnant women miscarried after the punishment.[28] Stowe cited a legal case in North Carolina from 1829 in which a white man, John Mann, shot and wounded an enslaved woman, Lydia, when she tried to escape a flogging. Mann had leased Lydia from her owner, Elizabeth Jones, for a specific amount of time and labor, which was a common practice within the Black enslavement system. Though Mann was initially found guilty, Stowe assailed the legal reasoning because Mann was found to have been in violation of his leasing rights to Lydia rather than excessive physical violence. The Supreme Court of North Carolina overturned Mann's guilty verdict "on the ground that the hirer has for the time being all the rights of the master." In the ruling, Associate Justice Thomas Ruffin delineated the necessity of protecting the rights of enslavers: "The power of the master must be absolute, to render the submission of the slave perfect."[29] Just as Drew identified the moral bankruptcy of a system in which the staking down of pregnant women was acceptable, Stowe argued that a system that required this level of repression to operate was inhumane and anti-Christian.

Ruffin somewhat acknowledged Stowe's argument. In the abstract, Ruffin conceded that any rational person would repudiate the notion of one human wielding absolute power over another human. But Ruffin, a wealthy enslaver who physically abused enslaved persons himself, maintained that the practice of Black enslavement required such extreme measures to function properly. In 1785, Thomas Jefferson made a similar observation about the tyranny of Black enslavement. Like Ruffin, Jefferson, as a wealthy enslaver, wrestled with the obvious moral contradictions when writing, "The whole commerce between master and slave is a perpetual exercise of the most boisterous passions, the most unremitting despotism on the one part, and degrading submissions on the other."[30] Jefferson was also troubled about the pernicious influences of Black enslavement upon white children in slave-owning families, because the very nature of children was to learn from and imitate their parents. Charles Stewart Renshaw, a white Congregationalist pastor in Quincy, Illinois, confirmed the veracity of Jefferson's concerns about the imitative dangers of slavery. During a visit to Kentucky, Renshaw saw several white teenage boys, ranging from twelve to fifteen years of age, cracking whips, and two enslaved boys crying. When Renshaw asked his companion, a member of a local Presbyterian congregation, about the awful scene, he was told, "Those boys have been whipping the niggers; that is the way we bring slaves into subjection in Kentucky—we let the children beat them."[31] In Stephanie E. Jones-Rogers's work on white slave-owning women, the historian documents the demands from enslavers when addressing their children. Enslaved persons were required to always refer to the white children as "master" or "mistress" and were punished when they did not. On some occasions, the white children doled out the punishments themselves.[32] Before Charles C. Jones became a slave-owning pastor in Georgia, he had doubts about the morality of Black enslavement while residing in the northern states. As a student at Andover Theological Seminary in Massachusetts, he wrote a letter to his fiancée expressing his view that slavery was a "violation of all the laws of God and man at once," "a complete annihilation of justice," and "an inhuman abuse of power."[33] Yet Jones, like Jefferson and Ruffin, found a way to reconcile what he himself believed was irreconcilable.

Formerly enslaved persons in Canada fled for their freedom because they could no longer stand the tyranny of slavery in the United States. The drudgery of uncompensated labor, with the accompanying regularity and severity of corporal punishment, was reason enough to escape. But many of the formerly enslaved persons in Drew's compilation explained that their greatest motivation to escape was the domestic slave trade from the upper southern states to the lower southern states. William Johnson was enslaved on a Virginia farm with a "quick-tempered overseer" and a slave-owning white man who did not provide sufficient rations. But Johnson explained, "The fear of being sold South had more influence inducing me to leave than any other thing. Master used to say, that if we didn't suit him, he would put us in his pocket quick—meaning he would sell us."[34] George Johnson was also enslaved in Virginia and recounted that the enslaved persons on his farm were "in more danger of being sold than of being whipped" and therefore they were "always afraid of being sold South."[35] The fears of William Johnson and George Johnson simultaneously reveal the importance of the domestic slave trade in Black enslavement and the trauma it produced within enslaved persons and families.

In 1787, the delegates of the Constitutional Convention in Philadelphia made several decisions regarding slavery. After much debate, they agreed to count three-fifths of a state's enslaved population in apportioning representation, require that "fugitive slaves" who cross state lines be surrendered to their enslavers, and ban the international slave trade in twenty years.[36] Paul J. Polgar traces the evolution of public opinion regarding the transatlantic slave trade in the United States and finds "in the late eighteenth century a broad condemnation of the international slave trade as an inhumane relic of the barbaric past."[37] By 1790, several states had enacted their own legislative measures against the transatlantic slave trade. But the lower southern states, such as South Carolina, railed against the agreement to end participation in the international slave trade by 1807 and considered the ban an attack on their sovereignty to govern as a state. In 1789, South Carolina legislator William Loughton Smith expressed how many politicians in the lower southern states felt especially betrayed by Virginia because it was also a slaveholding state. Smith called Virginia "our greatest enemy" because politicians from the commonwealth voiced moral criticism of the international slave trade and supported the ban.[38] But the white elite in Virginia did not have the same misgivings about the domestic slave trade. One effect of the ban on the international slave trade, which began on January 1, 1808, was the growth and expansion of the domestic slave trade. Between 1790 and 1860, approximately one million enslaved men, women, and children were sold and transported from the upper southern states to the lower southern states. From 1830 to 1860, approximately 300,000 enslaved persons were sold and transported from Virginia alone.[39] The domestic slave trade emerged as a lucrative economy with its own multilayered network of white investors, merchants, planters, sailors, and traders. And enslaved Black persons lay at the center of this web as the human merchandise.

In 1836, Ethan Allen Andrews, a white lexicographer, documented the domestic slave trade in his travels to some of its major sites, including the ports in Baltimore and Alexandria where many enslaved persons departed on ships for plantations in Arkansas, Louisiana, Mississippi, and Texas. A white Presbyterian pastor in Baltimore explained to Andrews how the domestic slave trade operated in a "circuitous manner" in which enslavers from the upper southern states sold their "older and more valuable" enslaved persons (likely between the ages of fifteen and thirty) and purchased younger enslaved children at a lower price. "In this way," Andrews learned, "such slaves especially as happen to be disliked by their masters, are sent out of the state, and their places supplied by younger ones, who, when they have attained to their full strength, will perhaps follow in the same path."[40] The pastor added that "family ties are often disregarded in this traffic."[41] The separation of enslaved families was common because the demand in the southwestern states was for field laborers. Infants and children were considered economically inefficient because they distracted enslaved mothers from their work and extracted short-term profits from white planters because of the costs to care for enslaved children. In one sale, an enslaver in Louisiana purchased a group of enslaved persons from a trader. Upon discovering a mother with an infant in the group, the enslaver immediately offered to return the infant to the trader at no cost. The cruel act of separating the mother and newborn child did not trouble him.[42]

Throughout his travels, Andrews also found the domestic slave trade was often talked about in hushed tones. It was a legitimate business, in the sense that the transactions were accurately recorded in ledgers and recognized by the law, and many white persons financially benefited from the domestic slave trade. Enslavers from the upper southern states invested in enslaved children to eventually sell at a profit. Planters from the lower southern states replenished their enslaved labor force every several years with a supply of new laborers from the upper southern states. Slave traders and shipping companies accrued revenue for their transporting services. But some white persons admitted to moral qualms about the painful experiences of enslaved persons when they were sold and transported. The domestic slave trade was called the "Second Middle Passage" because of the indignities it shared with the transatlantic slave trade. Enslaved persons were ripped from their families against their will, bound in ropes and chains, stripped naked during invasive examinations, and forced to travel in coffles to a foreign place where the most arduous agricultural labor awaited them. Enslaved persons in the upper southern states sometimes referred to slave traders as "soul drivers" because of the terrors of the Second Middle Passage. Harriet Tubman was confident in her assessment that slavery was "the next thing to hell" in no small part because two of her sisters were "carried away" in the domestic slave trade.[43]

In 1805, Charles Ball, an enslaved man in his mid-twenties, fell victim to the domestic slave trade in Maryland. His wife and child were enslaved persons belonging to another enslaver. Ball was physically strong, had many skills, and performed additional labor on Sundays for his own wages. Some enslavers permitted this practice, in which enslaved persons hired themselves out for temporary work so long as it did not interfere with their regular responsibilities and schedules. Ball hoped to make enough money to purchase his freedom from his enslaver and his family's freedom from their enslaver. But Ball's enslaver sold him to a slave trader, and Ball was ordered to cross his hands behind his back, where they were bound with rope. Ball asked if he could see his wife and child before departing, but the slave trader told him he would be able to find a new wife in Georgia. The only moment Ball was not bound was when the slave trader cut the rope around his hands to place him in a coffle with an iron collar around his neck and manacles around his hands and feet.

For approximately five weeks, Ball was forced to walk in step alongside fifty-one other enslaved persons behind a slave trader on horseback. The clothing on the enslaved persons tore and disintegrated, leaving some with barely any attire at all, as their coffle marched through the countryside and cities in Maryland, Virginia, North Carolina, and South Carolina. The journey was physically hard and psychologically humiliating. During the days, the sound of clinking chains rattled in Ball's ears and his eyes sometimes met the eyes of sad, curious, mean, and indifferent onlookers. In the night, Ball had nightmares about his weeping wife and child. In the middle of one nightmare, Ball remembered, "I awoke in agony and cursed my existence. I could not pray, for the measure of my woes seemed to be full, and I felt as if there was no mercy in heaven, nor compassion on earth, for a man who was born a slave."[44] Before arriving at the final destination of their Second Middle Passage, two pregnant enslaved women in their coffle were sold in South Carolina to a white bystander looking for "breeding-wenches" to increase the number of enslaved persons in his ownership.[45] The slave trader and bystander haggled over pricing, with the slave trader eventually agreeing to sell the two pregnant women at a slightly lower price because he thought they were walking too slowly and decelerating the pace of the coffle.

In his account of the domestic slave trade, Andrews was careful to note that the aim of his work was not to provide support for abolitionism. Rather, he sought to detail the features of the domestic slave trade to understand it more fully. Yet Andrews abandoned his caution on comparisons between the international slave trade and the domestic slave trade that suggested the former was entirely distinct from the latter. Andrews could not tolerate the dishonesty of white Americans critical of the barbaric evils of the transatlantic slave trade yet silent about the comparable atrocities that Ball and many other enslaved persons were suffering from the Second Middle Passage. Andrews identified the moral inconsistency of such thinking when he asked, "Why should it be piracy to purchase a cargo of slaves in Congo and offer them for sale in Charleston, while it is lawful to procure them in Alexandria or Washington and transport them to the same market?"[46]

Slave market of America (American Anti-Slavery Society, 1836)

Yet white Presbyterians like Adger evinced the very inconsistency that Andrews denounced as morally craven and intellectually meritless when some state legislators in South Carolina sought to reopen the transatlantic slave trade. One white politician, Robert Barnwell Rhett, told the British consul in Charleston that the decision to prohibit the international slave trade was a mistake because it was an admission that "the Institution of Slavery was an evil and a wrong."[47] Charles A. L. Lamar, a white merchant from Savannah, Georgia, with a financial interest in the outcome of the South Carolina debates on reopening the international slave trade, asked, "Did not the negroes all come originally from the Coast of Africa? What is the difference between going to Africa and Virginia for negroes?"[48] Adger disapproved of the callous rhetoric that Rhett, Lamar, and other white southern advocates employed in their efforts to reopen the international slave trade. He maintained that Black enslavement was a scripturally sanctioned institution but that it was unseemly to blithely ignore or minimize the terrors of the Middle Passage in the pursuit of economic gain. In 1858, Adger declared, "In the name of the Southern people, especially of the religious class at the South, and still more especially of Southern Presbyterians, we raise our voice of protest against the re-opening amongst us of the African slave trade, whether openly or in disguise."[49] But the proud spokesman of white southern Presbyterianism had little to say on behalf of his people concerning the evils of the domestic slave trade. Adger disapproved when white politicians dismissed the tragic separation of African families (referred to in one report as "involuntary separations") as a "supposed," rather than actual, evil. Yet the most he offered about the harsh realities of family separation within the day-to-day operations of Black enslavement domestically was that white slave-owning Christians did not treat it lightly: "Those 'involuntary separations,' when they occur amongst our slaves here, our community does not regard with anything like indifference."[50]

"The Contempt We Have Been Taught to Entertain for the Blacks": The Interconnected Power Structures of Slavery and Race

Adger understood that Black enslavement required two interconnected power structures to operate. The first structure entailed the near-absolute authority of enslavers over enslaved persons. Adger framed the power of enslavers with the topology of rights and duties. Enslavers had rights, including the right to sell their enslaved persons, as well as duties, to ensure they used their authority, which Adger argued was God-given, responsibly. The second structure was a racial hierarchy in which white persons were dominant over Black persons. Because the white race was superior to the Black race, the principle of equal rights between white and Black persons was "neither a possible nor a desirable form of the social state" and therefore Black enslavement was the "best form of society possible." Slavery was not only a "blessing both to master and slave," but it also provided the foundation for a highly regulated racial order in a white-dominant society that Adger believed was good for both white and Black persons.[51]

It was not surprising that relationships between enslavers and enslaved persons were antagonistic. These interpersonal tensions were inherent to any power structure pitting the oppressed against their oppressors across world history such that each party often hated the other. But the interconnected power structures of slavery and race added another layer of conflict between all white persons and all Black persons. In his travels throughout the United States in 1831 and 1832, the French political theorist Alexis de Tocqueville witnessed the enmity and fierce prejudice most white persons held against Black persons. John H. B. Latrobe, a white lawyer and president of the American Colonization Society, an organization that promoted the migration of free Black Americans to Liberia, told Tocqueville that it was not possible for the United States to become a racially integrated nation because "the black and white population are in a state of war."[52] The bitter racial prejudice of white persons against free Black persons in the northern states convinced Tocqueville that slavery in the United States had created a racial problem that even abolition would not solve. He believed that Black and white Americans were "fastened to each other without intermingling" in a precarious societal state in which "the two races" were "unable to separate entirely or combine."[53] Northern states passed legislation to either immediately or gradually abolish Black enslavement in the late eighteenth century, such as Pennsylvania's act of gradual emancipation in 1780, but Tocqueville encountered the ferocity and ubiquity of anti-Black racism among white persons in northern cities like Philadelphia in 1831 and 1832.

In 1779, Alexander Hamilton acknowledged the intensity of anti-Black prejudice among white persons during the American Revolution. In a letter to John Jay, president of the Continental Congress, Hamilton assessed the challenges of deploying military battalions with Black soldiers in South Carolina. "The contempt we have been taught to entertain for the blacks, makes us fancy many things that are founded neither in reason nor experience," Hamilton observed, "and an unwillingness to part with property of so valuable a kind will furnish a thousand arguments to show the impracticability or pernicious tendency of a scheme which requires such a sacrifice."[54] Hamilton elucidated how the interconnected power structures of slavery and race informed and fortified one another and anticipated the emergence of "a thousand arguments" defending Black enslavement with anti-Black racist reasoning. White slave-owning Christians like Adger illustrated Hamilton's point in their justifications for slavery with racial arguments regarding all Black persons as incapable of liberty because they belonged to an inferior and weaker race.

In the southern states, the education of white children reflected the interconnected power structures of slavery and race. Enforcing the requirement that enslaved persons refer to white children by honorific titles, such as "master" and "mistress," served more than one purpose. It reminded enslaved persons of their subservient positions to their enslavers and endeavored to reinforce a racial order of white superiority and Black inferiority.[55] Though many enslaved persons acquiesced to the practice, they refused to believe that their darker skin color meant they were inherently inferior to all white persons. But the practice had more success in teaching white children at a young age about the authority they wielded as enslavers over their human property and the racial superiority they possessed over all Black persons. Olmsted highlighted an encounter between a young white girl and an elderly enslaved man that demonstrates how thoroughly many white children learned these lessons: "I have seen a girl, twelve years old . . . stop the old man on the public road, demand to know where he was going, and by what authority, order him to face about and return to his plantation, and enforce her command with turbulent anger." When the elderly enslaved man hesitated, the young white girl threatened to "have him well whipped if he did not instantly obey." The elderly enslaved man relented and turned around. Olmsted was astonished at the young white girl's sudden and easy transformation from a "lovely child" to a dominant authoritarian exerting the power of her whiteness.[56]

The young white girl from Olmsted's southern travels in the 1850s displayed what George Bourne warned about slavery twenty years prior. The white abolitionist pastor made a direct link between Black enslavement and anti-Black racism in his theological investigation of "the natural effects of slavery on the slaveholders." Bourne maintained that the "primary and most permanent notion which an infant in a slaveholder's family imbibes" was a positional authority and racial superiority over enslaved persons, with the gravest sins deriving from the latter. He agreed with Jefferson that white children in slave-owning families learned to be despots and tyrants at a young age, but Bourne added that they also received a racist education training them to view Black persons as intrinsically inferior human beings and "no more than two-legged beasts." One of the inevitable pedagogical outcomes was the inculcation of a "marble-hearted insensibility" within white children as they absorbed racist ideologies and unjustly treated all Black persons as degraded creatures rather than as fellow human beings equally made in the image of God.[57]

William C. Gildersleeve, a white ruling elder in a Presbyterian congregation in Wilkes-Barre, Pennsylvania, confessed that he had become inured to the racist dehumanization of Black persons as a child in Georgia. Gildersleeve grew numb to the cruel punishments that Black persons endured. As one enslaved man was tied by his hands to a mulberry tree and struck with one hundred lashes on his naked body, Gildersleeve remembered watching the torture scene with no remorse and "feeling the least compassion" for the Black victim. "So hardening is the influence of slavery," Gildersleeve concluded, "that it very much destroys feeling for the slave."[58] John M. Nelson, a white lawyer in Ohio, also criticized how his rearing in a slave-owning family in Virginia had hardened his heart and corrupted his mind. Nelson's father was a ruling elder in a Presbyterian congregation in Augusta County with a reputation as a "good master" who provided sufficient food and clothing to his enslaved persons. Yet from his early childhood Nelson witnessed his father strip, tie up, and severely whip enslaved persons. Nelson initially begged his father to stop with pleading screams and weeping tears. But as he grew older, the young boy's natural feelings of horror and sympathy evolved into a blunt dullness and then a bestial fury as he inflicted the punishments alongside his father by the age of fourteen. Nelson deeply regretted his sins and deplored the "hardening nature" of an upbringing that taught him to mistreat Black persons "without remorse" and view them as subhuman on account of their race.[59] Within the interconnected power structures of slavery and race, some Black persons despised not only their enslavers but also all white persons. John Little, a formerly enslaved Black man from North Carolina, was sold at a public auction and separated from his mother and siblings. Because the distance between his previous and new enslavers was ten miles, Little went to visit his family one Sunday against his new enslaver's wishes. Though Little returned on time, he was punished with a whip and a cane. Afterward, salt was poured into Little's wounds, which was a common practice because it added more stinging pain to the punishment and helped the wounds heal faster to ensure an enslaved person could return to work. Little also had iron rings fastened around his ankles for several days to limit his physical movement and break his psychological spirit. Some enslaved persons were forced to wear an iron collar around the neck with protruding spikes or hooks, which was a tool intended to restrict activity and publicly humiliate. Recalling his life in slavery, Little explained, "The abuse a man receives at the South is enough to drive everything good from the mind. I sometimes felt such a spirit of vengeance, that I seriously meditated setting the house on fire at night, and killing all as they came out." He also observed that slavery "makes the feeling of dislike to color, leading the white to abuse a 'nigger' because he is a 'nigger,' and the black to hate the white because he abuses him." Little concluded that slavery was a curse for how it spawned a poisonous rancor between white and Black persons within and beyond the oppressive relations of enslaver and enslaved.[60]

In addition to a hatred of white people, many Black persons were deeply suspicious and fearful of them. Mary Younger, a formerly enslaved Black woman, was startled when some white persons on her journey to freedom through the northern states to Canada treated her kindly and did not call her a wench or other derisive terms for Black women. Younger's painful experiences under what she called the "barbarity of slavery" led her to believe that "all white people were alike" and possessed "no sympathy for colored people."[61] The recollections of two other formerly enslaved persons illustrate the absence of trust within Black persons in their encounters with white persons. William Grose remembered from his new residence in Canada: "I feel now like a man, while before I felt more as though I were but a brute. When in the United States, if a white man spoke to me, I would feel frightened, whether I were in the right or wrong."[62] William Wells Brown recalled his trepidation in the home of a white Quaker couple in Ohio who aided him in his escape to freedom: "I was not, however, prepared to receive their hospitalities. The only fault I found with them was their being too kind. I had never had a white man to treat me as an equal, and the idea of a white lady waiting on me at the table was still worse!"[63]

In his first days free from Black enslavement, Brown could not comprehend the idea of eating at the same table with white persons.

Alongside his discovery of humanity in white persons, Brown also recovered his own dignity in naming himself. Brown had lost his name, William, when his enslaver demanded he change it upon the arrival of a white nephew with the same name. Brown explained, "This, at the time, I thought to be one of the most cruel acts that could be committed upon my rights; and I received several very severe whippings for telling people that my name was William, after orders were given to change it."[64] Before departing the home of the abolitionists in Ohio, he affixed the name of his host, Wells Brown, "his first white friend," after his first name of William so that he would possess a surname, which many enslaved persons did not have.[65] Enslavers sometimes gave their enslaved persons surnames, but the intentional omission of surnames was another means to reinforce the interconnected power structures of slavery and race. Surnames were for free white persons, not enslaved Black persons. In court cases like *State v. Mann* in North Carolina, enslaved persons were differentiated by the absence of surnames. Elizabeth Jones, a white enslaver, sued John Mann, a white man who had leased the services of one of Jones's enslaved persons, Lydia, who did not have a surname. Eli Johnson, a formerly enslaved Black man, understood the significance of a surname: "In slavery, we are goods and chattels, and have no surname: but slaves generally take their master's name."[66] Some enslaved persons defied the intentions of their enslavers and resisted the larger power structures of slavery and race in giving themselves a surname as an assertion of their dignity and humanity. One historian finds that enslaved persons in the lower coastal plain and sea islands of South Carolina and Georgia all used surnames among themselves. A few took the surnames of their enslavers, but most chose surnames of other enslavers they knew.[67]

Enslaved parents also took seriously the naming of their children. William Wells Brown treasured his first name because it was given to him by his mother and not his enslaver. Enslaved children received their names either from their parents or their enslavers. In some cases, their parents and their enslavers named the children together in a complex process rife with coercion, domination, affection, and paternalism. One enslaver gave an enslaved child the same name as one of his own white children in an act meant to symbolize his desire to be a benevolent patriarch over a model plantation household comprising both the white and Black members of his "family." One historian observes that enslaved persons rarely used diminutives, such as Bessie instead of Elizabeth or Willie instead of William, for their first names and argues their rationale for the consistent use of full proper names was linked to their hatred of the white practice of referring to Black adults as "girl," "boy," or with diminutive names.[68] If enslavers were addressed as "Elizabeth" or "William," enslaved persons believed there should be no difference in their naming designations.

Some enslaved persons chose African names for their children or in renaming themselves as a means of retaining their African cultural heritage and resisting the white-dominant culture. Enslaved persons adopted an African day-naming practice in which children were named after the day they were born. For example, Quaco was a name given to men born on Wednesday, and Phiba or Phibbi was a name given to women born on Friday.[69] In Leslie M. Harris's recounting of free and enslaved Black Americans in New York City, the historian examines how the continued use of African names was a "double-edged sword" for Black persons. Black persons with African names such as Ambo, Cajoe, Mingo, and Zibia were connected to their African cultural heritage in a meaningful way, but they also experienced ridicule from white persons. Many white persons did not support African naming practices. Some, including abolitionists, interpreted the practice as one part of a larger problem—the failure of persons of African descent to assimilate to white culture in the United States. Others were more blatantly xenophobic and racist in deriding African names as strange, foreign, silly, and lowly. Harris explains how some African names, such as Sambo and Quaco, "evolved in the European consciousness and pronunciation as derogatory." White persons transformed the Hausa name Sambo into a "derogatory term for a black man, indicating laziness or stupidity."[70] Quaco was mispronounced and then mocked as Quack, which was thought to be an absurd proper name in a white-dominant culture.

The steady decline in African names among the free and enslaved Black populations from the beginning of the nineteenth century illustrates another tragedy of Black enslavement: the devaluing of African culture in both white and Black communities. In Adger's protest against the reopening of the transatlantic slave trade, one of his arguments was that two centuries of Black enslavement in the United States had "made the negro, in respect to his social feelings, a very far superior being to what the negro is in Africa."[71] Adger captured the racial and cultural hierarchies of many white persons in 1858 with his placement of white Americans at the top, Black Americans in the middle (though considerably lower than white Americans), and Black Africans at the bottom. The decline in African names was in part due to the closing of the transatlantic slave trade in 1808 and the subsequent decrease in first-generation Africans in the United States, but it also reveals how some Black Americans had internalized the devaluation of African culture themselves. Many formerly enslaved Black Americans migrating to West Africa viewed their Anglo-Saxon names as a marker of their cultural superiority over Black Africans.[72] The African name *Quaco* first evolved into *Quack* and then *Jack*.[73] At one level, this metamorphosis represents the resiliency of African culture in the United States when tracing the long history of the name *Jack*. But at another level, the change also illumines the diminution of African culture in the age of Black enslavement with the disappearance of its original root form. After Frederick Douglass escaped to freedom, a free Black family in New Bedford, Massachusetts, encouraged him to choose a new surname. Douglass gave his host, Nathan Johnson, the privilege of selecting it. Johnson was reading Walter Scott's *Lady of the Lake*, a narrative poem depicting an epic struggle from Scotland between King James V and a Highlander clan named Douglas in the sixteenth century, and suggested the surname of Douglas. Douglass agreed and added a second "s" for distinction.[74] Johnson and Douglass turned to European, not African, history for inspiration when looking for a new surname.

Seventeen years later, in 1855, Douglass wrote that Nathan Johnson had left a more inspiring legacy than Scott's Highlander clan.[75] Douglass admired Johnson's courage and generosity in risking his own life to aid "fugitive" enslaved persons in a northern state where Black Americans were free but not equal. Douglass experienced rampant anti-Black discrimination in Massachusetts, such as racially segregated seating on buses and trains, and even in churches. Although he found great hope in the Bible for the emancipation of enslaved persons and the eradication of anti-Black racism, Douglass did not see the proclamations of the gospel in the practices of many white Christians in the northern states. A few, such as John A. Collins, an abolitionist working with the Massachusetts Anti-Slavery Society, shared his convictions. In 1841, Collins loudly protested when a train conductor tried to eject Douglass from the seat next to him in a whites-only section.[76] But most were not interested in abolishing Black enslavement in the southern states or constructing a more racially just society in the northern states, which led Douglass to conclude that "the religion of the south" and "the religion of the north" were joined together "by communion and fellowship."[77]

Douglass's observation about the resolve and unity of white Christians in defending Black enslavement and perpetuating anti-Black racism was perhaps most evident among white Presbyterians in the United States. In a letter to Harriet Beecher Stowe, the Black Presbyterian pastor James W. C. Pennington wrote that slavery was "an awful system" because "it takes man as God made him; it demolishes him, and then mis-creates him, or perhaps I should say mal-creates him!"[78] Although Pennington was responding to Stowe's question about the accuracy of her portrayal of enslaved persons in *Uncle Tom's Cabin*, his reply also underscored the tyranny and tragedy that resulted from the interconnected power structures of slavery and race. He also answered Adger's question about whether there was anything very bad about white Presbyterian participation in Black enslavement. Pennington rightly defined slavery as a perversion of God's creating, redeeming, and sustaining order. Therefore, everything about slavery—the brokenness of Black bodies, the separation of Black families, the hardening of white hearts, and the devaluing of African culture—was very bad. Stowe also criticized the absence of Christian instruction to enslaved persons as grounds for abolition. Adger and other white Presbyterians partly agreed with Stowe. They too identified the lack of Christian instruction to enslaved persons as a problem, but their solution was not Black emancipation. Instead, they produced proslavery doctrines and presented these abominable teachings to enslaved persons and enslavers in the southern states as well as Black and white persons in the northern states. In doing so, white Presbyterians partook in a tragedy of their own making—the moral degradation and spiritual corruption of their Presbyterian Church.

PART II

The Indictment

4

"Is Jesus Christ in Favor of American Slavery?"

In 1831, the students and faculty at Western Reserve College in Ohio began debating abolition, colonization, and slavery. Charles Backus Storrs, the school's president and theology professor, had previously supported the colonization movement and was one of the founders of a local chapter of the American Colonization Society (ACS) in Ravenna, a city close to the college. White Christians affiliated with the ACS abhorred Black enslavement but also preferred the migration of free Black Americans to Liberia over the immediate emancipation and full integration of enslaved persons in the United States. But Storrs changed his mind and now supported abolitionism. Two other white faculty members, Beriah Green, a biblical studies professor and Presbyterian minister, and Elizur Wright Jr., a mathematics professor, endorsed immediate emancipation and denounced the colonization movement as racially discriminatory against Black Americans. In March 1832, approximately twenty students rallied together to advocate for immediate emancipation and declare their opposition to the majority of the student body favoring colonization. Green and Wright met privately with this small group of abolitionist students and other students wavering between immediate emancipation and colonization. The trustees of the college, as well as most local white Christians, opposed immediate emancipation and Black citizenship in a state that had passed several laws, known as Black Codes, to restrict the rights of free Black persons to establish residency, work, own firearms and property, and testify

79

against white persons. An insurrection in August 1831, in which an enslaved Black preacher, Nat Turner, led a group of enslaved persons in Virginia to revolt against their enslavers in one of the deadliest uprisings in U.S. history, further persuaded white persons in Ohio to support colonization instead of emancipation and integration.[1]

Green gave his students an assignment that would take the form of classroom debates on "the points which separate the patrons of the American Colonization Society from the advocates of immediate emancipation." Soon after the debates, Green preached four sermons himself at the college chapel in November and December 1832 on the same topic. Green denounced the "loathsome crime of slave-holding" as contrary to the gospel of Jesus Christ and colonization as sinful disobedience to the divine promise of racial equality. Green observed that abolitionists in the United States were like the Hebrew prophet Jeremiah, despised and rejected by his contemporaries for proclaiming an uncompromising message about God's justice. But Green encouraged the abolitionists at the college to continue speaking and mobilizing with hope and courage because their message, like the words of Jeremiah, was "clothed with divine authority."[2] Green's sermons created a tumult on campus and in the local community, but they also drew the attention of abolitionist leaders in the eastern states, such as William Lloyd Garrison, Gerrit Smith, and Arthur Tappan. Green resigned from Western Reserve College in 1833 to be the president of the Oneida Institute, a Presbyterian institution of higher learning that was the one of the nation's first racially integrated schools and that enrolled more Black students than any other U.S. college in the 1830s and early 1840s. Wright left the college shortly after Green to work with Tappan in New York City. Both Green and Wright were also involved in the American Anti-Slavery Society (AASS), an interracial organization and one of the most prominent advocacy groups for Black liberation.

In 1839, Green published a book with the AASS delineating how the "chattel principle" of Black enslavement contradicted the teachings in the New Testament and asked, "Is Jesus Christ in favor of American slavery?"[3] Green looked specifically at the arguments of white Presbyterians defending Black enslavement and accused them of committing the grave sin of blasphemy for presenting their proslavery and anti-Black racist doctrines as if they came straight from the mouth of Jesus Christ. Every American justifying slavery was wrong, but it was especially heinous for white Presbyterians, and other white Christians, to claim that Jesus Christ smiled upon American slavery.

In 1833, a committee of six Presbyterian pastors and four ruling elders from the Synod of South Carolina and Georgia delivered a report on the "religious instruction of the colored population" in the southern states. Two of the pastors on the committee, Moses Waddel and Charles C. Jones, were influential educators in addition to their leadership within their congregations. Waddel was president of the University of Georgia from 1819 to 1829, and Jones taught at Columbia Theological Seminary from 1836 to 1838 and 1848 to 1850. The committee perpetrated the sin that Green identified in their distortion of Christianity to defend their participation in Black enslavement. They advised enslavers to disregard abolitionists like Green because the witness of the New Testament, in the words of Jesus Christ and the apostles, sanctioned slavery. But the committee's primary focus entailed the glaring absence of Christian instruction to enslaved persons. They believed that God was not entirely pleased with the white members of their synod because of their inattention to the spirituality of the enslaved persons they owned as their human property. They found the New Testament also made clear that Christians had a duty to evangelize to all humans. In their context as slave-owning Christians, the task before them was to "impart the Gospel, with its accompanying blessings, in the first place, to such of our fellow creatures as are most dependent upon us for it;—to such as are most needy and accessible." Although evangelizing to enslaved persons was an important responsibility, these white Presbyterians acknowledged that they, and all slave-owning Christians, had "almost entirely neglected" this call from Jesus Christ. Because enslaved persons were "destitute of the privileges of the Gospel, and ever will be, under the present state of things," the committee advocated for increased efforts toward the evangelization of enslaved persons.[4]

However, the corrupted gospel that white Presbyterians tried to teach to enslaved persons, with its proslavery and anti-Black racist doctrines, had destructive consequences for both Black and white persons. White slave-owning Presbyterians were therefore guilty of committing two spiritual crimes. The first crime was one they freely admitted: they endeavored to withhold or restrict the access of enslaved Black persons to the means of God's grace, such as Christian worship and scriptural instruction. But the second crime may have been worse: they propagated a malicious re-formation of Christianity that sought above all else to reinforce their domination over enslaved Black persons.

"No Other God but Money":
White Resistance to Evangelization among Enslaved Black Persons

In 1842, Jones returned to the topic of white evangelization among enslaved persons and added a historical account beginning with the first British settlement of Jamestown in 1607 to the signing of the Declaration of Independence in 1776. Jones could not find a precise record with the overall Black population prior to the first U.S. census in 1790, but he traced various figures from colonial and state records to estimate that the Black population in 1776 was approximately 500,000 and comprised mostly enslaved persons. In 1790, there were approximately 60,000 free Black persons and 700,000 enslaved Black persons out of a total of approximately 3,900,000 persons. Jones also studied reports from the Society for the Propagation of the Gospel in Foreign Parts (SPG), a missionary organization of the Church of England founded in 1701. He summarized SPG efforts to evangelize to enslaved persons in the North American colonies as woefully insufficient, using frank assessments from SPG publications. One SPG account from 1730 admitted that the organization was sending too few missionaries and that the missionaries in the colonies were met with fierce opposition from planters. SPG missionaries baptized hundreds of enslaved persons, welcoming them into the Anglican communion, but their organization conceded "the instruction of a few hundreds in several years" paled in comparison to the "many thousands uninstructed, unconverted; living, dying, utter pagans" and identified the "greatest obstruction" to their ministry among enslaved persons as coming from enslavers.[5] Enslavers were not interested in the spirituality of their enslaved persons and actively resisted the evangelizing endeavors of SPG missionaries and other white clergy.

One initial reason for the resistance among enslavers was the possibility that enslaved persons could appeal to their Christian baptism as grounds for legal emancipation. In England, several enslaved persons made this claim in various courts. But the North American colonies passed laws, beginning with Maryland in 1664 and Virginia in 1667, that made clear that a profession of Christianity was not a means for emancipation. The preamble to the act in Virginia explained that the law was constructed to quell existing doubt among enslavers about the ramifications of baptism and encourage them to "more carefully endeavour the propagation of Christianity by permitting children, though slaves, or those of greater growth if capable to be admitted to that sacrament."[6] In 1727, the Anglican bishop of London, differentiating between the civil and the religious conditions of enslaved persons, further clarified in a letter "to the masters and mistresses of families in the English plantations abroad" that the baptism of enslaved persons did not result in their freedom. Changes in an enslaved person's religious condition were completely unrelated to that same person's civil condition. Enslavers did not have to fret, because the baptism of enslaved persons did not "make the least Alteration in Civil Property" or "in any of the Duties which belong to Civil Relations." The bishop declared that "the freedom which Christianity gives" was completely religious in nature—liberation "from the Bondage of Sin and Satan"— and had no effect whatsoever on an enslaved person's civil status.[7]

Yet several accounts from SPG missionaries and Anglican clergy in North America and the Caribbean in the seventeenth and eighteenth centuries reveal that the question about baptism and emancipation was hardly the reason for the lack of white evangelization among enslaved persons. In 1680, Morgan Godwyn, a minister who served in Virginia and Barbados, argued that the impetus behind the resistance of enslavers to evangelizing efforts among enslaved persons was economic greed. The planters offered other ostensibly high-minded rationales, such as linguistic challenges to enslaved Africans who did not understand English and racial arguments about the intellectual inferiority of the Black race, but Godwyn maintained these justifications were merely excuses to disguise their financial motivations. Godwyn observed that most planters desired for their enslaved persons to focus on their labor with no other distractions. Language was not a barrier to evangelization among enslaved persons, since the majority in the British colonies understood and spoke English by the middle of the seventeenth century. Godwyn also dismissed the "fiction of the brutality of the Negro's" as contrary to what he and other planters witnessed themselves in the abilities and capacities of enslaved persons as equal to white persons. His criticism of the sexual violence that slave-owning men perpetrated against enslaved women wryly noted the humanity of the Black race. White men surely would not be sexually attracted to monstrous beasts or inferior brutes; they only desired other fellow human beings. Godwyn concluded that the planters knew "no other *God* but *Money,* nor *Religion* but *Profit*" and preferred systemic obstacles to the evangelization of their enslaved persons, such as the legal ambiguities surrounding baptism and emancipation, because they provided cover for their sinful avarice.[8]

Godwyn also addressed one other significant hindrance to white evangelization among enslaved persons: the inescapable reality that the tyranny of Black enslavement pervaded white-dominant worship spaces. Enslaved persons were constantly subjected to harsh punishment and dehumanizing treatment from their enslavers and other white persons. For some, their only reprieve from the oppressive presence of white persons was on Sundays. White congregations practiced racial segregation in their sanctuaries, with designated pews for Black worshipers in a gallery raised above the main floor or in the back area of the main floor, which reminded Black worshipers of their fictitious but imposed racial inferiority. Godwyn observed the discontent in enslaved persons being forced to occupy the same worship space as their enslavers, even from "the most distant part" of the sanctuaries in their racially designated sections. He described the white church as a "prison" for some enslaved persons because the worship service absorbed a portion of their lone day to rest and more fully express themselves in the absence of white oppressors. Some enslavers deliberately saw the worship service as an opportunity for additional surveillance because it provided an opportunity to have their enslaved persons "always in their eye," even away from their plantations.[9]

Reports from SPG missionaries and Anglican clergy in the century following Godwyn's account from 1680 reveal no substantial changes in the religious attitudes of planters in North America and the Caribbean. In 1724, the Anglican clergy in the North American colonies completed a survey from the bishop of London about their ministries. One of the questions was about the evangelization of enslaved persons. A minister in one southern Virginia parish in Dinwiddie County answered that enslavers opposed his efforts: "I have several times exhorted their Masters to send such of them as could speak English to Church to be catechised but they would not."[10] Ministers of parishes in Gloucester County and Henrico County of Virginia shared that some enslavers permitted their enslaved persons to attend worship with them on Sundays but discouraged any further attempts from the clergy to offer Christian instruction to their enslaved persons.[11] A minister of another Virginia parish in James City County was frustrated that the slave-owning members in his church were "hardly to be persuaded by the Minister" to support any efforts to teach the Christian gospel to their enslaved persons, which meant "the poor creatures live and die without it" and were therefore consigned to an eternity in hell according to this minister's theology.[12] The secretary of the SPG,

David Humphreys, reported in 1730 that there were three prevailing reasons for why enslaved persons were not attending worship. Some enslavers allotted Sunday as the only time for their enslaved persons to prepare their weekly food rations, and therefore enslaved persons were fully engaged in the work of farming, planting, and cooking "to subsist themselves" for the upcoming week. The other two reasons were "popular arguments" from enslavers. One was the belief that "the negroes had no souls" and therefore could not comprehend the spiritual truths of Christianity. The other was the notion that Christian conversions made enslaved persons more prideful and less obedient because they saw themselves as equal to their enslavers. Humphreys dismissed these two arguments as absurd, with "no foundation in reason or truth," but even the SPG secretary could not deny the enduring power of these ideas throughout North America and the Caribbean.[13]

"There Is Room for You, Poor Negroes": A Re-formation of Christianity to Reinforce Black Enslavement and White Domination

White Presbyterians in the North American colonies did not detail their evangelization efforts among enslaved persons in the seventeenth century and the first half of the eighteenth century at anywhere near the level of the Church of England. Jones identified the ministry of Samuel Davies, a white Presbyterian pastor in Hanover County, Virginia, from approximately 1748 to 1759 as the first evangelization effort with some success in terms of Black church members.[14] What does the absence of documentation prior to Davies suggest? Although the first North American presbytery was founded in 1706, white Presbyterians were in North America before then, and some were enslavers. One historian of transatlantic Presbyterianism, Nini Rodgers, traces the journey of Francis Makemie, remembered as the founder of Presbyterianism in the United States, from Donegal, Ireland, to Maryland in the 1680s. Makemie was both a pastor and a successful merchant, funding his ministry with his commercial revenue. In the 1690s, Makemie left Maryland to reside in Barbados and encountered Black enslavement on sugar plantations there before returning to North America and marrying a white woman belonging to a wealthy merchant family in Accomack County, Virginia. Though records do not exist of Makemie regarding his ownership of enslaved persons, he was the largest landowner in Accomack County by 1704, with 5,109 acres of land at a time "when tobacco growing in the Chesapeake region was shifting from small farms to estates with extensive lands and a slave workforce." Rodgers convincingly argues that "Makemie's position inevitably suggests slave ownership," and the financial support he raised for the first presbytery in Philadelphia in 1706 was closely connected to profits from southern plantations.[15]

Davies's preaching and writing about white evangelization among enslaved persons also reveals the attitudes and actions of white Presbyterians prior to and during his life and ministry. In 1757, Davies preached a sermon on "the duty of Christians to propagate their religion among heathens" advocating for more participation from enslavers concerning the spirituality of their enslaved persons. His observation that enslavers gave insufficient attention to this matter, leaving in his view "crowds of neglected negroe slaves among us," hints at a widespread indifference among slave-owning Presbyterians regarding whether their enslaved persons received Christian instruction or not.[16] Davies also sought to debunk the same popular arguments from enslavers that Humphreys identified in 1730, which illustrates the presence of these pernicious myths in white Presbyterian congregations. "Some of you, perhaps, would object," Davies acknowledged, "that your negroes are such sullen perverse creatures, or stupid dunces, that it is impossible to teach them any thing that is good."[17] Davies contended that the notion that persons of African descent were incapable of understanding Christian doctrines was false. His own experiences with enslaved persons convinced him that they were as intellectually capable as white persons. But Davies also argued that the question of intellect did not have any bearing on evangelization since the Christian gospel, "as far as it is essential to salvation," was "not a difficult science" and more of a matter of the heart than the head.[18]

More than dismantling the myth of Black inferiority, Davies devoted his attention to the prevailing idea that exposure to Christianity affected the behavior of enslaved persons toward their enslavers. Davies understood that a considerable objection among slave-owning Presbyterians was the notion that baptizing and receiving enslaved persons as members in white Presbyterian congregations made them "proud and saucy" and led them "to imagine themselves upon an equality with white people." Davies assured slave-owning Presbyterians that enslaved persons possessing the "true Christian spirit" would be inspired to be more diligent in their labor and more submissive in their posture toward their enslavers. He went so far as to point out to slave-owning Presbyterians that supporting white evangelization efforts among enslaved persons directly served their economic interests because the Presbyterian kind of Christianity that Davies taught to enslaved persons urged them to be more honest, modest, and industrious.[19]

Several historians have noted the rarity and ambiguity of Davies's ministry among enslaved persons. In evangelizing to enslaved persons and encouraging them to be baptized and join his white congregation, Davies was doing something unusual and different from the normative patterns of white Presbyterian ministry in the North American colonies. Most slave-owning Presbyterians were likely resistant to, or indifferent toward, the evangelization of their enslaved persons. But historians characterizing Davies's ministry as ambiguous are missing, or misstating, the obvious aims, and sinful immoralities, of his preaching. One historian writes of "the ambiguity in Davies's evangelical encounter with slavery" because of Davies's "concern for spiritual over civil liberty" in his evangelizing efforts among enslaved persons.[20] The notion of ambiguity suggests inexactness or uncertainty. But Davies was both exact and certain in his proclamation of a corrupted gospel that taught enslaved persons and enslavers alike that Jesus Christ was in favor of Black enslavement. Enslaved Black Presbyterians were instructed to obey their white enslavers with the utmost humility and respect. Slave-owning Presbyterians were encouraged to bring their enslaved persons to worship with them because the objectives of Davies's ministry served their self-interests. Davies promised that enslaved persons who were baptized and received as members of a Presbyterian congregation would be more docile in relations with their enslavers and more diligent in their work.

Davies criticized Anglicans in Virginia for what he viewed as their theological laxity and spiritual declension. In 1750, he wrote a letter to Philip Doddridge, a white Congregationalist minister in England, complaining of the Anglican clergy in Virginia as "generally degenerated from the Calvinistic articles of their own Church" and inattentive to their sanctification in daily living.[21] Yet Davies himself shared several similarities with the Anglican clergy he was reprimanding. Davies, like many Anglican ministers, owned enslaved persons and was therefore economically invested in the clear separation of the civil and religious components of Black enslavement. His preaching that the conversion of enslaved persons to Christianity did not affect the "civil distinctions" of Black enslavement struck the same chords as the bishop of London's declaration in 1727 that the baptism of enslaved persons did not alter their legal status.[22] Davies also preached in white-dominant worship spaces with racially segregated seating for Black worshipers. In some of his sermons, he specifically addressed Black worshipers seated in galleries above or in the back pews, often referring to them as "poor negroes," and he called upon them to heed his words. In one sermon, Davies beckoned, "There is room for you, poor negroes; and for you, I hope, some vacant seats in heaven are reserved."[23] In another sermon, Davies referred to his enslaved persons as "my own negroes."[24] And in correspondence with his brother-in-law, Davies inquired about purchasing a "Negroe Wench."[25] Davies's slave ownership did not trouble his white Presbyterian contemporaries. Instead, he was recognized as one of their finest clergypersons and theologians. In 1759, after approximately eleven years of ministry among the "poor negroes" in Virginia, Davies accepted an invitation to be president of a Presbyterian college in New Jersey, Princeton University.[26]

In addition to the misstating of Davies's ministry as comprising an ambiguous position on slavery, some historians have overstated the results of his evangelizing efforts. Because Davies published sermons about his ministry among enslaved persons, which were reprinted in numerous editions during and after his life, there exists an underlying and untrue assumption that Davies dramatically turned the tides of white Christian resistance to the evangelization of enslaved persons.[27] In 1750, Davies wrote to Doddridge that there were approximately 1,000 enslaved persons in his vicinity and 100 were "the property of my people," meaning they were owned by enslavers in his congregation. Davies had baptized forty enslaved persons, seven or eight of whom were church members and thereby invited to "partake of the Lord's Supper."[28] Five years later Davies reported that there were approximately 150,000 enslaved persons in Virginia and that 300 enslaved persons regularly worshiped at his church, 100 of whom were baptized.[29] The highest estimate Davies provided was in 1756 when he surmised that a little more than one thousand enslaved persons attended his worship services.[30] Despite the growing number of enslaved worshipers at his church, Davies complained of "the almost universal neglect of many thousand poor slaves."[31] Davies's uncommon ministry among enslaved persons did not arouse a critical mass of white slave-owning Christians to be similarly attentive to the evangelization of enslaved persons. Therefore, Davies's accounts mirror the SPG report in 1730 lamenting the conversion of only a minuscule fraction of the enslaved population in the North American colonies.

The statistical figures from white Christians certainly do not capture the actual history of spirituality among enslaved persons in the North American colonies. Reports from Davies and SPG missionaries reflect their biased perspectives and often demean the religious cultures of Black persons from Eurocentric viewpoints. Enslaved persons expressed their spirituality with resilient creativity and assembled on their own in their living quarters, agricultural fields, and *hush harbors*—secluded spaces they built in dense forests or wooded areas—to worship in ways that affirmed their dignity, celebrated their intrinsic worth, and served as "acts of rebellion against the proscriptions of the master."[32] In 1903, W. E. B. Du Bois contended that Black folk music, which originated in enslaved communities, represented "the rhythmic cry of the slave" and constituted "the most beautiful expression of human experience" produced in the United States for its profound message of hope in the face of despair.[33]

But accounts by white Christians of their evangelizing efforts among enslaved persons illumine three significant transgressions. The first offense lies in their complete disregard for African and African American spirituality. Davies, like other white Christians in the eighteenth century, described African religiosity as ignorant heathenism and dismissed the possibility that enslaved persons could profess and practice an authentic kind of Christianity apart from white instruction. The second offense entails the promulgation of an abusive and perverted form of Christianity that justified and reinforced the unjust systems of Black enslavement and white domination. The third offense centers on the theological convictions of white Presbyterians and other white Christians in the North American colonies. Davies believed that enslaved persons, no different from white persons, were "candidates for the same eternal state" and thereby "bound for the same heaven or hell," which meant for them that the failure of white evangelization among enslaved persons had immortal consequences.[34] In other words, white Presbyterians believed that the enslaved persons who were not converted through their evangelizing efforts, or the ministries of other white Christians, were condemned to hell. Alexander Hewat confessed in 1779 that white evangelization among enslaved persons in South Carolina was virtually nonexistent. Hewat concluded, "One thing is very certain, that the negroes of that country, a few only excepted, are to this day as great strangers to Christianity, and as much under the influence of Pagan darkness, idolatry, and superstition, as they were at their first arrival from Africa."[35] Ezra Stiles, a white Congregationalist minister and president of Yale University from 1778 to 1795, estimated in 1772 that no more than 30 of the 1,200 Black Americans in Newport, Rhode Island, were members of Protestant congregations.[36] One historian finds that only 4 percent of the 306,193 enslaved persons in Virginia in 1790 were considered to be church members.[37] These reports from white Christians do not depict the realities of Black spirituality, but they list damning evidence against white Christians. White Christians believed that an overwhelming percentage of the enslaved population died as "great strangers to Christianity." And according to their own logic, white slave-owning Christians were the guilty party responsible for this grave sin.

"Is Not the Hard Yoke of Slavery Felt by Negroes as well as by White People?": A Racially Segregated Theology of Liberation

White Presbyterians maintained distinctions between the civil status and religious conversion of enslaved persons, but they combined civil and religious liberties for themselves in the American Revolution. John Witherspoon migrated from Scotland to New Jersey in 1768 to be president of Princeton University. He emerged as an influential leader in the revolutionary cause as both a preacher and a politician. In 1776, Witherspoon was elected as a delegate to the Continental Congress and strongly advocated for the passing of a resolution of independence from England. Eleven of the fifty-six signatories of the Declaration of Independence were Presbyterian, and Witherspoon was the only clergyperson to sign the founding document.[38] Approximately one month before his election to the Congress, Witherspoon delivered a fiery sermon at Princeton in support of the independence movement that was immediately published in Philadelphia and circulated throughout the North American colonies. Witherspoon noted in the sermon that it was the first time he had engaged a "political subject" from the pulpit, but he did so "without any hesitation" because "the cause in which America is now in arms, is the cause of justice, of liberty, and of human nature." He explained that there are occasions when it is appropriate to blend politics into Christian proclamation and that the revolution was such a moment because the "civil and religious liberties" of white Presbyterians, and all white persons, were at stake. Witherspoon declared, "There is not a single instance in history in which civil liberty was lost, and religious liberty preserved entire."[39] But Witherspoon's connection of civil and religious liberties did not extend to enslaved persons.

Although Witherspoon compared British colonial rule in North America to the oppressive conditions of slavery, he owned enslaved persons and resisted abolition efforts in the state of New Jersey. In 1790, Witherspoon was the chairperson of a committee that recommended New Jersey take no legislative action on slavery, which helped to delay the passing of a gradual emancipation law until 1804. In Scotland, Witherspoon baptized an enslaved Black man, Jamie Montgomery, in 1756. Like one of his presidential predecessors at Princeton, Samuel Davies, Witherspoon clarified that Montgomery's baptism did not grant him legal grounds for emancipation. At Princeton, Witherspoon privately tutored two free Black men, John Quamine and Bristol Yamma, in 1774 with the hope they would go to Africa as missionaries. Five years later, Witherspoon purchased two enslaved persons for agricultural labor on his 500-acre estate. One historian contends that Witherspoon had a "complex relationship to slavery" because he "advocated revolutionary ideals of liberty and personally tutored several free Africans and African Americans in Princeton" while also owning enslaved persons and opposing abolition.[40] But Witherspoon's relationship with slavery was straightforward, not complex. Throughout his life, Witherspoon consistently acted and argued in support of Black enslavement. He used his influence and power to promote white liberation from British colonial rule and defend white ownership of enslaved Black persons. Witherspoon's active participation in slavery was not unusual among white Presbyterians. But the notion of describing it as complex is deeply problematic because it suggests an ambiguity that did not exist in Witherspoon's life and invites an unearned sympathy for his indefensibly sinful actions and moral contradictions.

The preaching of Jacob Green, a white Presbyterian contemporary of Witherspoon in New Jersey, simultaneously illustrates and condemns Witherspoon's moral contradictions regarding civil and religious liberties. Green's support for the revolutionary cause, unlike Witherspoon's, extended to the emancipation of enslaved persons. In 1778, Green preached to his congregation in Morris County, approximately forty-five miles from Princeton, that it was unethical and against Christian principles to continue Black enslavement while fighting against England for civil and religious freedoms. He asked, "Can it be believed that a people contending for liberty should, at the same time, be promoting and supporting slavery?" Green plainly added that it was logically and morally inconsistent to "loudly complain of Britain's attempts to oppress and enslave" white Americans while "voluntarily holding multitudes of fellow creatures in abject slavery." Evoking the comparison between their colonial oppression to slavery, which was evident in Witherspoon's sermon and ubiquitous across political and religious revolutionary rhetoric, Green implored his white congregation to simply take the analogy to its most sensible conclusion: "Is not the hard yoke of slavery felt by negroes as well as by white people? Are they not fond of liberty as well as others of the human race?"[41]

Green deplored Black enslavement as a cruel and dehumanizing evil, identifying it as "the most crying sin of our land," for two reasons. Firstly, the institution of American slavery was contrary to the divine order because it destroyed the possibility of neighbor-love; it was impossible for enslavers to love their enslaved persons as their neighbors within an oppressive system in which the latter were the human merchandise of the former. Secondly, white Christian enslavers and defenders of Black enslavement were hypocrites guilty of "sinful self-interest" and "criminal partiality."[42] Green believed that white slave-owning Christians like Witherspoon knew of and accepted the moral contradictions of their promotion of one kind of freedom in the United States, white liberation from British colonialism, and their opposition to another kind of freedom, Black liberation from white ownership. Green added that white Christians had willfully made slavery a lesser sin in their own minds, as well as in their congregations, because of their economic interests.[43] Unlike the American Revolution, in which white Christians in the United States had a common foe in England, the cause of abolition required white Christians to call out their slave-owning neighbors and fellow church members as evildoers and the enemies of justice, humanity, and Jesus Christ.

Thus, it was easier for many white Presbyterians to profess that Jesus Christ was in favor of American slavery and work toward reforming the incidental evils of what they maintained was a divinely sanctioned institution. Green, Witherspoon, and other white Presbyterians made intentional choices. Green chose to be an antislavery pastor advocating for the gradual emancipation of enslaved persons in New Jersey. Witherspoon chose to be a proslavery pastor exerting his political and religious influence to defend and practice Black enslavement. No record of Witherspoon as an abusive enslaver exists, and it is likely that he treated the free and enslaved Black individuals he encountered with kindness, but he continually ignored and actively denied their yearning for freedom and pursuit of equal rights. Green was deeply concerned that military success in the American Revolution would not produce an enduring and effectual liberty for white Americans until they washed their hands "from the guilt of negro slavery."[44] There may not have been much difference in the actions of Green and Witherspoon toward the free and enslaved Black individuals they interacted with in their everyday lives, but to leave the comparative analysis at this interpersonal level omits the magnitude and significance of the unjust societal structures that Green, Witherspoon, and Black Americans inhabited. Green chose to preach against slavery so that the enslaved persons he saw every day in Morris County, along with the hundreds of thousands of enslaved persons in his nation, could be free from both their individual white oppressors and the oppressive system of Black enslavement. Witherspoon chose to be circumspect in his preaching about slavery. He thought it was imprudent to praise Black enslavement from the pulpit, but he found other ways, such as his leadership on a New Jersey committee recommending rejection of a gradual emancipation bill, to preserve the legality of slavery and protect his financial investments in human property.

In 1824, James Duncan, a white Presbyterian pastor in Indiana, contended that slavery was wrong because it contradicted the moral law. Duncan found in the opening question of the Westminster Larger Catechism (WLC) a summary of the moral law: "The great end for which God made man was, that he should glorify God and enjoy him forever."[45] But white slave-owning Christians could not fulfill these divine purposes because their participation in Black enslavement required them to openly disobey God's precepts and distort God's designs for creation. The legality of slavery in the United States did not mean it was in accordance with God's will. All persons had "the right to worship and serve God without being hindered by man, or any human authority," wrote Duncan. He continued that every person also retained "the right of all conjugal, parental, and filial duties" and civil government erred when they suppressed or denied these God-given rights.[46] Beriah Green made a similar argument in observing that American slavery contravened the principle that Christians worship a God who is no respecter of persons. Yet in slavery, Green noted there was a "respect of persons" that systemically reduced Black persons to slavery because of their skin color. In American slavery, Black persons were enslaved on account of God's creative act of giving them a "dark complexion." He charged, "But how can I be responsible for the incidents of my birth?—how for my complexion? To despise or honor me for these, is to be guilty of respect of persons in its grossest form, and with its worst effects." White Christian enslavers and enablers of slavery were guilty of the worst of sins because they presented a sadistic gospel "confounding all moral distinctions" in their glorification and enjoyment of a God who intentionally created Black persons to be enslaved by white persons.[47]

In their preaching to enslaved persons, some white pastors made their own theological distinctions about slavery and God's created order. In 1749, Thomas Bacon, a white Anglican minister in Maryland, published two sermons he had delivered to enslaved persons. Bacon distinguished between persons and offices. He began one of his sermons with this conviction: "God is no Respecter of Persons. He values no Man for his Riches and Power, neither does he despise or overlook any one for his Rags and Poverty." Therefore, every human was created with a spiritual soul and the same eternal worth. But Bacon explained that God also "appointed several *Offices* and *Degrees*," with some created as rulers and others as subjects. God created merchants, planters, ministers, teachers, masters, and slaves. Persons were responsible to fulfill the duties of the office God had assigned them. Bacon directed enslaved persons with the following instruction: "And while you, whom he hath made Slaves, are honestly and quietly doing your Business, and living as poor Christians ought to do, you are serving God, in your low Station, as much as the greatest Prince alive."[48] In another sermon, Bacon combined slavery, race, and God's providence, observing that enslaved persons were blessed with a "great Advantage over most White People" because they had fewer responsibilities. White persons experienced more stress because their duties included managing finances, budgeting, and other business matters. Enslaved persons only had to be concerned with "the Care of their daily Labour upon their Hands," which Bacon insisted was a praiseworthy illustration of God's wisdom.[49] Bacon's racist theology rested on the foundation that God created all Black persons with the same spiritual souls but lesser intellectual capacities as white persons.

In 1794, Cary Allen, a white Presbyterian pastor in Virginia, conveyed the same racist notions as Bacon from the pulpit. Toward the end of one sermon, Allen turned to the enslaved persons in attendance and remarked, "You negroes, I have a word for you. Do you think that such poor black, dirty-looking creatures as you can ever get to heaven?" Allen answered his own question in the affirmative, noting "that the blessed Saviour shed his blood as much for you as for your masters, or any of the white people." Like Bacon, Allen made the spurious claim that enslaved persons were more fortunate than white persons because they had fewer worldly temptations due to their restricted access to wealth and leisure. Unlike enslavers, enslaved persons were therefore blessed with a clearer pathway to heaven. Allen instructed them to be more concerned about their eternal destinations after death than the hardships in their daily lives: "Make God your friend, and take Jesus for your Saviour, and he will keep you through all your troubles here; and though your skins may be black here, you will hereafter shine like the stars in the firmament."[50] Allen's preaching endeavored to reinforce the oppressive system of Black enslavement with a racially segregated and multitiered theology of liberation. One tier professed the racist conception that all Black persons were intellectually inferior to white persons in God's creative order. A second tier maintained that slavery was a blessing to enslaved persons because they had fewer responsibilities and temptations in comparison to white persons. Thus, Black enslavement was a demonstration of divine goodness because it proved God did not test persons beyond their capacities. Allen and Bacon tried to convince their Black listeners that they would be ruined, in this life and the life to come, if they had to live like free white persons. A third tier directed attention away from the oppression of slavery and toward the anticipation of heaven. Allen connected the power structures of slavery and race in his recognition that the skin color of enslaved persons had everything to do with their oppression. But abolishing the system of slavery was not the remedy for the "troubles" of enslaved persons. Rather, Allen pointed toward the "firmament" and the promise of eternal structures.

After his sermon, Allen received commendation from some of the white worshipers for his message to the Black worshipers. There is no record of what specifically they appreciated about the sermon, but it is possible that some enslavers exhibited genuine concern for the salvation of their enslaved persons. Others likely approved of Allen's endorsement of Black enslavement from the pulpit. And these two rationales were not mutually exclusive, but they existed in tandem. Some slave-owning Presbyterians, like Witherspoon, desired for their enslaved persons to adopt the proslavery teaching that a person's skin color determined whether civil and religious liberties ought to be divisible or indivisible.

"The Most Obdurate Adherents of Slavery":
The Emergence of a New Catechism and the Entrenchment
of Black Enslavement in White Presbyterianism

Henry Pattillo was born in Scotland in 1726 and migrated to Virginia as a teenager. He initially set out to be a merchant but committed his life to pastoral ministry after several indelible spiritual experiences at revival meetings. With mentoring from Samuel Davies, Pattillo began preaching in Presbyterian congregations in Virginia and North Carolina in 1758. During the American Revolution, Pattillo became pastor of a congregation in Granville County, North Carolina. In 1787, he published a catechism for white slave-owning Presbyterian families entitled *The Plain Planter's Family Assistant*, with separate sections for the three hierarchical relations that Pattillo believed were of divine origin: husbands and wives, parents and children, and masters and slaves. In his message to slave-owning men, Pattillo pointed to the civil and religious liberties that had been won with American independence, which secured for them a vital principle in the Reformed tradition— freedom of conscience: "You have the honour to possess that soil, and breathe that air, where legislators have, for the first time, declared, that they have nothing to do with religion but to protect its professors; and that God alone is the Lord of conscience."[51] In addition to freedom of conscience, slave-owning men also enjoyed liberty from the unjust tyranny of British taxes. Taxation in the United States was different because the monies collected would remain at home to directly benefit American citizens instead of persons abroad in England. Thus, Pattillo urged white Presbyterian planters to "aim not at great wealth, but at a decent competency," meaning that a comfortable middle-class lifestyle, one in which they were able to provide for their families and contribute to their national government, was sufficient. It was unnecessary to imitate the "avarice of the British merchants" and continue their past sins, which included their abusive treatment of enslaved persons and their wanton participation in the transatlantic slave trade.[52]

Pattillo envisioned a different kind of Black enslavement and proposed reforms to ameliorate the oppressive system according to his interpretations of Christianity. He blamed England for leaving white Americans with a wicked inheritance in a system of slavery that prioritized profit over piety. Because enslaved persons were fellow human beings with spiritual souls, Pattillo criticized the ubiquity of excessive physical abuse and spiritual neglect among enslavers. God had given slave-owning Americans a fresh start and a new identity with national independence. They were no longer British colonists; they were American citizens. Therefore, Pattillo proposed "soft blows" and "hard arguments" in the discipline of enslaved persons. Like his mentor, Davies, Pattillo also identified the absence of white evangelization among enslaved persons as the worst tragedy of slavery. Pattillo conceded "that the omission of this duty of religious instruction to the slaves, is a great national evil; and the source of numerous others to society." His proposal entailed a reclamation of Sunday as a day of Sabbath rest and Christian instruction in which slave-owning families brought their enslaved persons to church for worship and taught them "psalms, hymns, catechisms, prayers, and the art of reading" at home. Pattillo was precise in his vision of the model Presbyterian plantation. He criticized enslavers for not giving sufficient Sabbath rest to some of their enslaved persons. Some enslaved laborers in the fields received a respite, but those responsible for household tasks like cleaning and cooking rarely did. Thus, Pattillo's instructions addressed this reality: "Remember, your cook has as good a claim to the holy rest of that day, as your other domestics, and cannot be deprived of it without injustice and oppression. So better a cold dinner, than an offended God, an angry conscience, and an oppressed servant." He asked planters to compare his understanding of the Sabbath with the "present graceless practice of our country" and decide which of the two was more in accordance with the Christian faith.[53]

Reception of Pattillo's vision among slave-owning Presbyterian families relied upon his instructions to enslaved persons more than his Sabbath recommendations. Pattillo constructed two catechisms, one for white children and another for enslaved persons. In the Reformed tradition, catechisms were designed to summarize and systemize Christian theology in an accessible format of short questions and answers. In 1647, the Westminster Shorter Catechism (WSC) was created in England "to provide a simple summary statement for young people of what was contained in the Larger Catechism and the Confession of Faith."[54] Pattillo's "Youth's Catechism" comprised ninety-two questions and was structured like the WSC. The first fifty-seven questions focused on beliefs, and the latter thirty-five questions addressed the duties of Christian youth. The twenty-sixth question emphasized the doctrine of original sin and detailed a threefold answer: The original sin of Adam "1. Involves all his posterity in the guilt of it. 2. It forfeits their primitive holiness and rectitude. 3. It pollutes and taints their whole nature with sin."[55] By comparison, Pattillo's "Negroes' Catechism" comprised fifty questions, with roughly half engaging beliefs and the other half entailing duties. Doctrines like original sin were explained in more simple language. Unlike his catechism for white youth, Pattillo's catechism for enslaved persons addressed race and slavery directly. The first seven questions were about "white folks and negroes." The answer to the second question confirmed that the Christian God was the "one father" of white and Black persons. The answer to the sixth question stated that white and Black persons both had spiritual souls because "we all love and hate the same things; and what gives pain or pleasure to the one, does to the other." Several questions detailed the Christian duties of enslaved persons. The answer to the thirty-seventh question about relations with their enslavers instructed enslaved persons "to be honest, diligent, and faithful in all things, and not to give saucy answers; and even when they are whipt for doing well, to take it patiently, and look to God for their reward." Like other white preachers, Pattillo accentuated haughtiness as an especially devilish sin for enslaved persons with the common admonition against "saucy" behavior toward their enslavers. Pattillo also discouraged any resistance from enslaved persons. Even when enslavers and overseers punished them unfairly, enslaved persons who were "whipt for doing well" were directed to seek eternal, not earthly, reparation. The answers to the thirty-ninth and fortieth questions encompassed the notion that enslaved persons were more blessed and "happier" than their enslavers because God had given to them fewer responsibilities.[56]

Pattillo's book reveals a significant omission when comparing the two catechisms: the absence of instruction about marital duties for enslaved persons. The catechism for white youth contained questions about choosing a spouse wisely and "their duties when married." Included in the answers were covenants "to stir each other up to love and to good works" and "to bring up their family to religion, learning, and industry."[57] The catechism for enslaved persons lacked marital covenants because of what one historian names as the "inability to convey kinship" for enslaved persons within an oppressive system in which white legislators and enslavers could not identify enslaved Black families as "something other than the expansion of someone else's estate."[58] Pattillo's Presbyterian vision of Black enslavement endeavored to protect the Sabbath rest of enslaved laborers but succumbed to the harsh realities of family separation in chattel slavery. Enslaved Black persons had the same spiritual souls as white persons, and loved just like white persons, but they did not have the commensurate marital covenants and kinship rights.

Pattillo's omission of marital covenants in his catechism for enslaved persons illustrated the sinfulness of American slavery to James Duncan, Beriah Green, and other abolitionists. Duncan appealed to the WLC in his criticism of slavery, in its denial of "all conjugal, parental, and filial duties" for enslaved persons, as antithetical to the moral law.[59] The WLC states that "the moral law is summarily comprehended in the Ten Commandments," and the "sins forbidden" in the Seventh Commandment are adultery and prohibiting lawful marriages.[60] Frederick Douglass lambasted white clergypersons like Pattillo as hypocrites for promoting marriage to white persons as among the greatest gifts from God while preventing enslaved persons from sharing in the sacred institution. Harriet Beecher Stowe disparaged white slave-owning Christians for altering the moral law to suit their purposes. Stowe pointed out how two local Baptist associations in the southern states changed their interpretations of the Seventh Commandment to permit second marriages among enslaved persons in cases of "involuntary separation" when "sold by his or her master."[61] These white Christians defied the immutability of the moral law and bent that which was written in stone, the Decalogue, to conform to their oppressive system.

In addition to the abolitionist appeal to the Seventh Commandment, George Bourne found that American slavery violated the Eighth Commandment and the Westminster Standards. Bourne drew attention to the 142nd question of the WLC regarding "man-stealing" as among the "sins forbidden" in the Eighth Commandment and highlighted the two scriptural verses, Exodus 21:16 and 1 Timothy 1:10, appended to the sin of man-stealing in the WLC, to argue that the "original import" of these verses meant slave-owning Presbyterians were guilty of stealing fellow human beings against their will in their practices of buying, selling, and retaining enslaved persons.[62] From the beginnings of the international slave trade, European and white American Christians defended Black enslavement with a claim that enslaved Africans were prisoners of war. They maintained that the Old Testament authorized the enslavement of military combatants. Prisoners of war, therefore, were in a separate category from civilians, because they relinquished their rights to liberty when entering the battlefield. But it became increasingly clear to merchants, planters, slave traders, and pastors that most enslaved Africans were abducted civilians and not prisoners of war. In 1786, Thomas Clarkson dismissed the notion that prisoners of war constituted the majority of enslaved Africans in North America and the Caribbean as a preposterous fiction.[63] Jacob Green also believed in 1778 that enslaved persons in the United States had "never forfeited their right to freedom" and therefore slave-owning Christians were committing the sin of man-stealing in their trafficking of innocent kidnap victims.[64]

In 1813 and 1815, Bourne was elected by his presbytery in Virginia to be a commissioner to the PCUSA General Assembly. But the Lexington Presbytery did not elect Bourne again after his attempt in 1815 to introduce an overture to a committee to study "the proper manner of dealing with members of the church who retain people of colour in slavery."[65] Bourne insisted that his denomination censure its slave-owning members for breaking the Eighth Commandment and defying the constitution of the Presbyterian Church. The following year he published *The Book and Slavery Irreconcilable,* a tome in which he criticized white ministers, ruling elders, and church members as "the most obdurate adherents of Slavery." He identified Black enslavement as the "acme of all impiety" and contended that it was "impossible" for an enslaver to be considered "a sincere Christian."[66] As a pastor in a slaveholding state, Bourne grew incensed with the perverse scale of piety that existed in his Presbyterian milieu. Sins like dancing, drunkenness, and gambling were denounced from the pulpit. Church councils, such as sessions and presbyteries, readily disciplined members for committing these sins. Yet the sins of Black enslavement were not remotely confronted. An impenitent church member who stole a horse from another church member would likely be excommunicated, but enslavers received no censure for their participation in an oppressive system of unjust human trafficking. Bourne believed his fellow white Presbyterians had their understandings of faith and piety all wrong and did not mince words in his rebuke of them: "It is the utmost Satanic delusion to talk of religion and slavery. Be not deceived: to affirm that a Slave-holder is a genuine disciple of Jesus Christ, is most intelligible contradiction. A brother of him who went about doing good, and steal, enslave, torment, starve, and scourge a man because his skin is of a different tinge!"[67] Bourne's presbytery was just as unequivocal in its rejection of his abolitionism. It indicted Bourne for "making injurious impressions in the Assembly against the Presbyterian Clergy in Virginia" and removed him from his ordered ministry.[68]

After his dismissal, Bourne moved to Germantown, Pennsylvania, to serve as pastor of a congregation there, but he also appealed the decision of the Lexington Presbytery. The commissioners of the PCUSA General Assembly initially voted in favor of Bourne in 1817, finding the charges against him were not "fully substantiated," before deciding against him one year later after the Lexington Presbytery conducted a new trial.[69] One biographer of Bourne argues that the reason for the different outcomes in the two General Assembly meetings was not because of any new findings from the Lexington Presbytery trial. Rather, an increasing number of white Presbyterians had read or heard of the abolitionist book Bourne published in 1816 and disapproved of his assault against their denomination for their unwillingness to censure slave-owning members.[70]

The General Assembly in 1818 engaged slavery beyond Bourne's appeal. The commissioners adopted a report from a committee studying "the subject of selling a slave, a member of the Church."[71] Should there be discipline for a white church member who sells an enslaved Black church member who is unwilling to be sold? The committee recommended that the "proper church judicature" suspend the white church member until he repented and made "all the reparation in his power to the injured party." The report also echoed some of Bourne's convictions. Slavery was "a gross violation of the most precious and sacred rights of human nature" and "utterly inconsistent with the law of God" because it created a "paradox in the moral system" that obstructed the practice of neighbor-love. They deemed that Jesus Christ was not in favor of American slavery. But the committee diverged from Bourne in its solutions. The report opposed immediate emancipation, endorsed the colonization movement, encouraged white evangelization efforts among enslaved persons, and warned against harsh opprobrium toward slave-owning members. The separation of enslaved marriages and families was recognized as abhorrent, but the strongest action the committee recommended was to "enjoin it on all church sessions and Presbyteries, under the care of this Assembly, to discountenance, and as far as possible to prevent all cruelty of whatever kind in the treatment of slaves."[72] The committee devised a way to denounce the evils of Black enslavement without rebuking the denomination's slave-owning members. Slavery was a crime with victims but no perpetrators. According to the General Assembly, Jesus Christ was unhappy about American slavery but not angry at white American enslavers. The word "sin" cannot be found among the 1,332 words in the committee's report on slavery.

Several historians contend that the adoption of this report in 1818 was connected to the vote to sustain the Lexington Presbytery's decision to defrock Bourne as a compromise measure to placate both proslavery and antislavery commissioners.[73] The action against Bourne's abolitionism appeased the demands of the former, and the report on slavery soothed the consciences of the latter. But the inaction of the PCUSA after 1818 contradicted its own words. In 1833, Bourne excoriated white Presbyterians for adopting an antislavery document that they had no intention of enacting whatsoever. The report had become less of a guide for the PCUSA and more of an indictment of the denomination's moral decline and spiritual hypocrisy. Bourne and other Christian abolitionists charged the PCUSA with the crime of capitulating to the power of American slavery and re-forming their faith to align with the desires of their slave-owning ministers and members. Bourne cited the empty rhetoric from the antislavery document in his accusation: "The American churches, and especially our own, wear the collar of the slaveholders, and are led captive by those who are constantly violating 'the most precious and sacred rights of human nature.'"[74] In 1836, Beriah Green also recognized that the PCUSA was choosing American slavery over Jesus Christ as evinced in the decreasing, rather than increasing, number of sermons from white ministers in the northern states touching upon the sin of slavery and the righteous struggle for racial equality. Green protested, "Must we see churches, built up by fraud and filled with adultery, without uttering a syllable! And religious teachers claiming for American slavery the stability and the sanctity of a Christian institution! And quoting texts from the Old Testament and the New to justify man-stealing!"[75]

Some of the delegates at the Constitutional Convention in 1787 hoped that slavery would be abolished over time. Thirty-one years later, some of the commissioners at the PCUSA General Assembly meeting in 1818 longed for the same. But slavery was expanding, and anti-Black racism was growing stronger. In the years and decades following 1818, the debates about slavery evolved and further exacerbated cultural, political, racial, and religious tensions in the United States. Individual Black and white Presbyterians helped to forge new pathways for abolitionist activism and Black liberation, but most white Presbyterian congregations and denominations turned Beriah Green's nightmare into a reality in leveraging their cultural and religious influence to justify Black enslavement and sanctify anti-Black racism.

5

"But What Do We See When We Look at the American Church?"

By the time the PCUSA General Assembly met in 1836, Charles Hodge had been a professor at Princeton Theological Seminary for over a decade and had acquired a reputation as one of the most renowned Christian theologians in his denomination and the United States. After graduating from the seminary in 1819, Hodge began pastoring but quickly discerned that his vocation was in the academy rather than congregational ministry, and so he returned to the seminary to teach. In 1825, he founded a theological journal that gained enormous influence among its Presbyterian readership as well as intellectual elites across many academic disciplines. Hodge traveled to Europe to study Semitic language and theology in Paris, Halle, and Berlin from 1826 to 1828. After his return, Hodge resumed teaching at the seminary, editing his journal, and writing numerous articles about biblical interpretation, Reformed theology, and ecclesiastical matters. Hodge also commented on contemporary religious developments, such as the controversies surrounding the emotionalism and populism of the revival movement. But Hodge had yet to write about slavery. Hodge, like several of his faculty colleagues at Princeton Seminary, was an enslaver. Hodge purchased Henrietta, an enslaved Black woman, for seventy-five dollars in 1828 and inherited another enslaved Black woman, Lena, a few years later from his family's estate.[1] The gradual emancipation bill in New Jersey was passed in 1804, but it guaranteed freedom for enslaved persons born after July 4, 1804, only when they turned twenty-one (for

103

women) or twenty-five (for men) years of age. Enslaved persons born prior to this date could also be freed, but the decision was incumbent on their enslavers with no legal mandate.

Hodge was able to remain publicly silent on Black enslavement for several years. He, like other white Presbyterians, took refuge in his denomination's nonbinding declaration against slavery from the General Assembly in 1818 that denounced it in principle but recommended no disciplinary action against enslavers. But the stirrings of Black liberation in the late 1820s and 1830s—with the establishment of abolitionist newspapers such as *Freedom's Journal* in 1827, edited by the Black Presbyterian pastor Samuel Eli Cornish, and *The Liberator* in 1831; the rise of organizations such as the American Anti-Slavery Society (AASS) in 1833; and the antislavery resolutions and addresses from the Chillicothe Presbytery and Synod of Kentucky in 1835—forced Hodge's hand. Hodge understood that abolitionists in his denomination saw the General Assembly meeting in 1836 as an opportunity to move the PCUSA toward a more actionable polity on Black enslavement, such as banning slave-owning members from the Communion table, so Hodge published his first essay on slavery one month before the General Assembly gathered. He argued that the debates concerning Black enslavement must be resolved according to the Bible, and therefore he sought to "ascertain the scriptural rule of judgment and conduct in relation to it." Hodge observed that while slavery existed throughout the first-century Greco-Roman world, Jesus Christ and the apostles neither denounced "slaveholding as necessarily and universally sinful" nor pronounced that "all slaveholders were men-stealers and robbers, and consequently to be excluded from the church and the kingdom of heaven." Instead, the apostles sanctioned and regulated slavery with specific precepts for masters and slaves. Hodge appealed to these mandates in the New Testament for slaves with "believing or Christian masters, not to despise them because they were on a perfect religious equality with them, but to consider the fact that their masters were their brethren, as an additional reason for obedience." Christian enslavers were likewise instructed to be kind and just in their slave ownership, but they were not taught to liberate their enslaved persons. Therefore, Hodge criticized abolitionists for incorrectly interpreting the Bible and forcing their agenda upon it to usurp the authority of Jesus Christ and the apostles, "the authors of our religion," in appealing to the New Testament in their struggle for Black liberation.[2]

Almost instantly, Hodge's article was widely circulated, frequently quoted, and reprinted in several formats, including in a pamphlet distributed on the floor of the General Assembly in 1836. One historian argues that "Hodge published in the *Princeton Review* and in separate pamphlets perhaps the most important and instructive contributions toward the formation of a national proslavery ideology of any nineteenth-century American."[3] White Presbyterians in the southern states praised Hodge for the theological clarity and scriptural precision they believed he had demonstrated in the article. They celebrated the fact that one of their denomination's finest thinkers and most respected leaders, a professor teaching at their flagship seminary in a northern state, defended Black enslavement.

Black and white Presbyterian abolitionists were enraged at Hodge for his proslavery publication. Because of the racial power structures in the Presbyterian Church, as well as the scourge of anti-Black racism in the northern states, white Presbyterians publicly protested Hodge's article whereas Black Presbyterians fumed and collaborated with their white allies privately. Gerrit Smith, a white Presbyterian scion of a wealthy family of landowners and merchants in New York, railed against Hodge in 1837 for defending American slavery on biblical grounds despite acknowledging its many sins of physical and spiritual abuse toward enslaved persons. He mocked Hodge for lending his authority as a "Professor of Theology" to support Black enslavement in his "polished, but pernicious, article on slavery."[4] Beriah Green disparaged Hodge's doctrine of a "perfect religious equality" between white Christian enslavers and enslaved Black Christians as a falsity because it permitted the former party to degrade and exploit the latter party. Green retorted, "Give perfect religious equality to the American slave, and the most eager abolitionist must be satisfied. Such equality would, like the breath of the Almighty, dissolve the last link of the chain of servitude." Green attributed the inaction at the General Assembly meeting in 1836 to the circulation of Hodge's article there and blamed him, derisively calling Hodge "our Princeton prophet," for his instrumental role in uniting the denomination against Black liberation.[5] Another white Presbyterian minister, Samuel Crothers, observed in 1837 that Hodge's article provided cover to white slave-owning ministers and proponents of Black enslavement. In the months following Hodge's article, Crothers found that these pastors opted to quote from Hodge's article rather than defend slavery in their own words.[6]

Elizur Wright Jr. also denounced Hodge's proslavery theology. In July 1836, Wright eviscerated Hodge's work in an article, "Slavery, and Its Ecclesiastical Defenders," charging Hodge with two offenses. The first offense shared the criticisms of Smith and Green. According to Wright, Hodge employed an inconsistent logic in his division between slavery in the abstract and in actuality. Hodge divorced all the sins within Black enslavement from the system so that he could simultaneously condemn the many abuses as unbiblical and defend the oppressive system as biblical. Wright lambasted Hodge's rationale as absurd without any semblance of a sound foundation, writing about Hodge, "But when pressed with the cruel practices, the wicked laws, the horrible results, he flies off, exclaiming, 'Oh! These are wrong to be sure, but then they are not necessarily any part of slavery itself.' This is the hole at which he is perpetually creeping out."[7] The second offense struck at the immorality of Hodge as a human being and a Christian. Wright accused Hodge of using his genius to be disingenuous about the obvious injustices of American slavery because Hodge refused to grapple with it "openly or honestly." Hodge, like too many white Christians, chose to turn his attention away from the brutal realities of Black enslavement and preferred instead to engage in intricate theological arguments about the definitions of slavery in the Bible. Wright was especially critical of white Presbyterians when asking, "But what do we see when we look at the American church?" When Wright looked at the Presbyterian Church, he saw "one of the largest denominations in America" that averred "to embrace the better sort of people" who "stand on the top of society" with emphases on doctrinal purity and spiritual piety. Yet for all their talk about purity and piety, Wright found that the Presbyterian Church was marked by "depravity and hypocrisy" for its deep participation in Black enslavement.[8] Why did Charles Hodge and other white Presbyterians oppose Black liberation? They said their primary reason was because they were bound to the authority of the Bible. But other powerful forces existed in their lives, their churches, and their nation. White Presbyterians, like all Americans, were captive to the economy of slavery. Therefore, they also defended Black enslavement because of its centrality to their financial prosperity and societal stability. Perhaps Wright's criticism regarding the shaky foundation of Hodge's proslavery theology was disputable, but the reality that slavery lay at the foundation of every facet of American life, including within its religious congregations, was incontrovertible.

"No Sect in the Land Has Done More to Perpetuate Slavery Than This": The Unique Place of White Presbyterianism and Its Terrible History with American Slavery

Why did abolitionists look to Presbyterians specifically? Some aboli-tionists did so because they were Presbyterians or closely connected to Presbyterianism. Black and white Presbyterians comprised at least half of the AASS executive committee in 1834, including Black pastors Samuel Eli Cornish and Theodore S. Wright, white pastors Samuel H. Cox and John Rankin, and white commercial merchants and broth-ers Arthur Tappan and Lewis Tappan.[9] For the first three years of the organization's existence, the annual meetings of the AASS were held in Presbyterian church buildings in New York City. Other abolition-ists appealed to Presbyterians because some of them were persons of financial means, cultural influence, and high social standing. Presby-terianism did not comprise the most members before the Civil War, but it was among the wealthiest Christian traditions in the nation. In the 1850 U.S. census, there were 13,280 Methodist churches, 9,375 Baptist churches, 4,824 Presbyterian churches, 1,706 Congrega-tional churches, and 1,459 Episcopal churches. Though Presbyteri-ans ranked third in the number of churches, they ranked second in the value of church property. The cumulative value of Presbyterian church property was $14,543,789, slightly below the value of Method-ist church property ($14,822,870). The value of Episcopal, Baptist, and Congregational church property was $11,375,010, $11,020,855, and $7,970,195, respectively.[10] When dividing the value of church property by the number of churches in these five traditions, Presbyte-rians ($3,014.88) ranked third behind Episcopalians ($7,796.44) and Congregationalists ($4,671.86) and ahead of Baptists ($1,175.56) and Methodists ($1,116.18).

The American Almanac for 1850 provided the following estimates for the numbers of adherents in each of the traditions: 1,230,069 Meth-odists, 952,693 Baptists, 435,377 Presbyterians, 227,196 Congrega-tionalists, and 67,550 Episcopalians.[11] Presbyterians occupied a unique place in the antebellum United States. They were simultaneously elitist and populist, with a diverse membership that comprised persons from the lower, middle, and upper classes, in contrast to the near uniform wealth among Episcopalians. Whereas most Congregationalists resided in the northern states, Presbyterians, like Methodists and Baptists, wor-shiped in congregations across the northern and southern states. There were fewer Presbyterians than either Methodists or Baptists but likely more middle- and upper-class persons in Presbyterianism compared to the two larger traditions.

Foreign observers took note of the distinctive influence of Presbyterians in the United States. In 1837, English sociologist Harriet Martineau gave special attention to Presbyterians as "a very large" body of Christians in a nation in which Christianity had a powerful influence in shaping the "habits of thought" and "habits of living" of its people. Martineau found that "some of the most noble of the abolitionists" as well as some of the most wicked defenders of slavery were Presbyterian.[12] Several years later, Scottish Presbyterian minister George Lewis noticed that white persons from the middle and upper classes in Washington, D.C., attended Episcopal and Presbyterian churches, whereas the "poorer whites" and Black persons worshiped at Methodist and Baptist churches.[13] In 1863, Georges Fisch, pastor of a French Protestant congregation in Paris, detailed his travels throughout the United States and agreed that Presbyterianism was "the back-bone" of the country, a popular notion shared with him by others and one he confirmed in his own observations about its middle-class ethos: "Accordingly Presbyterianism is the religious form preferred by the industrial and commercial classes, by men of enterprise and initiative."[14] Like Martineau, Fisch viewed Christianity as having a "preponderating influence" in the "morals, habits, and inmost thoughts" of Americans. Fisch therefore laid blame upon all white Christians, but especially Presbyterians, "who chiefly fabricated the system of biblical slavery," for upholding Black enslavement.[15]

Abolitionists in the United States also condemned white Presbyterians as the guiltiest perpetrators of Black enslavement and the fiercest opponents of Black liberation. Stephen S. Foster, a white Congregationalist and husband of Abby Kelley Foster, a prominent activist for abolitionism and women's rights, accused white Presbyterians in 1843 of leveraging their considerable influence to commit the utmost evils. Because white Presbyterians were not content with participating as enslavers but also constituted the "most active and energetic" enemies of the abolition movement, Foster stated of Presbyterianism, "No sect in the land has done more to perpetuate slavery than this."[16] Foster's assessment about Presbyterianism was put to the test in the following two years. In 1844 and 1845, Methodists, Baptists, and Presbyterians all confronted the question of whether their respective denominations would discipline slave-owning members for their enslaving sins.

Like Presbyterians, Methodists and Baptists had resisted the abolitionists within their denominations seeking unequivocal condemnations of Black enslavement until 1844. Early Methodist leaders, such as the white pastors Francis Asbury and Thomas Coke, opposed slavery, and they led their denomination to adopt firm policies against slaveowning clergy. In 1780, Methodists required a pledge from their slaveowning preachers to emancipate their enslaved persons and declare that "slavery is contrary to the laws of God, man, and nature." But they suspended this rule five years later after significant protest. In 1798, Asbury lamented the compromises he had made in his leadership because of slavery: "O! to be dependent on slaveholders is in part to be a slave and I was free born. I am brought to conclude that slavery will exist in Virginia perhaps for ages; there is not a sufficient sense of religion nor of liberty to destroy it; Methodists, Baptists, Presbyterians, in the highest flights of rapturous piety, still maintain and defend it."[17] One historian finds that "slavery haunted Asbury to the end of his life." In the last two years of his life, until his death in 1816, Asbury frequently thought and talked about Black enslavement. Asbury was convinced that the economic wealth produced by slavery was the actual motivation behind the many biblical and theological justifications of it from white Methodists and other white Christians, and he died believing what many enslaved and free Black Christians surmised: it was not possible for an enslaver to enter the kingdom of God.[18] In 1844, there was sufficient agitation from Methodists in the northern states to demand that one of their bishops in Georgia, James Osgood Andrew, withdraw from his work until he divested himself of the enslaved persons he had acquired through marriage. White Methodists from the southern states were incensed, and the largest Methodist denomination, the Methodist Episcopal Church, split along regional lines that year. In 1845, white Baptists from the southern states removed themselves from their national Triennial Convention and formed the Southern Baptist Convention in protest of a decision in 1844 to deny the appointments of enslavers as missionaries.[19]

The Scottish minister George Lewis was present in Louisville when the General Assembly of the largest Presbyterian denomination, the PCUSA (Old School), met in 1844. Lewis was grateful for the warm welcome he received on the floor of the General Assembly as a visitor representing the Free Church of Scotland. But he was soon "cast down by the reception which the Assembly gave to the question of slavery."[20] On the eighth day of the proceedings, the commissioners supported a motion to abort discussion of their denomination's position on slavery by a vote of 115 in favor, 70 in opposition, and 1 abstention.[21] Lewis was aghast at the refusal of even a discussion on slavery and conferred privately with one of the commissioners. Lewis asked whether the matter of U.S. laws prohibiting the education of enslaved persons was a part of the discussion and divulged that he thought this was an obvious injustice antithetical to Presbyterianism because it denied persons access to read the Bible for themselves, one of the bedrock principles of the Reformed tradition. The commissioner sadly agreed with Lewis but replied that some white clergy in the southern states were "content to acquit our consciences by disobeying privately" through offering scriptural instruction to enslaved persons. The commissioner also added that the white Presbyterians in Louisville were simply not prepared to speak publicly about slavery.[22]

The commissioners at the PCUSA (Old School) General Assembly meeting one year later in Cincinnati understood that the actions and schisms among Methodists and Baptists made it nearly impossible for them to further prevent or postpone a decision on slavery. A special committee was appointed on the third day of the proceedings to make a recommendation. Three days later, the committee submitted a report dividing the abolitionist protests within their denomination into "three classes." The first class entailed "those which represent the system of Slavery, as it exists in these United States, as a great evil, and pray this General Assembly to adopt measures for the amelioration of the condition of the slaves." The second class desired for the General Assembly to "allow a full discussion" of slavery and encourage members of their denomination in the southern states "to seek by all lawful means" the repeal of laws that "forbid the slaves being taught to read." The third class called upon the General Assembly to enforce ecclesial discipline on members "maintaining or justifying the relation of master to slaves."[23] This group advocated for Presbyterians to move from words to actions. The General Assembly in 1818 had already approved a report stating that slavery was evil, so the next step was to censure the enslavers and enablers of slavery in their denomination, not to produce another report. But a report was precisely what was forthcoming.

As the committee met to prepare the report, its members agreed that church unity was their most important commitment and consulted with several commissioners from the southern states. James Henley Thornwell, a commissioner from the Charleston Presbytery and professor of biblical studies and theology at the University of South Carolina, emerged as one of the leading voices in these gatherings. Thornwell was respected as one of the brightest thinkers among white Presbyterians in his region. In 1847, he was one of the founding editors of a theological journal, *Southern Presbyterian Review*, and he joined the faculty of Columbia Theological Seminary in 1855. Thornwell wrote his wife, Nancy Witherspoon Thornwell, from Cincinnati to share about his crucial work staving off the implementation of a firmer position against Black enslavement: "The question of slavery has been before the house, and referred to a special committee of seven. Though not a member of the committee, I have been consulted on the subject, and have drawn up a paper, which I think the committee and the Assembly will substantially adopt; and if they do, abolitionism will be killed in the Presbyterian Church, at least for the present."[24]

Thornwell's paper, which the committee advanced as its own, emphasized the spirituality of the church, which meant that the General Assembly's jurisdiction pertained only to the "religious faith" and "moral conduct" of its members. Presbyterians were not permitted to "legislate where Christ has not legislated."[25] Six years later, Thornwell argued in 1851 that the Bible addressed slavery in "cool, dispassioned, [and] didactic" language and treated it as a hierarchical relation alongside husbands and wives, parents and children, and magistrates and subjects.[26] Thornwell also preached in 1850 that slavery was "a part of the curse which sin has introduced into the world" and compared it to poverty and war as earthly phenomena that would persist until the eschaton.[27] As a commissioner to the General Assembly in 1845, Thornwell devised a way to reorient the "three classes" of abolitionist appeals into a single question that was less about the atrocities of Black enslavement and more about interpretations of the doctrine of scriptural authority. The committee recommended that the General Assembly address the following question: "Do the Scriptures teach that the holding of slaves, without regard to circumstances, is a sin, the renunciation of which should be made a condition of membership in the church of Christ?"[28] In presenting the decision on slavery in this manner, Thornwell built on Hodge's proslavery contention from 1836 that Presbyterians lacked explicit biblical warrant to declare slavery as sinful to advance his own argument restricting the authority of the Presbyterian Church to doctrinal matters, like the debates around revivalism and original sin, and not civil and political issues such as slavery. The boundaries on what constituted political matters remained in flux, such that supporting temperance and resisting women's rights from the pulpit were permissible, but Thornwell helped to shape a consensus among white Presbyterians about slavery as a civil institution outside of their church's authority. The commissioners almost unanimously sided with Thornwell and the committee: 168 voted with them and only thirteen voted against them, along with three abstentions.[29] Thornwell also exulted to his wife about the significance of defeating abolitionist efforts in a city he called "the stronghold of abolitionism" because of the formidable presence of antislavery activism there.[30] Although Thornwell did not receive public recognition for his leadership, since he was not a formal member of the special committee, he received a greater honor two years later when he was elected moderator of the General Assembly in 1847 at the age of thirty-four, making him the youngest person to hold the position to that point in the denomination's history.

"And the Business of the North, as well as the South, Has Become Adjusted to It": The Economic Centrality of Black Enslavement in the United States

What made white Presbyterians in the northern states more captive to slavery than white Methodists and Baptists? A majority of white Methodists in the northern states refused to allow an enslaver to hold the office of bishop and exercise leadership over important ecclesial affairs. A sufficient number of white Baptists in the northern states resolved to oppose the hypocritical act of commissioning slave-owning missionaries to proclaim the gospel message throughout the world. Yet the white members of the PCUSA (Old School) from the northern states honored the enslavers and proponents of Black enslavement within their denomination and entrusted them to be their ministers, missionaries, and moderators. There is nothing inherent in the Reformed faith, such as its doctrines of human depravity or original sin, or distinctive about Presbyterian approaches to biblical interpretation, to explain the capitulation of white Presbyterians to American slavery. Presbyterians in Ireland and Scotland shared in the same Reformed heritage as white Presbyterians in the United States, as well as similar approaches to reading the Bible, yet they overwhelmingly supported abolition. One historian of abolitionism in Scotland, a nation steeped in Presbyterianism, argues that "by 1830, disapproval of slavery could be assumed in all respectable and literate Scots homes."[31] White Methodists and

Baptists in the southern states also adhered to literalist approaches to biblical interpretation in justifying Black enslavement. In 1841, the white Baptist pastor Thornton Stringfellow maintained that a plain and commonsense reading of the Bible revealed that the institution of slavery was "recognized, and its relative duties regulated, by Jesus Christ."[32] Hodge, Stringfellow, Thornwell, and other white Protestant proslavery thinkers added their own accents, but they all generally based their scholarship around the same underlying principle about the divine sanction for slavery in the Scriptures.

White Presbyterians were likely more susceptible to the corrosive moral influence of American slavery because of its economic centrality. Eli Whitney's invention of the cotton gin in 1793 and technological advances within the textile industry in the early nineteenth century made cotton one of the most profitable plants to cultivate. Whitney's cotton gin made the process of separating cotton from seed far more efficient, and the development of new weaving and spinning machines transformed cotton manufacturing. The rise of slavery in the United States was directly related to the increasing profitability of cotton. Between 1790 and 1810, Georgia's cotton production grew from 3,138 to 177,824 bales and its enslaved population increased from 29,000 to 105,000 persons.[33]

In addition to the cotton industry, the rapid growth of the rice industry also created more demand for enslaved labor. By the start of the Civil War, two-thirds of the wealthiest Americans lived in the southern states. In 1860, 80 percent of the nation's gross national product was connected to slavery, and the twelve wealthiest counties were below the Mason-Dixon Line.[34] In the 1860 U.S. census, there were over 100,000 more enslaved Black persons (402,406) than white persons (291,300) in South Carolina. In 1825, Whitemarsh B. Seabrook, a white planter and politician from South Carolina, argued that the economic viability of the United States in the global marketplace relied almost entirely on enslaved agricultural labor by pointing out that the production of cotton, rice, and tobacco from the southern states accounted for 60 percent of all U.S. exports. Seabrook also estimated that the total value of the enslaved population was between $300,000,000 and $600,000,000 and suggested the cost of emancipation to the annual budget of the federal government alone would be at least $40,000,000.[35] Presbyterians in Scotland understood that their textile industry was dependent on U.S. cotton, but their economy was also diversifying as middle-class Scots turned away from the Caribbean plantations and looked toward financial opportunities in England, Canada, Asia, and Oceania.[36] But white Presbyterians in the United States knew that their wealth and well-being were inextricably linked to Black enslavement, which remained at the center of their economy.

Abolitionists in the United States acknowledged that the economy of slavery made it difficult for white Christians to support Black liberation, in part because that was what they heard directly from white Christians themselves. In 1835, Samuel J. May, a white Unitarian minister working with the New England Anti-Slavery Society, encountered a white merchant at a Presbyterian church in New York City. The merchant asked May to walk out of the church with him so they could converse more freely. Once outside on the street, the merchant explained, "Mr. May, we are not such fools as not to know that slavery is a great evil, a great wrong. But it was consented to by the founders of our Republic. It was provided for in the Constitution of our Union. A great portion of the property of the Southerners is invested under its sanction; and the business of the North, as well as the South, has become adjusted to it." The merchant shared that his opposition to abolitionists like May therefore was not over "a matter of principle" but rather revolved around "a matter of business necessity."[37] Charles C. Jones admitted that an economy reliant on enslaved labor led some planters to treat enslaved persons as "creatures of profit" rather than as human beings made in the image of God.[38] But Jones, like Hodge and Thornwell, insisted that the economic exploitation within Black enslavement, along with its other incidental evils, did not disprove their biblical justifications for slavery. In 1835, a committee from the Synod of Kentucky disagreed with this literalist interpretation of the Bible and found that the New Testament surely condemned American slavery with a striking metaphor about a physician diagnosing a patient. The committee argued that it would be ludicrous for a patient, after being told by a physician that "every limb and organ was diseased," to declare the body was not unsound because the physician had not "said in *express terms* that my body is unsound."[39] When weighing the morality and economy of Black enslavement, the committee's members decided that they, and other white Presbyterians, must choose the principles of abolition over the business necessities of slavery, no matter the financial cost.

In 1837, the AASS, an organization with wealthy white industrialists and merchants in its ranks, recognized the financial stakes involved in slavery. It stated that "the desire to get the most riches for the least labor" was not unique to American slavery but a common phenom-enon throughout world history after the original sin of Adam.[40] But one distinct aspect of American slavery was its foundational nature and the ways it took root and grew within every branch of the national economy. In Caitlin Rosenthal's economic history of American slavery, Rosenthal observes that a profitable business in the antebellum United States required land, labor, and capital. One advantage in the southern states was that enslaved persons counted as both labor and capital. In addition to their agricultural production on cotton, rice, and tobacco fields, enslaved persons were valuable human capital whose value could appreciate through maturation and reproduction.[41] In 1860, the annual household budget of a middle-class family in the United States was approximately between $1,200 and $1,500.[42] At a slave auction in the same year, the price of one enslaved man and one enslaved woman in the prime of their lives ranged from $1,550 to $1,625 and $1,375 to $1,450, respectively.[43] Enslavers also used their enslaved persons as collateral for loans; approximately 40 percent of all southern mortgages were secured with human collateral.[44] Another historian of slavery and American capitalism, Bonnie Martin, finds that "capital raised using human collateral was likely a major driver of economic development" because of the increased access it granted to enslavers for bank loans and mortgages they otherwise would not have been able to obtain with their cash alone.[45] In 1860, the wealth per capita (free persons) in the South Carolina Lowcountry was $2,253.60, significantly higher than in Massachusetts ($625.19), New York ($596.99), and Pennsylvania ($570.92). But the human capital of enslaved persons accounted for approximately 50 percent of the South Carolina Lowcountry's wealth. In 1870, five years after the Civil War, the mean per capita wealth had decreased to $347.96.[46]

John Hartwell Cocke, a white Presbyterian planter in Virginia, criti-cized the tyranny of Black enslavement and supported the American Colonization Society (ACS). Cocke hoped for a future in Virginia free from the institution of slavery and all Black Americans. In the early 1840s, Cocke purchased two plantations in Alabama and transported forty-nine of his enslaved persons there to prepare them for emanci-pation and migration to Liberia. Cocke had them covenant to earn through their agricultural labor the equivalent of their value (approxi-mately $1,400 each) and be honest and obedient, abstaining from alco-hol, cursing, fighting, and sexual promiscuity. If they fulfilled these promises, Cocke would emancipate them and pay for their migration to Liberia.[47] Cocke's plan mostly failed, with only six enslaved persons meeting his expectations by 1853, but his effort to support the ACS with his own human capital was uncommon.

As much as Cocke detested Black enslavement, he also recognized that slave ownership was the surest pathway to the middle class for white farmers in the southern states because enslaved persons provided multiple revenue streams. In the seasons when the price of tobacco was low in the marketplace, or when the crop production was diminished, white farmers could either sell or lease their enslaved persons for additional income. Their investment in human capital was also collateral for additional loans and mortgages. Cocke observed that these "enterprising cultivators who have accumulated their own Fortunes" within the "middle class" of white Virginians comprised the most ardent defenders of Black enslavement.[48] In 1818, another white planter, James Steer, likewise observed, "For a young man, just commencing life, the best stock, in which he can invest Capital, is, I think, negro Stock." Steer was convinced that slave ownership proved a more secure investment than "any Bank dividend."[49] In 1859, Jones advised his son, Charles C. Jones Jr., to hire a "reliable manager" for his new plantation and to be mindful of the prices of cotton, produce, and enslaved persons, noting that there was "much inflation at present in the value of Negro property."[50] Cocke and Jones were wealthy enslavers. In 1860, Cocke owned 135 enslaved persons and Jones owned 129.[51] Their fortunes were yoked to Black enslavement, but they also understood the precarious centrality of slave ownership for the white middle class. Within the class diversity of Presbyterianism, some of its members were white middle-class farmers. With less land, fewer enslaved persons, and lower agricultural output than wealthy planters, the livelihoods of these white farmers revolved entirely around the value of their human capital.

Some white Presbyterian abolitionists acknowledged the obvious unwillingness of enslavers to support Black liberation because it went against their financial interests, and so they turned their attention to the lower-class white persons in the southern states who did not participate in slave ownership. In 1843, Lewis Tappan appealed to "non-slaveholders" in the southern states in an essay detailing his economic rationale for abolition. Tappan explained that his aim was not to convince them that slavery was "cruel and unjust" toward the Black race. Instead, his purpose was to illustrate how Black enslavement created and perpetuated a vicious cycle of wealth inequality and crushing poverty for white persons. He estimated that only 248,711 of the 1,016,307 white men over twenty years of age in the southern states were enslavers. Therefore, approximately 75 percent of the white population did not have access to this lucrative source of human capital. The institution of slavery only benefited the wealthy because of the price of enslaved persons, which was beyond the means of most white persons. "When an infant will bring one hundred, and a man from four hundred to a thousand dollars in the market," Tappan noted, "slaves are not commodities to be found in the cabins of the poor."[52] In Keri Leigh Merritt's work on poor white persons in the antebellum southern states, the historian finds that in 1860 "slightly more than a thousand families accounted for nearly half of the Deep South's wealth," and "the region's poorest half of the population held only 5 percent of its wealth." Merritt also identifies the financial barriers that made it nearly impossible for lower-class white persons to become enslavers and suggests that it required $130,000 in 2011 U.S. dollars (roughly $157,000 in 2021 U.S. dollars) to purchase an enslaved person in 1860.[53] In addition to the cost of slave ownership, another barrier was the prevalence of a credit-driven economy with few cash transactions, which favored white persons with existing holdings in land and human capital.[54] Tappan also compared the higher rates of white population growth in the northern states versus the southern states and attributed the difference to the contrasting regional economies. The primary industry in the southern states was agriculture, but it did not create jobs for white persons because of enslaved labor. In the northern states, the growth of the manufacturing industry presented more job opportunities for lower-class white persons.

In 1847, Henry Ruffner, a white Presbyterian pastor and the president of Washington College (now Washington and Lee University) in Virginia, agreed with Tappan's economic assessment. Ruffner was an enslaver and no proponent of Tappan's abolitionism, but he supported gradual emancipation and the removal of free Black persons in western Virginia (West Virginia in 1863, when it became a state) because of the plight of lower-class white persons there. Ruffner lamented the limited employment opportunities for lower-class white persons amid the dominance of an agricultural economy with an enslaved Black workforce. He conceded that the northern states had a healthier and more diversified economy of agriculture, commerce, and manufacturing. Over six decades of U.S. history had proven that the system of "free labor" was superior to "slave labor" in terms of prosperity for the overall white population. Ruffner contended, "It is a truth, a certain truth, that slavery drives free laborers—farmers, mechanics, and all, and some of the best of them too—out of the country, and fills their places with negroes."[55] Ruffner also criticized the deleterious effects of slavery on the morality and work ethic of white persons. White persons associated work in the fields and kitchens as "negroes' work" and rebuffed many types of agricultural and domestic labor opportunities even though their refusal was at odds with their financial well-being. Ruffner was also the rare white Virginian to openly concede the reality of slave breeding in his state—not as a "chosen occupation" but rather as a "dire necessity" when the agricultural economy was in decline—as another reason to gradually abolish slavery in western Virginia.[56] In 1848, several months after the publication of Ruffner's essay, which became known as the "Ruffner Pamphlet," he was forced to resign from the presidency of the college, due in no small part to his public criticism of slavery and advocacy for gradual emancipation.[57]

Despite the economic concerns of Tappan and Ruffner, the two wealthy men clearly did not share the same social context as lower-class white persons in the southern states. How many lower-class white persons were Presbyterian? Several historians suggest the number is slight. Though it is "incredibly hard to estimate how many poor whites attended church," Merritt argues that a meager percentage of lower-class white persons in the southern states worshiped in a congregation because of their inabilities to purchase and read the Bible, their residences in backwoods or outskirts away from church buildings that were often in the heart of a town, and social stigmatization.[58] Some lower-class white Christians lacked churchgoing attire, and many more were uncomfortable in middle- and upper-class worship spaces.

When lower-class white persons went to church, it was likely to a Methodist or Baptist one. The white abolitionist Moncure Daniel Conway observed in 1864 that lower-class white persons had "nothing that can be called religion or education" and that the few who were Christian occasionally went to "a Methodist or Baptist" camp meeting "once or twice in three months."[59] Some white Presbyterians, notably in Kentucky and Tennessee, embraced camp meetings and the populist spirit of revivalism in the early nineteenth century, but most white Presbyterians were resistant to the revival movement and insistent on a formally educated clergy. In 1810, three white Presbyterian pastors—Finis Ewing, Samuel King, and Samuel McAdow—established a presbytery in Tennessee that developed into a separate denomination (Cumberland Presbyterian Church) diverging from the

PCUSA on revivalism and ordination standards.[60] But white Presbyterians generally preferred more orderly worship services with sermons from seminary-trained preachers who knew how to parse Greek and Hebrew verbs. In Bruce Collins's history of white religious cultures in the antebellum southern states, Collins traces the origins of many white rural spirituals to early emigration from heavily Presbyterian regions in Scotland and Ireland. But with the religious changes in the first half of the nineteenth century, these songs were primarily heard among Methodists and Baptists, not Presbyterians.[61]

White slave-owning Presbyterian clergy seldom spoke publicly about the economic benefits of Black enslavement. In 1836, James Smylie acknowledged that one could not preach about abolition in the southern states because of its direct financial implications. In the ears of a slave-owning man, a sermon about Black liberation would sound as follows: "It is the tendency of the Gospel, to make him so poor, as to oblige him to take hold of the maul and wedge himself—he must catch, curry, and saddle his own horse. . . . His wife must go, herself, to the wash tub—take hold of the scrubbing broom, wash the pots and cook, all that she and her rail mauler will eat."[62] Smylie was wrong about this outcome for wealthy white planters after the Civil War, because they hired Black and white laborers to perform all of these domestic tasks, and he was engaging in hyperbole to make his point, but he captured the unspoken reality that permeated throughout the sanctuaries where he and other white clergy preached: Black liberation went against the economic interests of enslavers, especially in terms of human capital. Jones wrote infrequently about the economy of slavery, but he and every other slave-owning Presbyterian meticulously tracked the value of their human capital. Just as they tracked the prices of cotton, rice, tobacco, and other produce, they also knew how much their enslaved persons were worth in the slave marketplace. In 1854, Jones advised his sister, Susan M. Cumming, "Cotton is low, and you must *practice economy to keep out of debt.*"[63] Two years later, he wrote letters to his son about the forthcoming sale of eight of their enslaved persons. Jones made the following estimates: "C. Sr. Father. Age 45. Good field hand, basket-maker, and handy at jobs (I put him at that; Mother thinks it too low): $800"; "P. Mother. Age 47. Accomplished house servant in any and every line: good cook, washer and ironer, and fine seamstress: $1,000"; "P. Son. Field hand. Handy fellow. Age 16: $800"; "V. Daughter. Age 14. Smart, active field hand: $800."[64] These estimates were listed in private correspondence, but nobody in the age of Black enslavement would have thought Jones's practice was unusual. The enslaved adults in Jones's letter likely knew their own valuations with the same precision as Jones because they too kept a constant eye on the slave marketplace.[65]

In addition to their silence regarding the economic benefits, white clergy were just as reticent about the social meanings of slave ownership. In Dale Evans Swan's study of the antebellum rice industry of coastal South Carolina and Georgia, the historian discovered that the rates of return for planters with over thirty enslaved laborers in 1859 were between 7.7 percent and 18 percent.[66] Although the rates of return were lower for planters with fewer enslaved laborers, white persons pursued slave ownership for several reasons, some of which reflected the cultural and emotional dimensions of wealth and class. Slave ownership, like homeownership or wearing fashionable clothing, was a visible social marker signifying success. In the northern states of Connecticut, Massachusetts, and Rhode Island, one initial obstacle to abolition was this social component. In a region where the profitability of slave ownership was nowhere near as high as in the southern states, many middle- and upper-class white families in the seventeenth and eighteenth centuries owned enslaved persons for domestic labor. One historian of slavery in colonial New England finds that "no prominent household was complete without its retinue of black servants" throughout Boston, Hartford, New Haven, Narragansett, and other similar cities.[67] In 1687, one French Protestant visitor observed, "You may also own Negroes and Negresses; there is not a house in Boston, however small may be its means, that has not one or two. There are those that have five or six, and all make a good living."[68] In the southern states, slave ownership continued to represent social respectability and provide the psychic benefits accompanying wealth and class.

In addition to tracing the centrality of Black enslavement to the economy of the southern states, the AASS explained why some white Christians in the northern states were simultaneously antislavery and antiabolition. As much as these white Christians despised slavery, they did not support abolition because they feared its financial consequences as much as slave-owning Christians. At one level, white manufacturers and exporters in the northern states relied upon raw materials produced by enslaved labor in the southern states. In 1860, Thomas Kettell made connections between the two regional economies in his book *Southern Wealth and Northern Profits* and linked the natural resources of the southern states with the industrial capacities in the northern states.[69]

For example, the former sold their raw cotton to the latter and the latter turned it into clothing to sell in the global market. At another level, the economy in the northern states was also heavily dependent on consumers from the southern states. In 1860, the *Boston Post* estimated that the "aggregate value of Boston merchandise sold to the South annually" was $60,000,000, which included $20,000,000 in shoes alone.[70]

In 1837, the AASS noted these "interwoven" economic dynamics when identifying the stakeholders of Black enslavement: "northern merchants, northern mechanics, and manufacturers, northern editors, publishers, and printers, northern hotels, stages, steamboats, rail-roads, canal boats, northern banks, northern schoolmasters, northern artists, northern colleges, and northern ministers of the Gospel."[71] The organization used the example of the acquiescence of the New York–based Harper and Brothers publishing house to complaints from white readers in the southern states regarding Anne Marsh-Caldwell's book *Tales of the Woods and Fields* in 1836. These readers protested because they interpreted one of the book's chapters as advocating for abolition. In response, the company immediately apologized and republished an edition of the book without the chapter, writing a letter to a bookseller in South Carolina emphasizing the new edition "in which the offensive matter has been omitted." The AASS highlighted this decision from Harper and Brothers, an ostensibly "honorable business" seeking to "bring into the world the creations of thought," as a perilous indication of how "the idol of slavery has been set up and the burning wrath of the South has been proclaimed as the penalty for refusing to fall down and worship."[72] A plethora of white individuals and institutions in the northern states made moral compromises to accommodate enslavers and thusly exhibit their complicity in Black enslavement.

The Power and Peril of the "Bible Argument"

The college in Princeton where Charles Hodge and his father, Hugh Hodge, were nurtured as students, and the seminary where Charles Hodge taught as a professor, were among the most complicit educational institutions. During the presidency of John Witherspoon from 1768 to 1794, Princeton University welcomed white students from elite slave-owning families and had an unusually high percentage of its enrollment from the southern states. In Craig Steven Wilder's history of slavery and higher education in the United States, Wilder finds that at Princeton "the percentage of young men from the South more than doubled during Witherspoon's tenure, while the proportion from elite backgrounds more than tripled."[73] Another historian, Allen C. Guelzo, notes that as much as one-third of the student population at the college was from the southern states between 1800 and 1860, and debates on slavery among students at Whig Hall, an on-campus society with a predominantly southern membership, which Charles Hodge joined as an undergraduate, resulted in condemnations of abolition in 1802, 1817, 1819, 1839, and 1851. Guelzo adds that "the climate of opinion at Princeton Theological Seminary was just as heavy with proslavery influence." Students from the southern states comprised 21 percent of the seminary's enrollment in 1828. This proportion increased to 24 percent in 1838.[74] Hodge may not have delved into his seminary's economic ties to Black enslavement in his proslavery writings, but it is wrong to ignore or minimize the social context in which Hodge defended Black enslavement. Hodge was exceedingly aware of the southern currents at his northern institution, with a considerable number of students and donors from slave-owning families.

Hodge was also an attentive observer of his denomination's General Assembly and began writing meticulous and lengthy articles reviewing its annual meetings from 1835 through 1867. Hodge's article on the meeting in 1835 was over forty pages, and his subsequent articles from 1836 and 1837 exceeded sixty and seventy pages, respectively. Though it is not in his article, the minutes of the General Assembly in 1836 included a financial report from the denomination's board of trustees showing that the trustees moved $81,402.28 from banks in the northern states to banks in the southern states of Alabama ($11,000), Kentucky ($10,500), Mississippi ($34,677.28), Tennessee ($15,225), and Virginia ($10,000) in April 1835 because of higher interest rates. The report explained, "The above investments were deemed by the Finance Committee to be safe, two of the members of the Committee having invested in several of the above banks large portions of their private funds."[75] Like other white Americans in the northern states, these two members of the finance committee transferred much of their cash holdings to banks in the southern states with the full understanding that the growth and expansion of the domestic slave trade was the primary reason for the more profitable returns. William Goodell, a white member of the AASS executive committee, charged the PCUSA with abject hypocrisy for moving its funds to southwestern banks offering the best interest rates in the nation "on account of the unprecedented briskness of the domestic slave trade."[76] In 1818, Presbyterians attested that slavery was a violation of human rights "totally irreconcilable with the spirit and principles of the gospel of Christ," but seventeen years later their board of trustees did not hesitate to move $81,402.28 (over $2,400,000 in 2021 U.S. dollars) to financial institutions connected to human trafficking practices they had denounced for a "higher rate of interest."[77] Abolitionists like Goodell howled in protest, but Hodge and most white Presbyterians remained silent.

Gerrit Smith contended in 1837 that most white Christians in the northern states believed slavery was immoral but appealed to U.S. laws and politics to help soothe their consciences. In 1835, the white merchant defending Black enslavement to Samuel J. May took refuge in the legality of slavery to reconcile his participation in an obviously sinful system. Smith explained that "a large proportion" of white Christians in the northern states "refuse to take a stand" against slavery for economic and social reasons. Slavery was a foundational reality in their lives; they preferred the world as they knew it, even with the many evils of slavery and anti-Black racism, over the uncertainties of deconstructing their world and reconstructing a new one in closer accordance with the teachings of Jesus Christ. Smith argued that the response of white Christians to slavery therefore revealed that the governing principle of their faith was the "doctrine of expediency." They obeyed the Bible only to a certain point and made compromises whenever it was inconvenient or difficult to apply the principles of the gospel. Smith compared the direct ways white Christians enforced discipline on other sins such as drunkenness with their reluctance to act for Black liberation: "But, in relation to slavery, they flatter themselves that they have discovered 'a more excellent way'—that of leaving the sin untouched, and simply hoping for its cessation, at some indefinite period in the distant future." When Smith looked at white Christians, he doubted that they even prayed about slavery. His word choice of "simply hoping for its cessation" was intentional: "I say hoping, instead of praying, as prayer for an object is found to be accompanied by corresponding efforts."[78]

The evolution of Henry Watson Jr., a lawyer and planter born in Connecticut in 1810 and educated at Harvard University before moving to Alabama in 1834, illustrates the prevalence of the doctrine of expediency. During his initial months in Alabama, Watson abhorred slavery. Yet within fifteen years, Watson had changed his mind and wrote to his wife, Sophia Peck Watson, "If we do commit a *sin* owning slaves, it is certainly one which is attended with *great conveniences*."[79]

Hodge, Jones, Thornwell, and their denomination's General Assembly never described slavery as a convenient or expedient sin, but the actions of most white Presbyterians suggest that was precisely how they understood it.

Hodge's proslavery article in 1836 also troubled Smith for another reason. Smith was concerned that Hodge's claim that there was nothing inherently sinful about slavery represented a dangerous turn in white Presbyterianism and Christianity in the United States. The silence of white Christians on slavery, and their inaction on abolition, was problematic, but they at least believed in the sinfulness of slavery and did not publicly defend their complicity. The doctrine of expediency was enacted quietly because there were at least some pangs of guilt among white Christians for their inaction. But Hodge's proslavery theology presented white Christians with another pathway on slavery— the doctrine of biblical authority. Unlike the doctrine of expediency, Hodge's doctrine of biblical authority justified both Black enslavement and white complicity without concessions to convenience or confessions of sin. Hodge argued, "We may admit all those laws which forbid the instruction of slaves; which interfere with their marital or parental rights; which subject them to the insults and oppression of the whites, to be in the highest degree unjust, without at all admitting that slaveholding itself is a crime."[80] White Presbyterians simply had to frown upon the injustices of Black enslavement and hope that enslaved persons would be treated more justly in an oppressive system that stripped them of all their dignity and rights. Unlike Smith's doctrine of expediency, which required white Christians to at least acknowledge the compromises they were making for economic and social reasons, Hodge's doctrine of biblical authority made it possible to push aside any consideration of slavery as a foundational sin that corrupted the world they inhabited. The only foundation that mattered was the existence of slavery throughout the Bible.

In Kenneth M. Stampp's history of slavery in the United States, Stampp contends that proslavery writers did not sufficiently deploy the most persuasive argument in their arsenal—the economic one. Whereas their philosophical, racial, and religious proslavery arguments were contestable, the evidence supporting the profitability of slavery was hard to dispute on economic grounds alone. In the 1850s, it was clear that "the slave was earning for his owner a substantial, though varying, surplus above the cost of maintenance" and that slavery continued to produce significant financial gains for many white persons

throughout the northern and southern states.[81] The centrality of slavery in the U.S. economy helps to explain why so many white Presbyterians defended Black enslavement and opposed Black liberation, but
it does not excuse them of their crimes and sins. The AASS rightly castigated white Presbyterians for completely abandoning their Christian
principles and choosing a false peace over truth and justice: "Here then
we see the state of things in which the men who preside over our highest theological schools, the mints of public opinion on religious and
moral subjects, would leave in quiet peace, like the stagnant sea over
the slime of Sodom, the Presbyterian Church!"[82]

White Presbyterians were responsible for many of the regnant religious proslavery arguments. Although slavery was abolished in 1865,
the harmful interpretative practices and theological frameworks that
emerged in the age of Black enslavement stoked the fires of anti-Black
racism in the era of Reconstruction and reverberate in the United
States today. White Presbyterians seldom engaged the economics
of slavery for several reasons. Middle- and upper-class Presbyterians
generally did not like to talk or think about their money at church.
Many also did not want to probe the unjust systems, especially Black
enslavement, that lay at the foundation of their society. Thus, proslavery Presbyterian thought centered on what Robert Lewis Dabney, a
professor at Union Presbyterian Seminary in Virginia and Austin Presbyterian Theological Seminary in Texas, called the "Bible argument."
In 1851, Dabney wrote a letter to his brother musing about whether
the question of slavery would again arise before the General Assembly of the PCUSA (Old School). If it did, Dabney recommended that
"the proper way to argue this ethical question is to put the Bible arguments" first because the doctrine of biblical authority had proven effective in the past. Dabney explained, "This policy is the wiser, because
we know that on the Bible argument the abolition party will be driven
to unveil their true infidel tendencies. The Bible being bound to stand
on our side, they will have to come out and array themselves against
the Bible." Dabney also assured his brother that there would not be an
ecclesial schism. He opined, "I know the temper of my own denomination." When Dabney looked at his church, what he saw in its northern
membership was "a vast, powerful and usually sober body of Presbyterians, in the abstract anti-slavery, but not abolitionist," which meant
that slave-owning members would not be confronted about their sinful participation in Black enslavement. Dabney thought the southern
membership could push the denomination into a more pronounced

proslavery witness to "compel the whole Christianity of the North to array itself on our side."[83] Some white antislavery Presbyterians maintained that their interregional unity was advantageous because they, unlike the Methodists and Baptists, could continue to persuade their slave-owning members when gathering together for worship and fellowship. But this promise of persuasion only existed in the abstract. In actuality, the commitment to ecclesial unity emboldened proslavery Presbyterians and further dismayed and repelled Black Presbyterians.

PART III

The Reckoning

6

Anti-Black Racism in a World without White Fragility

In 1897, Matthew Anderson, a Black pastor in Philadelphia, explained why he was Presbyterian. Anderson latched onto Reformed doctrines emphasizing an interconnected understanding of God's purpose for humanity to flourish in "soul and body," which meant that Presbyterians sought to enact ministries exhibiting divine care for the whole person through evangelism and social reform. As a pastor, Anderson interpreted the *missio Dei* as integrating spiritual teachings with social realities to fulfill the call of the gospel. Black Americans were freed from slavery, but Anderson observed the tenacity and ferocity of anti-Black discrimination throughout the nation: "In the South, they are shot down for the slightest provocation, deprived of their votes, cheated out of their honest earnings, while in the North they have closed against them nearly every avenue to skilled labor." Anderson added that ministry among Black Americans therefore required "more than sermons on the Sabbath," because it also involved "encouragement in everything that will tend to the development of the true man and womanhood; they need help in the practical things of life."[1] Anderson saw in Presbyterianism a comprehensive vision for effective ministry, but he also experienced how the racism of white Presbyterians blocked and betrayed the theology and ecclesiology of their Reformed heritage.

In his assessment of Black Presbyterianism in Philadelphia, Anderson identified the causes of its struggles to grow and expand. White Presbyterians were apathetic to the Black population in their city

129

because of residential segregation and their social distance from Black persons. The only contact most elite white laypersons had with Black persons was "from the colored help in their families." Most white pastors had no contact with Black persons and "knew practically nothing about them, not even the condition of those who lived in the little streets under the very eaves of their churches." Black residents were weary of Presbyterianism for these reasons, as well as remembering the tradition's history of active participation in slavery, and judged the Presbyterian Church as "cold, aristocratic, pharisaical, and which had no use for the Negro more than to use him as a servant." Anderson loathed soliciting financial support from white Presbyterians, but he endured the aggravation and humiliation accompanying the task for the sake of his new church. In one encounter, a wealthy railroad tycoon chastised Anderson and told him that Black pastors should stop "begging" among white persons and pay for their own churches. Anderson retorted that the staggering racial wealth inequalities in their city and the country were not the result of a lagging work ethic within Black Americans but the lack of comparative access to education and employment due to ongoing practices of anti-Black discrimination that originated in the age of Black enslavement. Ultimately, Anderson concluded that the question for his predominantly white denomination was "not whether the Negro wants the Presbyterian Church, but whether the Presbyterian Church wants the Negro" and would be willing to confess its sins of anti-Black racism and re-form its ministries to confront the racial prejudices within its white congregations and work toward the eradication of discriminatory laws in society.[2]

Anderson's insightful and incisive criticism of white Presbyterianism also had roots in the antebellum history of Black Presbyterianism. Earlier Black Presbyterians such as Samuel Eli Cornish, James W. C. Pennington, and Theodore S. Wright helped to establish a tradition of racial justice and social activism within Presbyterianism in the United States. These Black pioneers had some white Presbyterian allies, but these collaborations occurred in efforts and organizations outside of the mainstream denominations. In 1837, the PCUSA ruptured over a theological controversy related to the imputation of Adam's sin. Some within the PCUSA challenged the belief that the result of Adam's sin, as the "federal representative" of humankind, was the inheritance of original sin from infancy. They disagreed with the implication that humans were deserving of divine punishment due to Adam's sin being imputed, or ascribed, to them. Rather, these Presbyterians maintained that humans were only responsible for the sins they committed. In 1829, Albert Barnes contended that humans were not "personally answerable for the transgressions of Adam" as soon as they were born because of guilt by association, which presented Christianity as a "most clearly unjust" religion.[3] Barnes and other Presbyterians adhered to the Reformed doctrine of human depravity and agreed that all humans were sinners, but they diverged from the tenet that God counted Adam's sin against all humankind. These Presbyterians became known as the "New School," and some of them were connected to Congregationalists in an ecumenical cooperation between the two denominations established in 1801. In 1837, the PCUSA General Assembly commissioners excommunicated roughly 60,000 members for denying the imputation of Adam's sin and advancing what they interpreted as false doctrine regarding the fall of humankind.[4] These exscinded members formed the PCUSA (New School) denomination in 1838.

Although the PCUSA (New School) had more outspoken abolitionists than what became known as the PCUSA (Old School), its southern members, as well as its proslavery and antiabolition members in the northern states, deterred it from adopting a clear position against slavery and a firm church polity excluding enslavers. In 1857, the white PCUSA (New School) pastor Frederick A. Ross published a book, *Slavery Ordained of God*, arguing that all Black persons were racially inferior to white persons and the "most degraded in form and intellect" of all the human races because of divine sanction in the Noahic curse of Ham and the scorching equatorial climate in Africa.[5] After reading Ross's book, Abraham Lincoln lambasted it for contributing to the wicked bastion of racial and religious proslavery arguments that propagated the notion that God predestined Black persons for perpetual slavery.[6]

"The Direful Effects of Noah's Curse": The Rise of Biblical Arguments to Justify Perpetual Slavery and Black Inferiority

Antebellum Black and white Presbyterians in the Old School, New School, and other denominations lived in a world of anti-Black racism without white fragility. Robin DiAngelo defines "white fragility" as a state in which white persons resist conversations about race because "the mere suggestion that being white has meaning often triggers a range of defensive responses," such as fear, guilt, and rage, and compels an unwanted exploration into the racial hierarchies that grant them privilege and power based on the color of their skin.[7] White Presbyterians, along with other white Americans, openly, and sometimes happily, acknowledged that the white race was naturally superior to the Black race. Most white Americans did not think it was wrong that they had more rights than Black Americans. Among the few who protested the prevailing attitudes of white domination and racially discriminatory laws against Black persons, there existed a posture of passivity and a spirit of acquiescence. In 1828, the Connecticut Colonization Society did not hesitate to address the pervasiveness of white prejudice against Black persons. It believed that the racial notions of white superiority and Black inferiority were morally wrong and lacked evidentiary grounds, but it also conceded that "the habits, the feelings, [and] all the prejudices" of white society were so deeply ingrained and widespread to make the eradication of anti-Black racism impossible. White Americans had established a broad and impassable "line of demarcation" between themselves and Black Americans, which "neither refinement, nor argument, nor education, nor religion itself" could overcome, which left free Black Americans in the following predicament: "The African in this country belongs by birth to the very lowest station in society; and from that station he can never rise, be his talents, his enterprise, his virtues, what they may."[8]

Many white Americans approached the realities of white supremacy and anti-Black racism in their world without a hint of fragility. They may have possessed twinges of guilt over the virulent anti-Black racism of white persons, but the overwhelming sentiment they conveyed was acceptance, not remorse. One historian argues that "the belief in black inferiority" was so prevalent among white persons that many Christian defenses of slavery "never really took the trouble to prove it, and instead merely assumed that it was one of those social and moral axioms which competed with the law of gravity for credibility."[9] White Americans did not suppress their racial domination or whisper about it in private conversations. Instead, they publicly recognized and reinforced the racial hierarchies that governed over their lives.

In 1841, Pennington published a book entitled *A Text Book of the Origin and History of the Colored People* to rebut the regnant discourse justifying Black enslavement and anti-Black racism on scriptural and scientific grounds. Pennington began with a lament about the pervasive reach of the spurious and racist scholarship in the United States, which poisoned white and Black minds. He was both saddened and infuriated that some Black Americans had absorbed and believed the lies about their racial inferiority. Pennington continued with refutations of two biblical arguments: the curse of Cain and the curse of Ham. Some European and white American thinkers maintained that the Black race began with Cain, who had killed his brother Abel, with an interpretation that the unspecified mark that God put on Cain in Genesis 4:15 was black skin. In 1620, the English poet Thomas Peyton connected Cain's mark to the black skin color of Africans in calling them "the cursed descendant of Cain and the devil." The Anglican minister Morgan Godwyn acknowledged in 1680 that some European Christians believed enslaved Africans bore the mark of Cain in their black skin but that this was not among their most common proslavery biblical arguments.[10] In 1824, the white Presbyterian abolitionist John Rankin acknowledged and refuted popular scriptural arguments linking the "blackness of the African" to "the horrible mark of Cain" and "the direful effects of Noah's curse."[11] Pennington provided a more forceful and thorough repudiation of black skin as the supposed curse of Cain. He wished he did not have to respond to such a "stupid saying," but he deemed it was necessary because the racist interpretation was "trumpeted about by bar-room and porter-house orators, with as much gravity as a judge charges a jury who are to decide in a case of life and death." Pennington observed that the genealogical lineage of Noah omitted Cain and Abel and instead began with Adam's son Seth, then proceeded through seven subsequent generations from Enosh to Lamech. He argued that the posterity of Cain therefore perished in the flood, according to Genesis 7:21–23, and made it impossible for persons of African descent to inherit the mark of Cain.[12]

Pennington devoted more attention to the argument that the curse of Ham justified perpetual Black enslavement. Like Rankin, Pennington believed this approach to biblical interpretation was unsound, but he recognized the prevalence of appeals to the Noahic curse throughout the United States. European and white American interpreters employed the curse of Ham from Genesis 9:24–27 because it simultaneously justified Black enslavement and Black racial inferiority. In David M. Goldenberg's study of the reception history of the Noahic curse, Goldenberg traces how "blackness and servitude were combined in interpreting the biblical narrative" as a "dual curse of Ham" when expositors argued that Ham and his son, Canaan, were divinely punished with both black skin and perpetual slavery after Ham sinfully looked at his father, Noah, in his drunken and naked state.[13] Goldenberg identifies forty-eight works from 1700 to 1998 in the United States where the blackness of Ham's descendants is explicitly addressed. The overwhelming majority, forty of the forty-eight, employ the notion that Ham's descendants were not created with black skin until after Ham's sin.[14] In 1575, the Spanish missionary Francisco de la Cruz defended the transatlantic slave trade by appealing to the curse of Ham: "The blacks (*negros*) are justly captives by just sentence of God for the sins of their fathers, and that in sign thereof God gave them that color." The Spanish bishop Diego de Yepes added seventeen years later that the Noahic curse changed Ham's red skin color to black. The curse of Ham gained popularity across Europe in the seventeenth century, but it was refuted as often as it was promoted. The English physician and philosopher John Bulwer noted in 1653 that the two most common theories for the black skin of Africans were "the heat and the scorch of the Sun" and the Noahic curse, but he denied the latter proposition as unverifiable and improbable.[15] In North America, one of the first published abolitionist tracts, a work in 1700 entitled *The Selling of Joseph* from the Massachusetts judge and Puritan Samuel Sewall, refutes the curse of Ham theory on three grounds: the uncertainty surrounding the extent and duration of the curse; the ethnological argument that enslaved Africans in the North American colonies were descendants of Cush, not Canaan; and questioning the veracity of a curse that would attribute a perversely vindictive wrath to the Christian God.[16]

Yet the biblical justification for Black enslavement from the curse of Ham endured and found new life in the antebellum United States, especially after 1830. As the abolition movement gained momentum in the late 1820s and 1830s, the proponents of slavery advanced more forceful arguments in response. They muted their concession that Black enslavement was a necessary evil and instead advanced the notion that it was a positive good for white and Black Americans. In 1836, Charles Hodge traced this evolution in proslavery thought as a "very great change" in public sentiment: "It is not long since the acknowledgment was frequent at the south, and universal at the north, that [slavery] was a great evil. It was spoken of in the slaveholding states, as a sad inheritance fixed upon them by the cupidity of the mother-country in spite of their repeated remonstrances."[17] Hodge recalled the debates in the state legislature of Virginia from 1831 to 1832, in which many of the delegates were opposed to slavery and some advocated for gradual emancipation in concert with the colonization movement to send free Black Americans to Liberia. Although the legislators ultimately voted against any laws for Black liberation, their ambivalence about slavery illustrated the recognition of its intrinsic evils.[18]

In the other southern states, the response to the surge of abolitionism involved abandoning a defensive posture and instead going on the offensive with arguments that slavery was a positive good and a divine blessing. Stephen Decatur Miller, a white Presbyterian and governor of South Carolina in 1829, urged his fellow white citizens to no longer speak of their slave ownership "in a whisper" or as a "national evil." Rather, Miller declared that slavery was "a national benefit."[19] In 1835, the proslavery journalist Duff Green worked from his office in Washington, D.C., to build a national campaign to sway the minds and soothe the consciences of white Americans: "We must satisfy them that slavery is of itself right—that it is not a sin against God—that it is not an evil, moral or political."[20] The evolution from slavery as a necessary evil to a positive good was encapsulated on the floor of the U.S. Senate in 1837 in a speech from South Carolina senator John C. Calhoun, when he declared, "I hold that in the present state of civilization, where two races of different origin, and distinguished by color, and other physical differences, as well as intellectual, are brought together, the relation now existing in the slave-holding States between the two, is, instead of an evil, a good—a positive good."[21] One historian argues that the new wave of proslavery propaganda after 1830 was successful, especially in shaping the attitudes of white persons in the southern states. Over the next thirty years, most of them became convinced that slavery was a positive good and rejected all mentions of the evils of Black enslavement as falsities from the mouths and pens of lying abolitionists.[22]

The biblical argument defending Black enslavement with the Noahic curse was connected to the larger campaign of praising slavery as a positive good because it provided a clear and definitive explanation for the racial superiority of white persons and the racial inferiority and perpetual slavery of Black persons. Of all the biblical arguments for Black enslavement, the curse of Ham was the simplest. Ross summarized its appeal to white Americans when writing in 1857: "When Ham, in his antediluvian recklessness, laughed at his father, God took occasion to give to the world the rule of the superior over the inferior. . . . Shem was blessed to rule over Ham. Japheth was blessed to rule over both. God sent Ham to Africa, Shem to Asia, Japheth to Europe."[23] White Americans, as the descendants of Japheth, had God's sanction and blessing to enslave Black Americans because they were the descendants of Ham. In 1843, a white harness maker in New

York, Josiah Priest, published a popular proslavery book employing the Noahic curse. Priest proposed outlandish claims that had no basis in either the biblical or scientific scholarship of his day, such as the notion that God turned Japheth white and Ham black while they were in the womb "in an extraordinary and supernatural manner." According to Priest, all humans prior to Japheth and Ham had red skin, including their parents. God's blessing on Japheth and God's curse of Ham, therefore, did not occur at the moment Ham saw their father, Noah, in his drunkenness and nakedness, but the divine outcomes were predestined from their births: "It is not our opinion that for this *one act* of Ham that dreadful curse fell upon him and his race. It was not for that *one act* alone, but on account of his *whole character* and *nature* (which one act was, however, in awful keeping with his previous life), that the curse of slavery was entailed on his race."[24] Hodge and other white Presbyterian faculty in higher education did not endorse Priest's book and would not assign it in their classrooms, but Priest's racial theory nevertheless resonated with many white Presbyterians, and other white Christians, in the pews of local churches. His book was reprinted in numerous editions over the next several years, and white Presbyterian clergy, such as Ross, integrated some of Priest's unfounded racial claims, often without attribution, in their own proslavery preaching and writing.

Thus, Pennington and other Black Christians were forced to grapple with the preposterous scriptural arguments about the dual curse of Ham. Pennington meticulously traced the genealogy of Ham's sons in the Old Testament to argue that free and enslaved Black persons in the United States were the descendants of Cush and Mizraim, not Canaan. In addition to genealogy, Pennington appealed to Reformed theology in contending that the ubiquity of the dual-curse-of-Ham interpretation revealed "the depravity of the human heart" in "men's fondness for theory to justify their sins." He denounced white clergy for turning the Bible into a weapon to oppress and racially abuse Black persons: "They have not only thus desecrated their holy profession, but they have taken a part of God's word and construed it into a commission to shed the innocent blood of his creatures. Noah cursed his grandson Canaan, and this *dooms* the black man to slavery, and *constitutes* the white man the slaveholder! Astounding!"[25] Pennington also refuted the notion that the Noahic curse implied the perpetual enslavement of an entire race of humans. Apart from the four verses in

Genesis 9:24–27, there was scant evidence in the Old and New Testaments to support the everlasting duration of the curse. Reflecting his theological convictions as a pastor within the Congregational and PCUSA (New School) denominations over his career, Pennington expressed his strong disagreement with the doctrine of imputation. He thought the implication that humans were responsible for the sins of their ancestors, such as Adam and Ham, ran contrary to the spirit of Christianity and contradicted the divine proclamation in Ezekiel 18:20 regarding children as not being held liable for the iniquities of their parents.[26]

Yet white Presbyterians continued to appeal to the dual curse of Ham as scriptural evidence of their racial superiority. In 1857, James A. Sloan, a white pastor from Mississippi belonging to the Associate Reformed Synod of the South, argued that white Americans were among the descendants of Japheth in a lineage including the rulers of the Grecian and Roman Empires and their European ancestors.[27] Ross praised God for bestowing unto white slave-owning Americans—belonging to the "noble family of Japheth"—the responsibility to supervise enslaved Black persons, the benighted and helpless descendants of Ham.[28] Two white members of the PCUSA (Old School) serving as justices in the Supreme Court of Georgia cited the Noahic curse in their rulings to uphold Black enslavement. In 1851, Eugenius A. Nisbet wrote in his ruling on *Neal v. Farmer*, "The curse of the Patriarch rests still upon the descendants of Ham. The negro and his master are but fulfilling a divine appointment." Two years later, Joseph Henry Lumpkin invoked the dual curse of Ham in his ruling on *Bryan v. Walton* when noting that "the social and civil degradation" of enslaved persons was the result of "the taint of blood" as "the descendants of Ham." Shortly after writing this opinion, Lumpkin wrote a letter to his daughter sharing how he had "just finished reading a most interesting Book—a work on negro slavery—by a man named Priest" and that Priest's book aided him in writing his "opinion on the status or condition of a free negro in Georgia." Lumpkin added that Priest had "incontestably" convinced him that Jezebel, introduced into the biblical narrative in 1 Kings 16:31 as the wife of King Ahab, was "a negro wench with a black skin and wooly head."[29] In 1858, Thomas R. R. Cobb, a white lawyer, politician, and member of the PCUSA (Old School), cited Priest's interpretation that "all the Canaanites were black" as supporting evidence in his survey of the legality of Black enslavement.[30]

"What Shall We Do with the Free People of Color?": Anti-Black Racism at the Heart of the American Colonization Society

White Presbyterians, along with other white Christians, clung to the dual-curse-of-Ham interpretation because it also helped to justify their racial hostility against Black Americans. Other prevalent racial theories offered reasons for the physiological differences between the two races, but the notion of the descendants of Japheth and Ham at enmity with one another, despite its false and unproven premise, provided a scriptural rationale for the anti-Black racism of white Americans. In 1799, the white abolitionist, physician, and Presbyterian Benjamin Rush argued that the disease of leprosy caused the dark skin color of Black persons. In his epidemiological study, Rush contended that leprosy had a long history in the African continent because of the "greater heat," "more savage manners" of Africans, and the spread of "bilious fevers" across the population. He highlighted how some of the symptoms of leprosy, such as a darkening of the skin, a swelling of the lips, a flattening of the nose, and a distinct "smell" emanating from the body, were present in Black Americans. According to Rush, Black Americans had contracted a mostly noninfectious variant of leprosy that did not reduce their life expectancy but explained their physical appearance and sexual promiscuity. (Rush believed insatiable sexual desire was another symptom of leprosy.)[31] Rush's medical contemporaries roundly dismissed his theory—one biographer of Rush identifies it as "the most spectacularly wrong-headed address of Rush's career"—but others likely rejected the hypothesis because Rush argued that his epidemiological rationale disproved "all the claims of superiority of the whites over the blacks, on account of their color" and countered that the differences between the two races originated in disease rather than a divine curse.[32] Pennington devoted only a few sentences in his book on Rush's theory. He was reluctant to malign "such a man as Dr. Rush" but discounted the physician's proposition as implausible.[33]

Pennington wrestled more deeply with the racial theorizing of Samuel Stanhope Smith, a white Presbyterian pastor and president of Princeton University from 1795 to 1812. In 1787, Smith published a book on the racial differences between Black and white persons. At the onset of the book's second edition in 1810, Smith explained why he would "devote so much time to studies which seem to be only remotely connected with the offices of piety peculiarly belonging to a Christian minister"—to refute scientific theories that proposed the non-Adamic origins of the Black race and defend the Christian doctrine of human monogenesis (all humans of every race were descendants of Adam and Eve).[34] In 1774, the Scottish philosopher Henry Home, Lord Kames, gave credence to the notion that the various races of humans were not all united as the same human species. Because "different races of men" were "fitted by nature for different climates," Kames mused about the possibility that there were "different species of men" not unlike different kinds of animals and plants. Kames, perhaps mindful of the prevailing Christian ethos in his context, stopped short of a full endorsement of human polygenesis, the theory that some races were created before or after Adam and Eve and therefore did not have their roots in the biblical narrative from the first three chapters of Genesis. But Kames nonetheless gave momentum to the polygenesis school with his scholarship.[35]

Smith therefore argued for "the unity of the human race, notwithstanding the diversity of colour" as a doctrine proven in both the divine revelation of the Bible and the principles of natural philosophy. Smith maintained that the physical and intellectual features of Black persons were explained by three main factors: climate, social conditions, and diet. Smith diverged from Rush and did not suggest that the black skin of persons of African descent was a symptom of disease, but Smith's theory connoted notions of racial superiority and inferiority. Persons from temperate climates, such as Europeans, were more civilized than persons from equatorial or polar climates, such as Africans, because they were not exposed to the "injurious effects" of extreme heat or cold. In the case of Africans, their "rude habits" as an "uncultivated people" magnified their intellectual degradation. Smith stressed that many white Americans in the southern states suffered from the heat and humidity of the region and contracted more diseases than Black Americans because of the different physiologies of the two races due to their respective climatic genealogies.[36] Other white proslavery writers utilized this connection between climate and race to justify Black enslavement by arguing that Black persons were divinely created to perform the arduous agricultural labor in the hot and moist climate of the southern states. Josiah Priest wrote that God designed Black persons to thrive in the climatic conditions of the southern states and therefore it would not be possible for white persons to produce commensurate crops of cotton, indigo, rice, sugar, and tobacco.[37] Thomas R. R. Cobb agreed that it was not possible to substitute white laborers for enslaved persons because of "climate and disease, which bring death to the

Saxon, and health and immunity to the African."[38] Pennington agreed with Smith on the obvious influence of climate on human complexion, but he rejected Smith's suggestion that darker skin implied intellectual inferiority. Pennington also dismissed the attention that Smith and other white persons devoted to whether the skin color of Black persons could become lighter in future generations with interracial marriage and further exposure to the temperate weather conditions in the northern states as unimportant.[39] More important to Pennington and other Black Presbyterians was removing the racial hatred of white Americans against Black persons because of their skin color.

Pennington consistently argued that the theological stakes of anti-Black racism were more significant than the disputations between racial theorists about the origins of Black and white Americans. Theories about the natural inferiority of the Black race were an affront to the doctrine of divine creation because they dared to portray God as either unjust or impotent. Pennington emphasized the reign of God as the moral governor of the world, which meant that all humans were created equally in the image of God with the same capacities. The notion that God designed different races with different capacities, with some races bearing inherent deficiencies leaving them defenseless against other more dominant races, was a monstrous blasphemy contrary to the moral law of God. Pennington condemned the anti-Black ideologies of white Christians as "absurd" attacks against both Black Americans and God: "But why has God, who is moral Governor, and also the Creator of man done this act? Is it credible to say that he has put a difference between men in point of intellect, whilst he has put none in point of obligation? The supposition is not incredible only, but it is also inadmissible."[40] The sin of racial prejudice amounted to hating the image of God and defiling the character of God. And the reluctance from white Christian clergy who agreed with Pennington but remained silent revealed what they really believed about God's administration of justice. God's rule as the moral governor was partial or deferred. In the antebellum United States, even the Almighty God could not defeat the powerful forces of anti-Black racism until the Parousia.

Some Presbyterians did not want to wait until the second coming, but they were also pessimistic about the eradication of anti-Black racism among the white population. In 1802, Alexander McLeod, a white pastor of a congregation in New York City belonging to the Reformed Presbytery of America (which became the Synod of the Reformed Presbyterian Church in America in 1809), a denomination connected to the Reformed Presbyterian Church of Scotland, published *Negro Slavery Unjustifiable*. McLeod's denomination, also known as the Covenanters, diverged from the mainstream Presbyterian denominations in its resolute antislavery position and firm church polity excluding enslavers from its ecclesial membership. Some white Covenanters participated in the Underground Railroad and openly sympathized with John Brown's insurrection attempt at Harper's Ferry to liberate enslaved persons in 1859. But there were significantly fewer Covenanters (approximately 10,500 in 1844) than Presbyterians in the mainstream denominations.[41] In addition to advocating for Black emancipation, McLeod addressed the unease and anti-Black prejudice of most white Americans, including some abolitionists, regarding the end of slavery. What should be done once enslaved Black persons were liberated? The three prevailing plans among white Americans were a process of forced migration to Africa, the establishment of a separate colony in North America, and amalgamation (full integration into U.S. society). In McLeod's assessment, none of the three proposals were optimal: "To export them to Africa would be cruel. To establish them in a separate colony would be dangerous. To give them their liberty, and incorporate them with the whites, would be more so." But McLeod maintained that it was better to "adopt any one of those plans than continue the evil" of Black enslavement.[42]

In a lecture published in 1812, Samuel Stanhope Smith engaged the same three plans anticipating the gradual emancipation of enslaved persons. Like McLeod, he found the desire among some white Americans to forcibly transport Black Americans to Africa as unconscionable and no less immoral than the international slave trade. "All men condemn the barbarity of dragging the simple Africans from their native country," Smith observed. "But America is the country of their descendants, and it would now be equally cruel to tear them from the soil in which they have grown up, and to send them back to Africa."[43] But Smith also dismissed the full integration of Black Americans in the United States because of anti-Black prejudice in white society. Smith went as far as to suggest that it was "impossible to amalgamate the two races" due to the racial animosities of white persons against Black persons. Thus, Smith proposed the creation of a separate territory from the "unappropriated lands of the United States," perhaps looking westward at the land acquired in the Louisiana Purchase in 1803, in which every Black person would receive a "certain portion of land" but with white persons holding every position of governing authority to supervise the colony. Smith also encouraged interracial marriages and families with an incentive of a "double portion of land" for "every white man who should marry a black woman" and "every white woman who should marry a black man" in the hope that these unions would help to chip away at the tenacity of anti-Black racism in the white-dominant culture over time.[44]

McLeod and Smith criticized the cruelty in the plan to forcibly transport Black Americans to Africa, but it emerged as the preferred option among white Presbyterians between 1820 and 1860 after one significant alteration to the proposal: the addition of a foreign mission component. In 1816, Robert Finley began mobilizing support for the creation of an organization that would become the American Colonization Society (ACS). Finley's father emigrated from Glasgow, Scotland, to Princeton at the encouragement of his friend, John Witherspoon, and Finley studied at the school where Witherspoon was president, Princeton University, before pastoring a Presbyterian congregation in Basking Ridge, New Jersey, and serving on the board of trustees at his alma mater. Finley shared many of Smith's convictions about the impossibility of racial integration in the United States because of anti-Black racism, but Finley believed the migration of Black Americans to Africa presented an opportunity for world mission and evangelization. In a letter to John P. Mumford, a white lawyer in New York City, Finley explained the "three-fold benefit" to his plan. The first benefit was that white Americans would not have to live together with Black Americans. The second positive outcome was the prospect of increased evangelization in Africa. The third advantage was that Black Americans would migrate to a land where they would not be discriminated against because of their race.[45]

Finley expanded on his plan in an essay, *Thoughts on the Colonization of Free Blacks*, which he began by asking, "What shall we do with the free people of color?" Finley contended that anti-Black prejudice among white persons was "too deep rooted to be eradicated" and that there was no part of North America, even westward territories, where Black Americans would be sufficiently free of white contempt to flourish. He added that Black enslavement had thoroughly corrupted the hearts and minds of white Americans and created in them a spirit combining indolence and arrogance. Many white persons saw all Black persons, whether free or enslaved, as menial laborers to serve their wishes and perform the undesirable tasks in society that they did not want to do. Although the monetary cost to finance the migration of Black Americans to Africa was much higher than the establishment of a separate colony in North America, Finley believed it was a better investment for several reasons. A colony in North America would entice enslaved persons to seek their freedom because it "would furnish great facility to the slaves in the nearest states, to desert their masters' service, and escape to a land whether their own race was sovereign and independent." The complete expulsion of Black Americans from North America was also the only way to obliterate the sinful prejudices of the white population in the United States. As a white person, Finley believed "our contempt" of Black persons "would gradually die away" if they were "removed far from our sight." Finally, Finley appealed to the cause of world mission and the plight of "those benighted regions" on the African continent where millions were perishing without the gospel.[46] In his private correspondence, Finley conceded that Black Americans, as a "partially civilized and Christianized" people in his estimation, were not the finest candidates for foreign missionaries.[47] But in his published essay, Finley muted this concern and emphasized the promise of evangelization. Finley solicited donations from white Christians with an appeal to divine providence. He presented his colonization plan as a part of God's purposes to turn evil into good. According to Finley, God permitted "so great an evil to exist as African slavery" in the United States, "a land of civil liberty and religious knowledge," so that Black Americans could convert to Christianity and "at the appointed time, be prepared to return, and be the great instrument of spreading peace and happiness" in Africa.[48]

In 1817, Finley contracted an illness while traveling to the University of Georgia to assume his new duties as the school's president and died within months of his arrival there. But he saw his dream come to fruition on December 21, 1816. The ACS held its inaugural meeting in Washington, D.C., with the white Kentuckian legislator Henry Clay presiding over the affairs as the chairperson and many other prominent white elites joining Finley, including Elias Boudinot Caldwell, a graduate of Princeton University and clerk of the U.S. Supreme Court; Francis Scott Key, a lawyer, enslaver, and lyricist of the national anthem, "The Star-Spangled Banner"; and Alexander McLeod, the Covenanter who had previously thought it was cruel to encourage the migration of Black Americans to Africa.[49] Between 1820 and 1860, roughly 560 enslavers sent approximately 6,000 of their enslaved persons to Liberia. Fewer Black Americans from the northern states went to Liberia because they possessed an agency as free persons that enslaved Black

Americans did not have (their enslavers tied the promise of emancipation to colonization), and many Black and white abolitionists criticized the ACS for perpetuating anti-Black racism in its efforts to remove Black Americans from the nation. Between 1834 to 1847, only fifty-six Black Americans from the northern states migrated to Liberia. The juxtaposing attitudes of Sarah Louisa Forten Purvis, a Black abolitionist poet from Philadelphia, and Margaret Mercer, a white slave-owning woman from Maryland who freed some of her enslaved persons under the condition they go to Liberia, illumine the centrality of anti-Black racism in the colonization movement. Purvis summarized Black attitudes toward the ACS: "I despise the aim of that Institution most heartily—and have never yet met one man or woman of Color who thought better of it than I do." Mercer captured white motivations for supporting the ACS: "I would rather die with every member of my family than live in a community mixed up of black & white."[50]

Cornish and Wright helped to lead Black opposition to the ACS. In 1840, they coauthored a work rebutting several of the main thrusts of the colonization movement as immoral, irrational, and anti-Christian. They began with a searing rebuke of the exclusively white membership of the ACS. The ACS was an organization professing to work on behalf of the interests of Black persons, but it did not consult or include any Black persons in its work. The ACS therefore propagated racist and false ideas that Black Americans universally denounced. ACS members spuriously claimed that Black Americans "yearned in their hearts for Africa" and therefore welcomed the opportunity to migrate to Liberia. Cornish and Wright noted that several months after the inaugural meeting of the ACS, approximately 3,000 Black persons gathered in Philadelphia to discuss the ACS and "there was not a single voice in that vast assembly which was not raised for its decisive, thorough condemnation."[51] If consulted, Black Americans would tell the ACS that what they yearned for in their hearts was equal rights and equitable access to education and employment in the United States.

Cornish and Wright also challenged the ACS for accommodating, rather than combating, the anti-Black racism of white Christians. Wright was the first Black graduate of Princeton Theological Seminary in 1828 and pastored a Black Presbyterian congregation in New York City afterward. One of his professors, Archibald Alexander, advocated for the ACS, declaring, "It is in vain to declaim about the prejudice of colour; however unreasonable, it will long continue to exist, and will prove an effectual bar to the possession and enjoyment of the same privileges and advantages which the white population enjoy."[52] Cornish and Wright charged the ACS with promoting a powerless gospel that surrendered to anti-Black racism as an unconquerable sin. They took the racial claims of the ACS to their theological conclusion: "To this end . . . there is in the white man an inherent prejudice against his colored brother, so fixed, that its removal, whilst the latter remains *in this country*, is not only beyond all human power, but beyond Christianity itself, '*the power of God*'; but that it might surely be mitigated at least, if not extinguished, provided the Atlantic Ocean could be made to roll between them."[53] The solution to anti-Black racism was the repentance of white Christians, not the removal of Black Americans. Three years earlier, Cornish, writing in his newspaper, the *Colored American*, called the colonization movement a "subterfuge of Satan" for lulling the consciences of white Christians to sleep and seducing them to believe they were not accountable for their racial prejudices.[54] One former ACS member, James A. Thome, a white Presbyterian pastor in Ohio, lamented in 1834 that his participation in the colonization movement intensified his feelings of anti-Black racism and noted how the ACS was especially dangerous because the organization was able to "sanctify" his racial prejudice with its missionary rhetoric of evangelization in Africa.[55]

"The Stronghold of an Unholy Prejudice against Color": Black Resistance to the Surge of Anti-Black Discrimination in White Presbyterianism and White Society in the United States

Neither Cornish nor Wright were naive about the prevalence of anti-Black racism among white Christians. They encountered it daily as Black clergy in a predominantly white denomination. Cornish and Wright were often subjected to racist treatment from white colleagues in their presbytery in New York. Cornish recalled attending presbytery meetings in which white Presbyterians refused to sit in the same pew as him and witnessing racially segregated practices of Communion in which Black worshipers were invited to the table only after all the white worshipers had been served. Sometimes the racial discrimination was more subtle. On numerous occasions, white worshipers did not know they were sitting in the same pew as Cornish or other Black worshipers until several minutes into a worship service, but they immediately departed the pew once they realized who was in their pew and acted as if the Black worshipers "were infected with the plague." At one presbytery meeting, Cornish was told that all of the traveling members would receive lodging and food accommodations from various families belonging to the host church, but he was "left by himself in the church, for three successive days, without dinner or tea, because no Christian family could be found in the congregation, who would admit him to their table, on account of his color."[56] Cornish also protested the absence of invitations from white congregations in his presbytery to preach, either as a guest speaker or as "[pulpit] supply of vacant churches," and his exclusion from serving as a commissioner to the General Assembly.[57] Although his presbytery voted to appoint every member as a commissioner on a rotating basis, Cornish had waited with what he described as "Job-like patience" for over fifteen years without an opportunity. Cornish understood this appointment was "the highest honor the Presbytery could confer upon a member—the Assembly being the Upper Court in the Church," but the Black pastor saw time and again white members who had joined the presbytery after him chosen in his place, leading him to conclude in 1837: "Prejudice against color—the spirit of caste in the Church of God, and among her ministry, has prevented our appointment."[58]

Alexander observed the phenomena that Cornish experienced, but from the perspective of a white Presbyterian. And Alexander was no ordinary Presbyterian, but a white man with influence as a seminary professor and moderator of the PCUSA General Assembly in 1807. Yet rather than advocate for Black Presbyterians like Cornish, which entailed directly confronting the macroaggressions and microaggressions that members of his white Christian community perpetrated against Black Christians, Alexander maintained that the sin of racial prejudice was unreasonable but inevitable. Alexander likely would not have disagreed with Cornish's assessment that white Christianity was "the stronghold of an unholy prejudice against color."[59] But Alexander did not act with any urgency, even though Black Presbyterians like Cornish and Wright testified about the painful consequences of white Presbyterian racism. In a highly publicized speech to the New York State Anti-Slavery Society, which was reprinted in numerous newspapers, Wright contended that the racial discrimination Black Christians encountered in white congregations, such as the frowns they were met with when entering a sanctuary and the segregated practices of Communion, afflicted their spirits and injured their souls.[60] Cornish and Wright identified white Christian racism as one of the most destructive and evil sins because it demonstrated to both Black and white Americans that the religion of Christianity either endorsed anti-Black prejudice or was not strong enough to vanquish it.

One white Presbyterian ally of Cornish and Wright, Arthur Tappan, joined in their struggle against racial prejudice in their denomination. In 1834, Tappan invited Cornish to sit with him at the white Presbyterian church that Tappan attended on Laight Street in New York City. Tappan was frustrated with the racial discrimination that existed in white congregations in the northern states, with their "negro pews" in galleries above or rear sections behind the "white pews" and their segregated practices of Communion. Thus, he believed the act of worshiping together with Cornish in the pew he rented would serve as a visible representation of the Christian vision he and others in the abolitionist movement were proclaiming. Others at his church vehemently disagreed. Some of the ruling elders confronted Tappan to accuse him of disrupting the worship service and warn him to desist from inviting Cornish, or any other Black person, to sit in his pew in the future. Reflecting the intersections of race, color, and class in his social and religious context, Tappan thought there would be less resistance to Cornish at his church because Cornish was a well-dressed and educated biracial man with light black skin.

But the ferment over Tappan's decision percolated over the next several days within the congregation, and the pastor, Samuel H. Cox, addressed the controversy by siding with Tappan and addressing the sin of racial prejudice. Cox noted to his white congregation that Jesus Christ was a man of color from Palestine, bearing a skin complexion that was likely closer to Cornish's than to that of anyone in their white congregation, and wondered if they would similarly oppose the notion of Jesus sitting in one of their pews designated for white worshipers. Cox's message did little to sway the sinful attitudes of many in the congregation, but it did turn their anger away from Tappan and onto Cox. Tappan's brother, Lewis Tappan, recalled that one local newspaper assailed Cox for "having stated that the Saviour was a colored man."[61] One white merchant angrily denounced Cox: "And would you believe it? he called my Saviour a nigger! God damn him!"[62] Only weeks after Cornish and Tappan worshiped together in the same pew, in July 1834, a mob of white persons destroyed the homes of both Tappan and Cox and damaged their church property during one of the largest riots in the antebellum history of New York City. Following a racially integrated celebration of Emancipation Day at the Chatham

Street Chapel, an occasion to mark the anniversary of the eradication of slavery in the state of New York in 1827, white mobs decrying the abolition movement for its promotion of amalgamation, interracial marriage, and Black citizenship razed the homes of prominent Black and white abolitionists, several Black and white churches, and Black-owned businesses over three days of rampant violence.[63]

The extensive mob violence in New York City, along with similar riots from white mobs against abolitionists in Boston in 1835 and Black residents in Cincinnati in 1836, revealed the depth and severity of anti-Black racism among the white population in the northern states. They were vile components of a larger reckoning. The various racial theories and religious interpretations to justify Black enslavement and purport Black inferiority, as well as the colonization movement and the reluctance of white Christian clergy and lay leaders to confront the glaring sin of racial prejudice, produced an escalating surge of anti-Black racism across the nation that has yet to be vanquished. Antebellum white Americans did not exhibit fragility regarding racial discourse. Rather, many of them welcomed the opportunity to talk about race. The positive good theory of slavery required that white Americans subscribe to the myth that Black Americans were inherently inferior and lacking the mental capacities to live as free citizens alongside the superior white race.

In 1860, Benjamin Morgan Palmer preached from the pulpit of First Presbyterian Church in New Orleans that God predestined white persons to enslave Black persons for the sake of a stronger race protecting a weaker one. Palmer ridiculed abolitionists from the northern states as "the worst foes of the black race" because they did not interact with Black Americans as closely as he and other white persons in the southern states did: "We know better than others that every attribute of their character fits them for dependence and servitude. By nature, the most affectionate and loyal of all races beneath the sun, they are also the most helpless: and no calamity can befall them greater than the loss of that protection they enjoy under this patriarchal system." Palmer predicted that abolition would be a death knell for enslaved Black Americans, as they would surely wither and waste away "in the presence of the vigorous Saxon race" without white enslavers as their "providential guardians."[64] The white author Richard H. Colfax explained in 1833 that "the almost unanimous voice of our white population" opposed the abolition movement because of its insistence on exposing and eradicating anti-Black racism. Colfax did not dispute the existence of anti-Black racism among white Americans, but he justified this "rancorous hatred against the negroes" as a product of nature. Superior creatures, whether human or animal, inherently detested inferior creatures and did not want to dwell among them. Colfax made the following analogy: in the same way that Black persons naturally would not want to live together with "orang-outangs," white persons were repulsed by the notion of amalgamation and intermarriage with Black persons.[65]

Even white abolitionists grappled with their own racial prejudices and questioned whether their advocacy for racial equality deterred their efforts to persuade their fellow white Americans. In *Uncle Tom's Cabin*, Harriet Beecher Stowe endorsed the colonization movement through one of her fictitious characters, George Harris, a formerly enslaved Black man. Stowe presented Harris with a yearning in his heart for Africa and "no wish to pass for an American."[66] Stowe also revealed her racial biases in writing biracial characters who were less docile and more independent than fully Black characters on account of their white ancestry. Harris's relentless pursuit for freedom and discontent with slavery are the product of the half of his lineage belonging to the "hot and hasty Saxon," not the meek and childlike African. In Stowe's book, Harris serves as both archetype and advertisement for the ACS vision when he declares, "As a Christian patriot, as a teacher of Christianity, I go to *my country*,—my chosen, my glorious Africa!"[67] Some Black abolitionists, such as Martin R. Delany, publicly criticized Stowe for her promotion of the ACS, which she denied, but others chose to forbear their displeasure with the white author because of Stowe's allyship in the cause for Black liberation.

Pennington acknowledged that one of the strategies of Black Christians required a spirit of forbearance among racist white persons, even though so many of them were cruel and remorseless in their discrimination against Black persons. Pennington did not promote a passive acceptance of anti-Black racism, for he experienced the injury and misery of racism "almost at every step" of his life, but he, like other Black abolitionists, knew that Black Americans did not have the same emotional license as white persons.[68] They were not permitted to display their raw fury like the white mobs, or even like the lone white woman, man, or child spewing racial epithets at them on the street, because of the different and discriminatory cultural mores in the northern states. In 1839, Andrew Harris, a Black Presbyterian pastor in Philadelphia and the first Black graduate of the University of Vermont in 1838, described how the "deadly poison" of racist justifications of slavery "disseminated from the torrid regions of the South to the frigid North" in the ways that white persons ascribed racial judgments upon the actions of Black individuals: "Yet, with all this, if the colored man is vicious, or if he is not educated, it is set down to his natural stupidity and depravity, and the argument is raised that he belongs to an inferior race."[69] The criticisms of a small group of angry, indolent, or drunk persons varied according to race. When the group was white, the scorn was mostly directed at their individual morality with isolated hints of racial connotations if the persons were more recent immigrants from certain European nations, such as Ireland or Italy. When the group was Black, the contempt revolved entirely around the myth of inherent Black inferiority and the insinuation that all Black persons were better suited for slavery than freedom.

Some white abolitionists confessed their sins of anti-Black prejudice. In 1849, Lewis Tappan recognized that he and other white abolitionists were "the enemies of caste" in the abstract but did little in their daily lives to prove that they were "the practical opponents" of anti-Black discrimination. Angelina Emily Grimké asked her Black colleagues in the abolitionist movement to be patient with her and other white persons because they would not be able to overcome their racial prejudice apart from continued fellowship with Black persons.[70] In addition to the macroaggressions and microaggressions that Black abolitionists endured, they grew increasingly frustrated with white abolitionists urging a slower pace for racial equality. In 1834, immediately after the mob violence subsided in New York City, the American Anti-Slavery Society posted notices throughout the city stating that it did not promote "intermarriages between white and colored citizens."[71] Arthur Tappan later regretted sitting next to Cornish in worship and believed it was a strategic blunder because of its rashness and nonconformity to the "fastidiousness of the age." Tappan was motivated to be a practical opponent of anti-Black racism and enact his belief "that as Christians we were bound to treat the colored people without respect to color," but he refrained from any further outward displays of racial integration with Black persons until "the public mind and conscience were more enlightened on the subject."[72] Cornish, Pennington, and Wright disagreed with any approach that marginalized the pursuits of Black citizenship and civil rights. Black liberation in the United States could not be divided into two separate parts. The drive for racial equality could not be divorced from the push for the abolition of slavery. Wright criticized the desire of some white abolitionists to "first kill slavery, and leave prejudice to take care of itself" and countered that "prejudice is slavery" because Black Americans could not be truly free from oppression until they had equal access to education, employment, and public transportation.[73]

In 1850, Pennington delivered a speech before the Young Men's Christian Association in Glasgow, Scotland, during his travels throughout Europe. Prior to his visit to Scotland, Pennington was awarded an honorary doctorate in 1849 from the University of Heidelberg, with the faculty there proudly announcing, "You are the first African who has received this dignity from a European University, and it is the University of Heidelberg that thus pronounced the universal brotherhood of humanity."[74] In Scotland, Pennington argued that Black Americans tested the egalitarian promises of democracy in his home country. Was the United States indeed a nation in which all persons were born free and equal with the inalienable rights of life, liberty, and the pursuit of happiness? "If we, born in America, cannot live upon the soil upon terms of equality with the descendants of Scotchmen, Englishmen, Irishmen, Frenchmen, Germans, Hungarians, Greeks, and Poles," Pennington declared with his comparison between persons of African and European descent, "then the fundamental theory of the American Republic fails and falls to the ground; and the door once opened to kick out the people of colour, let others be prepared for their turn."[75] When Cornish began his newspaper, the *Colored American*, in 1837, he made a similar appeal in noting that Black Americans were no less "American" than any of their "white brethren" and made significant civic, cultural, economic, and religious contributions to support their nation. Cornish therefore argued that Black persons should be called "Colored Americans" instead of "Negroes, Africans, and blacks," because the latter three identifying markers had been maliciously "stereotyped" as "names of reproach."[76] In Manisha Sinha's history of abolitionism in the United States, Sinha credits Wright as the "most responsible for raising the issue of racism" in the righteous struggle against slavery, as he and other Black abolitionists "made antiracism, at a programmatic as well as intellectual level, an essential part of the abolitionist project."[77]

Just as Wright and other Black Presbyterians endeavored to make racial justice a central component of the abolitionist movement, Palmer and other white Presbyterians in the southern states made anti-Black racism a foundational element in their perpetuation of slavery. In 1861, the Confederate States of America provided its final answer to the question about whether Black Americans were entitled to equal rights. On March 21, 1861, Alexander H. Stephens, the vice president of the recently formed Confederate States, delivered a speech in Savannah, Georgia, making clear that Black persons were not created free and equal to white persons. Stephens was a member of a Presbyterian congregation in Washington, Georgia, and nurtured in a proslavery faith that imbibed the positive good theory to justify slavery and propagated biblical interpretations with divine sanctions for white superiority and Black inferiority. Stephens explained how the Constitution of the United States erred in its "assumption of the equality of races" and that the new Constitution of the Confederate States had settled "all the agitating questions" about slavery: "Our new government is founded upon exactly the opposite idea; its foundations are laid, its corner-stone rests upon the great truth, that the negro is not equal to the white man; that slavery—subordination to the superior race—is his natural and normal condition."[78] Stephens added that white persons were right to enslave Black persons either because of the laws of nature or "the curse against Canaan." He was also confident that their system of Black enslavement was "in conformity with the ordinance of the Creator."[79]

Several months later, white Presbyterians from the southern states gathered at First Presbyterian Church in Augusta, Georgia, on December 4, 1861, for the first General Assembly of their new denomination, the Presbyterian Church in the Confederate States of America (PCCSA). According to one PCCSA pastor, Robert Quarterman Mallard, the various presbyteries, "realizing the gravity of the situation, had sent their oldest, wisest, most experienced, and, in a word, most suitable men" as commissioners, and nearly all of them were enslavers.[80] As they met, a committee was appointed, with James Henley Thornwell serving as the chairperson, to write an address clarifying their denomination's position on slavery. A portion of the address was in agreement with Stephens, sharing in his convictions and echoing some of his same words about the "normal condition" of Black persons: "We are profoundly persuaded that the African race in the midst of us can never be elevated in the scale of being. As long as that race, in its comparative degradation, co-exists, side by side, with the white, bondage is its normal condition."[81] The commissioners passed a resolution to file the original copy of the address in their archives with the signatures of all the commissioners. Mallard described the ritual as "a deeply interesting spectacle," as each commissioner, when he heard his name in the roll call, solemnly walked to the desk where the address lay and proudly affixed his signature to the document.[82] The moment was designed to represent the beginning of a new journey in faith, but what it really marked was a funereal ending. Perhaps the battle between good and evil had long been decided among white Presbyterians in the southern states, with the evil of American slavery triumphing over the good news of the Christian gospel, but the commissioners verified the outcome with their own signatures.

7

The American Captivity of the Presbyterian Church

In 1845, months after the publication of his autobiography, Frederick Douglass traveled across the Atlantic Ocean to continue his abolitionist activism in Europe. White allies in the United States, such as William Lloyd Garrison, encouraged Douglass to expand his lecture circuit and partner with foreign abolitionist groups in a transnational strategy that would ultimately create more pressure on enslavers and enablers of slavery from abroad. Though Douglass's influence and stature grew in the United States, he retained the legal status of a "fugitive slave" and therefore also found the trip gave him a respite from the constant threat of recapture.

During these nineteen months abroad, Douglass underwent a personal transformation as he pursued his vocational goals of building momentum for the eradication of slavery in the United States. In a letter to Garrison from the Victoria Hotel in Belfast on January 1, 1846, Douglass shared about the freedom and joy he felt from the comparative absence of anti-Black discrimination. Unlike his precarious experiences in the northern states, Douglass recounted being "treated at every turn with the kindness and deference paid to white people" when visiting churches, riding on public transportation, and dining at restaurants: "Instead of the bright blue sky of America, I am covered with the soft grey fog of the Emerald Isle. I breathe, and lo! the chattel becomes a man."[1] Douglass was also making great strides in his social activism. Richard D. Webb, an Irish abolitionist who published Douglass's autobiography in Ireland, wrote in a letter to a colleague that Douglass's lectures had "occasioned deep interest in the anti-slavery cause, and many who never thought on the subject at all, are now convinced it is a sin to neglect."[2]

Thomas Smyth, the white pastor of Second Presbyterian Church in Charleston, South Carolina, received a letter from Mary Cunningham, a friend in Ireland, about Douglass. Smyth was born in Belfast in 1808 and migrated with his family to the United States in 1830. After graduating from Princeton Theological Seminary, Smyth became the pastor at Second Presbyterian and married Margaret Milligan Adger, a member of the congregation who belonged to one of the wealthiest families in the city. Smyth also maintained close relations with clergy in Ireland and Scotland. He emerged as one of the most prominent American supporters of the Free Church of Scotland (FCS), founded in 1843 after a group of Scottish Presbyterians protested the Church of Scotland's polity of patronage, which granted a local congregation's landowning patron the sole right to select the pastor, and he hosted representatives from the FCS during their fundraising tour across the United States in 1844. Smyth sought strong bonds of fellowship between the FCS and his denomination. But the FCS was under pressure to cut ties with and return monetary donations from the PCUSA (Old School) because the American denomination included enslavers in its membership. Several months before Smyth's own trip to Ireland, Scotland, and England, Cunningham asked Smyth on January 14, 1846, whether Douglass's firsthand account of the "heart sickening horrors" was true and questioned how white American Christians, especially clergy, could participate in the "dreadful system" of slavery.[3]

Cunningham's letter was a foretaste of the far more harsh and unrelenting criticism Smyth would experience in Ireland. "On reaching Belfast, my native city," wrote Smyth, "I found the General Assembly in Session and the city in a hub-bub about this said Douglass."[4] Irish Presbyterians disparaged Smyth's defense of slavery, and abolitionists in Ireland, as well as Douglass himself, challenged Smyth to public debates. One newspaper reported that Smyth had been excluded from a Presbyterian meeting in Belfast, where he ordinarily would have been seated as an honored visitor, because he was an enslaver.[5] In the same city where Douglass testified the chattel had become a man, Smyth found himself the minister who had become a villain. In Europe, Douglass utilized freedoms he did not have in the United States to directly criticize Smyth. Douglass was not a Presbyterian, but he focused his abolitionist efforts on a Presbyterian controversy in Scotland. He lent his voice to the campaign calling for the FCS to cut all ties, including financial ones, with the PCUSA (Old School). Because Douglass understood slavery as an evil incompatible with genuine Christianity, he argued that Christian congregations and denominations, the FCS in this case, must unequivocally separate from any association with slavery. Douglass observed that one of the strongest obstacles to abolition was the close connection between slavery and the "garb of Christianity" in the United States: "The church and the slave prison stand next to each other; the groans and cries of the heartbroken slave are often drowned in the pious devotions of his religious master."[6] Therefore it was important to expose Smyth as emblematic of the larger problems of hypocrisy and immorality among white American Christians. In his lectures, Douglass called out Smyth by name as "the Minister, at least, of a slaveholding Church" and ridiculed Smyth's claim that the pastor was not actually an enslaver because the enslaved persons in his family belonged to his wife and were the result of marriage.[7]

Smyth was taken aback, as his moral integrity and Christian standing were being interrogated in unfamiliar ways. No longer in the safe confines of Charleston, or in the familiar company of ecclesial colleagues in his proslavery denomination, Smyth resorted to a personal attack against Douglass. In David W. Blight's biography of Douglass, the historian recounts how Smyth "worked with other anti-abolitionist supporters of the Free Church to circulate a rumor that Douglass had been seen leaving a house of ill repute in Manchester, England." Blight characterizes this rumor as a "scurrilous effort to discredit" Douglass, likely because of the insinuations of sexual impropriety, proven false after Douglass threatened to sue Smyth for defamation and Smyth offered an apology through lawyers.[8]

"That It Was Not the Gospel": The Willful Compliance of White Presbyterian Clergy in the Southern States

Smyth's miserable experience abroad illumines the stark differences between Presbyterianism in the United States and Presbyterianism in Ireland and Scotland. In 1520, the German reformer Martin Luther published a treatise entitled *The Babylonian Captivity of the Church* excoriating the Roman Catholic Church in Europe because of his opposition to its sacramental teachings, especially about Communion. Luther compared the influence of the Roman papacy over European Christians to the captivity of the Jewish people when they were forced to migrate from Jerusalem under the rule of the Babylonian Empire. Luther called upon Christians to remove what he believed were distractions that had been added to the celebration of the Lord's Supper, "such things as vestments, ornaments, chants, prayers, organs, candles, and the whole pageantry of outward things," and administer the sacrament as he interpreted it had been done in the New Testament, for "in that word alone, reside the power, the nature, and the whole substance of the mass." But Luther also acknowledged that he was touching upon a "difficult matter" and addressing a practice that was "perhaps impossible to uproot" because it had been established over a long duration of time and was "firmly entrenched" in the hearts and minds of Christians as what was customary and right.[9]

In the antebellum United States, much of white Presbyterianism was under the captivity of American slavery. After 1830, white slave-owning Presbyterians and other proponents of slavery responded to the growth of the abolitionist movement with a ferocious flurry of literature in periodicals, pamphlets, and books to justify Black enslavement. One historian estimates that white clergy produced "almost half of all defenses of slavery published in America," and Presbyterian pastors were responsible for more proslavery writings than clergy from any other Christian tradition.[10]

In the southern states, it was difficult for a white Presbyterian pastor to be anything other than proslavery. The few who were not, such as John D. Paxton, who emancipated and sent the enslaved persons he received from his wife's family to Liberia in 1826 while pastoring a congregation in Virginia, were forced to leave their ministries. Paxton and his wife, Elizabeth Carr, made this decision together. They had previously professed that slavery was "morally wrong," but the acquisition of enslaved persons compelled them to do more because they believed that "actions speak louder than words."[11] In 1833, Francis R. Goulding, the son of Thomas Goulding, the first professor of Columbia Theological Seminary, was forced to shut down the Sabbath school he had founded for enslaved persons in South Carolina. Initially, enslavers chastised Goulding for employing pedagogical methods, such as displaying illustrations of biblical narratives and distributing slips of paper with scriptural verses on them, that might produce literacy among his enslaved students. Goulding therefore restricted his lessons to nothing other than oral instruction, but he ultimately lost the trust of the white community when they learned of his support for the colonization movement.[12] Abolitionists criticized the colonization movement for promoting the removal of free Black Americans to Liberia; enslavers detested it because they saw the campaign as a subversive means to make them feel guilty and relinquish their valuable human property.

After his travels across the southern states in 1844, the FCS pastor George Lewis was disappointed in white Presbyterians for their paltry ministries among enslaved persons, especially in comparison to the Methodists and Baptists: "I regret to say here, as elsewhere, the Presbyterian Church is doing little for the coloured population, and that little without any system, dependent entirely upon individual zeal and favourable circumstances. The Methodists and Baptists seem to have done almost all that has been done." Lewis continued, "The number of planters, in connection with the Presbyterian and Episcopal Churches, seem to paralyze the clergy."[13] Because white Presbyterians likely published more pages about their catechisms and sermons among enslaved persons than the Methodists or Baptists, historians have highlighted and overemphasized the efforts of Presbyterians such as Charles C. Jones. One historian's effusive and embarrassing praise of Jones illustrates the tendency to incorrectly exaggerate his ministry: "In promoting the spiritual welfare of the [enslaved] population in Liberty County and throughout the South no man was more active or zealous than the Rev. Dr. Charles Colcock Jones, 'Apostle to the Blacks,' a lifelong member of Midway Church . . . a rich planter, a gentleman of liberal education, and a Presbyterian clergyman of radiant Christian character."[14] In addition to Lewis's observations, one of Jones's white contemporaries, John Robinson, also provides numerical data to contradict this rendering of Jones's work and legacy. In 1852, Robinson confessed that white Presbyterians had "fallen far below the standard of duty" in their ministry among Black Americans and compared the slight Black membership "of about 7,000" in his denomination with the 237,528 Black members in the southern Methodist (137,528) and Baptist (100,000) denominations.[15]

Jones and Smyth attended a meeting in Charleston in 1845 regarding "the religious instruction of the negroes" convened by a committee of white planters and politicians with Daniel Elliott Huger, a wealthy U.S. senator who owned roughly 200 enslaved persons, serving as the chairperson.[16] The committee's aims illustrated why there were fewer enslaved Black Presbyterians in the southern states: Jones and other white Presbyterian clergy were presenting a religious message that was antithetical to the Christian gospel and insulting to Black Americans. The committee only permitted Christian instruction that enhanced the discipline on plantations and inculcated a spirit of subordination within enslaved persons. One white Presbyterian planter was pleased that some of his enslaved persons had become more diligent and obedient upon converting to Christianity, noting, "The deeper the piety of the slave, the more valuable is he in every sense of the word." A white Episcopal planter agreed: "My most orderly negroes are those connected with the church."[17] Jones boasted that the results of his ministry had proven beneficial for planters: "Their management has been made more easy: discipline is less frequently administered, and the people, generally speaking, are remarkably subordinate."[18]

Before escaping from his enslaver, Henry Bibb was subjected to the horrible kind of Christianity that Jones was championing, which tried to stifle his yearning for freedom with piety instead of punishment. The white preacher was no less cruel than an overseer with a whip in his hand, and perhaps more sinister than the overseer, because he threatened enslaved persons with the prospect of eternal damnation. Bibb detested when his enslaver told prospective buyers that he was a worthy investment because he was a Christian: "He tried to make it appear that I was so pious and honest that I would not run away from ill treatment; which was a gross mistake, for I never had religion enough to keep me from running away from slavery in my life."[19] Bibb lamented that white evangelization among enslaved persons produced two terrible outcomes: enslaved persons either converted to a false version of Christianity, or they rejected Christianity altogether as the religion of the white enslavers. In 1864, Jacob D. Green, a formerly enslaved Black man, regretted believing the lies of white evangelization: "From 18 to 27 I was considered one of the most devout Christians among the whole Black population, and under this impression I firmly believed to run away from my master would be to sin against the Holy Ghost."[20] After Green's wife was viciously sold to a slave trader, he recanted his faith in this spurious doctrine and made plans to escape.

Jones himself was aware of the limitations of his ministry among enslaved persons. In 1845, he recalled an occasion when he was preaching to a large group of enslaved persons from the Epistle of Philemon and "insisted upon fidelity and obedience as Christian virtues in servants" and emphasized the apostle Paul's condemnation of running away. Upon his proscription against escaping from slavery, half of the group immediately walked off, and "those that remained looked anything but satisfied, either with the preacher or his doctrine." After Jones finished his sermon, some enslaved persons refuted his message by declaring "that there was no such an Epistle in the Bible" and "that it was not the Gospel." Others accused Jones of preaching "to please the masters" and objected to Jones's slave ownership, telling him "that they did not care if they ever heard me preach again."[21]

In 1846, Albert Barnes highlighted Jones's account as clear evidence and "a very affecting illustration" against white scriptural interpretations of Philemon to justify Black enslavement based on "the innate conviction of the slaves themselves" in rejecting Jones's preaching as unbiblical and immoral. Barnes, like Bibb, criticized Jones and other white Christians for adulterating the Bible to defend their unjust slave ownership.[22] One reckoning that Barnes feared was the diminishment of Christian witness in the United States. White Presbyterians, and other white Christians, were not only destroying their reputations but also the appeal of Christianity among the broader population with their steadfast deployment of the Bible as a weapon of oppression and anti-Black racism. In 1858, the white Congregationalist pastor Abram Pryne cited an article from the *Baltimore Sun* deriding proslavery Christians for their stubborn insistence on scriptural justifications as an example of popular sentiment turning against Christianity: "Slavery is recorded in the Bible, and approved, with many degrading characteristics. War is recorded in the Bible, and approved, under what seems to us the extreme of cruelty. But are slavery and war to *endure* forever because we find them in the Bible?"[23] Barnes rightly predicted, "Future generations will look upon the defences of slavery drawn from the Bible, as among the most remarkable instances of mistaken interpretation and unfounded reasoning by the perversities of the human mind."[24] Barnes disagreed with every proslavery argument, but he preferred that white Christians refrain from using the Bible and allow the debate over abolition and slavery to be fought on economic, political, and social grounds.

It is also incumbent upon future generations to assess why white Presbyterians misused the Bible and failed the biggest moral test in their lives. As we look back into the past today, we are like Mary Cunningham, Thomas Smyth's friend from Ireland, and we share Cunningham's revulsion that white American Christians justified and participated in slavery. We, too, are horrified, but many of us turn away from the age of Black enslavement too quickly and are reluctant to examine precisely why white Presbyterians committed such abhorrent sins. Yet in the words of the historian Joyce Appleby, "History is powerful because we live with its residues, its remnants, its remainders and reminders." Appleby compares historians to cultural translators. Historians immerse themselves in the past, just as a cultural translator studies the customs and environs of a foreign country, "in order to sustain our connection to it" and help to "minister to the confusion and cynicism rampant today."[25]

"Just as Liable to Be Swayed by Interest": The Captivity of the White Pulpit

One sobering lesson is that many white Presbyterian clergy succumbed to economic, political, and social forces. Although their proslavery preaching and writing focused on religious arguments, the financial livelihoods of white Presbyterian pastors in the southern states were dependent on slavery. Presbyterian clergy were well-educated and respected figures in their local communities, but their salaries were low. In 1855, the average annual ministerial salary was $400 in an era in which a middle-class lifestyle began at roughly $1,200.[26] Presbyterian clergy sometimes earned more than clergy in other traditions, with larger congregations providing anywhere from $1,200 to $6,000, but pastoral ministry was generally not a lucrative career choice. In 1855, Robert Quarterman Mallard received an annual salary of $800 from a Presbyterian congregation in Walthourville, Georgia. D. L. Buttolph was offered an annual salary of $1,200 in 1867 from a Presbyterian congregation in Marietta, Georgia.[27] Even when pastors were ministering in small congregations without many enslavers, they were cautious in their preaching because they hoped to be in a larger and wealthier congregation someday. In 1837, Harriet Martineau observed that many white clergymen married into wealthy families because of social mores in the United States: "It is common, not to say usual, that young clergymen, who are almost invariably from poor families, marry ladies of fortune. Where there are several sisters in a rich family, it seems to be regarded as a matter of course that one will marry a clergyman."[28] One of the first Presbyterian pastors in the North American colonies, Francis Makemie, married a woman from a wealthy Virginia family. When marrying Margaret Milligan Adger, Thomas Smyth became exceedingly wealthy. Adger's inheritance after her father died in 1858 was $100,000 (roughly $3,400,000 in U.S. dollars today).[29] Smyth had one of the largest private libraries in the country, with approximately 20,000 books and a theological collection that ranked among the finest anywhere.[30]

The economic realities of slavery do not excuse white Presbyterian pastors in the southern states for their moral failings. Martineau complained that white Protestant clergy, especially Presbyterians and Episcopalians, were the "worst enemies of Christianity" and the "most guilty class" because they justified slavery on religious grounds. Pastors were more sinful than planters and merchants because they claimed to be Christ's ambassadors and "pledged themselves to declare the whole counsel of God" without consideration of "pecuniary interest." Thus, Martineau detested what she saw of white Presbyterianism: "But the bulk of the Presbyterian clergy are as fierce as the slave-holders against the abolitionists."[31] Eli Washington Caruthers, a white pastor in North Carolina forced to leave his congregation in 1861 after a public prayer acknowledging the southern states were "engaged in a lost cause," surmised that his ministerial colleagues ardently defended slavery because many of them participated in slave ownership and were "just as liable to be swayed by interest, custom and the influence of politicians" as other white persons.[32] For many white Presbyterian clergy in the southern states, the severity of their sins centered on their dishonesty. They almost never divulged their own economic ties to slavery and instead professed to be impartial interpreters with their gazes completely fixed on proclaiming the truths of the Bible. Why didn't more of them follow the example of John D. Paxton and emancipate their enslaved persons? It was probably because of the financial ramifications. The value of one enslaved person was likely equivalent to one year's salary. In freeing their enslaved persons, the Carr-Paxton couple forfeited a financial amount comparable to several years of Paxton's salary. Even wealthy pastors with many enslaved persons did not want to surrender income. The "Apostle to the Blacks" Charles C. Jones owned 129 enslaved persons in 1860 and did not emancipate any of them.

In 1838 and 1839, the white British actress and author Frances Anne (Fanny) Kemble lived on her husband's family plantation in coastal Georgia for eighteen months. Kemble was born in London and married a white American man in Philadelphia in 1834. She and her husband, Pierce Butler, relocated to a plantation near Jones after her father-in-law died. Kemble, like Jones, was convinced while residing in the northern states that slavery was inhumane and unjust. But unlike

Jones, Kemble's experiences of slave ownership confirmed, rather than dissuaded, her abolitionist convictions. Kemble was most disturbed by the religious justifications of slavery and white evangelization efforts among enslaved persons because of their deception and malice. Upon being thrust into her new life as an enslaver, Kemble immediately understood that white persons in the southern states defended slavery because it was financially profitable. "If the majority of Southerners were satisfied that slavery was contrary to their worldly fortunes," Kemble observed, "slavery would be at an end from that very moment." She believed that the "only obstacle to immediate abolition" was "the immense value of human property." Toward the end of a lengthy debate with a wealthy enslaver from South Carolina, Kemble was told, "I'll tell you why abolition is impossible: because every healthy negro can fetch a thousand dollars in the Charleston market at this moment."[33] Thus, Kemble abhorred the ways that white clergy participated in a massive cover-up of the obvious economic motivations of enslavers with pernicious appeals to God instead of mammon. If white clergy could not publicly confess that they suppressed their convictions about the evils of slavery for financial reasons, it would be better if they simply remained silent instead of misconstruing the Bible to make abusive and false arguments about the racial inferiority of Black Americans.

Kemble also criticized the practice of Communion, with white worshipers served before Black worshipers, as "a shocking mockery" of Christ's teachings in his farewell discourse from the Gospel of John. However, Kemble also recognized that some white worshipers took great pride in the sacrament as an illustration of their faith commitments because it was unusual to welcome enslaved persons to the same table and food as them. In their own homes, slave-owning Christians never allowed enslaved persons to sit at their dining tables.[34] Frederick Douglass was similarly repulsed at the theological claim that the practice of racial segregation during Communion was a confirmation, rather than a contradiction, of the gospel. In his abolitionist speeches, Douglass recalled one of his first worship experiences in a white congregation after escaping from slavery. He mocked how the white pastor looked up to the "negro pew" where he was sitting and exclaimed with outstretched arms, after all the white worshipers received the Communion elements, "We now invite our colored friends to come down and partake of this holy feast, for the Lord is no respecter of persons!"[35] Black and white listeners often laughed with Douglass at this point in his address because of the irony in the divergence between the white pastor's words about God's intention for racial equality and the racially segregated action.

Yet American slavery had so corrupted the hearts and twisted the minds of some white Presbyterians that they believed their racially segregated practice of Communion was a beautiful sign and faithful seal of divine grace. George Howe, a white professor at Columbia Theological Seminary, praised the ministry of Smyth at Second Presbyterian Church in Charleston because the Black worshipers were invited to receive the Communion elements "after the tables had been successively filled by the whites." Howe even asserted that the "communion occasions" at Second Presbyterian testified to the scriptural teaching in Galatians 3:28 proclaiming that humans of all races, classes, and genders were unified as one in Jesus Christ.[36]

White Presbyterian clergy also borrowed popular proslavery arguments from their larger culture. In 1860, Smyth delivered a sermon about how the institution of slavery did not originate in the southern states but was authorized in the Scriptures. But Smyth also employed a simplistic economic analogy that would have been familiar to his congregants because of its ubiquity in print culture. Smyth declared that slavery had proven to be in the best interests of enslaved persons because they were "healthier and happier than any other laboring class on the face of the earth" due to the "fostering care of these Southern States" and white evangelization efforts on southern plantations.[37] Smyth's criticism of the economic injustices in free (contra enslaved) labor capitalism in the northern states and Europe was a common argument from white proponents of slavery. Richard Nisbet argued in 1773 that enslaved persons in the Caribbean enjoyed better lifestyles, in terms of food, shelter, security, and leisure provisions, than the working classes of Ireland and Scotland.[38] Popular political cartoons in U.S. newspapers compared the fictional merriment of enslaved persons in the southern states with the misery of white industrial laborers in the northern states and England. Formerly enslaved Black authors often countered this ludicrous myth that Smyth was regurgitating from the pulpit by stating that every human obviously yearned to be free and earn fair pay for their labor. The solution to poverty was wage justice, not slavery.

Benjamin Rush's criticism of clergy reveals how white Presbyterian pastors in the northern states were just as susceptible to economic, political, and social impulses. In 1773, Rush implored white pastors to adjust their ministerial priorities. He was frustrated in their preaching

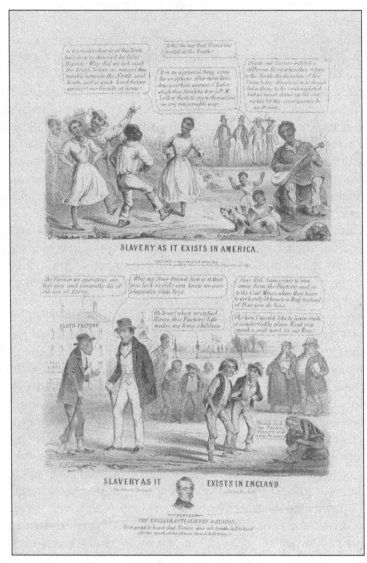

Slavery as it exists in America. Slavery as it
exists in England (Boston, 1850).

because the sermons focused almost entirely on the duties of "tithe and cummin" in the pursuit of an individualistic piety defined as much by social mores as scriptural precepts. White preachers neglected "the weightier laws of justice and humanity."[39] Thus, Rush called upon white clergy to turn their homiletical attention toward the grave sins and atrocious abuses of slavery. But white pastors in the northern states ignored Rush's counsel because they knew that their congregations were not interested in hearing about slavery and anti-Black racism. In 1852, William Henry Ruffner, the white pastor of Seventh Presbyterian Church in Philadelphia, acknowledged that white persons in the northern states tried hard to convince themselves that slavery was "not such a bad thing after all" because they preferred the order and stability of their present lives over the uncertainty of abolition and division of their nation.[40]

Therefore, Rush's assessment was morally right, but his prescriptions were difficult for clergy to put into practice. White pastors did not preach about slavery mainly because they wanted to keep preaching in their congregations. Some white Presbyterians in the northern states hated slavery, but even they did not want their pastors to compel them to grapple with the injustices of slavery and anti-Black racism on Sunday mornings. Most white Presbyterian congregations in the northern states paid their pastors to preach about the lesser sins and encourage a piety that they could enact without any tangible disruption to their everyday lives.

Many white Presbyterian clergy in the northern states were also wary of the increasing intersectionality of some abolitionist organizations. In 1840, the American Anti-Slavery Society (AASS) elected a white woman, Abby Kelley Foster, to its business committee and added three other white women—Maria Weston Chapman, Lydia Maria Child, and Lucretia Mott—in its executive committee.[41] It was the first time in the organization's existence that white women were given prominent leadership roles alongside Black and white men. The election of Kelley Foster was contentious, with 557 votes in favor and 451 votes in opposition, and nearly all voting in opposition left the meeting to form a separate organization, the American and Foreign Anti-Slavery Society (AFASS).[42] The white Presbyterian merchants Arthur Tappan and Lewis Tappan helped to form the AFASS because they resisted the presence of women in leadership. The Tappans also believed that the abolitionist movement should focus solely on Black liberation and not get entangled with the burgeoning women's rights movement. Other Black and white abolitionists agreed that an intersectional commitment integrating abolition and women's rights was a poor strategy, regardless of individual convictions, because it would repel one of the primary groups they were seeking to persuade—white Christians.

The mainstream Protestant denominations in 1840 restricted ministerial ordination and ecclesial leadership responsibilities to men. Some Black abolitionists were unhappy about the schism because they felt it diverted energies away from advocacy for Black liberation and toward internal organization building.[43] The abolitionist movement also did not take full advantage of one of its greatest strengths, its racial and gender diversity, because the leaders were slower to empower Black women despite their pivotal work as community organizers, public speakers, social activists, and writers.

The Tappans were wrong in their stance opposing women in their organization's leadership, but they were right about the temper of their Presbyterian tradition. White Presbyterian clergy in the northern states denounced the abolitionist movement because of its intersectional pursuit of Black liberation and women's rights. In 1850, Joseph C. Stiles, a white Presbyterian pastor in New York City, delivered a speech before the PCUSA (New School) General Assembly, which met in Detroit, opining that the abolitionist movement "destroys the foundations of the Bible" and "sets up a Bible of humanisms in the place of the Word of God" because of its support for women's rights. Stiles believed the Bible clearly taught "that the head of the woman is the man, for woman was made second, and is the weaker vessel." Stiles accused abolitionists, with their "doctrine of Womanism," of participating in a perilous crusade seeking to overturn the natural order and biblical foundation of their churches and wider society. He also disagreed with one of the theological implications of the women's rights movement: scriptural interpretation required a deep understanding of the social contexts in which the books of the Bible were written and how oppressive patriarchal customs influenced certain proscriptions against women. Stiles was enraged at the idea that the "Scriptures were penned in a dark and barbarous age" unable "to bear the revelation" of God regarding "the perfect development of woman's capacities, relations, and rights."[44]

Structural Fragility, the Machinery of Slavery, and the "Noble History" of American Democracy

A second lesson is that most white Presbyterians were either uncomfortable with structural change or downright resistant to systemic reforms. In 1833, Paxton worried that Black enslavement was destroying the moral fabric of white society in the southern states. As a resident of Virginia, Paxton understood that planters had little accountability because of their remote location, considerable distance from neighbors, and the larger social conditions. One historian explains how the open physical space, close kinship ties within white families, and lack of government restraint in the southern states shaped a regional identity with a weak institutional framework. In 1860, one in five Americans lived in a town of 2,500 persons or more, but there were far more of these towns in the northern states. For example, nearly two-thirds of all persons in Rhode Island and roughly 40 percent of all persons in New York resided in towns. Less than 6 percent of all persons in seven southern states lived in towns: Alabama (5 percent), Florida, Tennessee, and Texas (4 percent), Mississippi and North Carolina (3 percent), and Arkansas (1 percent).[45] The white-owned plantation, in the absence of a bustling town with apparel shops, banking branches, and grocery stores, provided the main support structures for lower- and middle-class white farmers and residents. When they needed to learn about the prices of various crops, receive informal banking services, and barter for clothing and food, these farmers and residents went to one of the larger plantations. Wealthy planters also offered employment opportunities as overseers, which was one of the few pathways for lower-class white persons to earn decent wages. Between 1850 and 1860, the number of overseers increased by 80 percent in North Carolina and 50 percent in South Carolina.[46] Other lower-class white persons worked as slave patrollers or pursued enslaved persons who had escaped for the monetary rewards that their enslavers promised for their return. One example is from an advertisement in a local newspaper in Lexington, Kentucky: "$50 Reward—Ran away from the subscriber, a negro girl, named Maria. She is of a copper color, between 13 and 14 years of age—bare headed and bare footed. She is small of her age—very sprightly and very likely. She stated she was going to see her mother at Maysville."[47] Advertisements for "fugitive slaves" were ubiquitous, and many newspapers relied on the income from these advertisements to sustain their businesses.

Thus, many white Presbyterians in the southern states may not have disagreed with Paxton's observations about the detestable features of Black enslavement—such as the separation of enslaved families, the excessive physical abuse, and unchecked sexual violence—but they were more wary of the structural ramifications of abolition. Paxton highlighted the prevalence and tacit acceptance of sexual violence as one demonstration of the moral deterioration in white communities:

"That the vice prevails to a most shameful extent is proved from the rapid increase of mulattoes. Oh, how many have fallen before this temptation: so many, that it has almost ceased to be a shame to fall!"[48] Other white clergy simply did not mention these abuses, but white laity like Thomas R. R. Cobb more readily acknowledged that slavery was an imperfect system with "unquestionable" evils, including "immorality in the white males" for raping enslaved Black women. But Cobb maintained that every human society was governed under structures that had benefits and blessings as well as injustices and inequities.[49] Because slave-owning Presbyterians received the benefits and blessings of slavery, they aggressively resisted structural changes and adopted a hostile posture toward any systemic reforms that disrupted their way of life, especially Black liberation. Lower-class white persons were, in the words of one historian, "cogs in the machinery of slavery, performing much of the dirty work for the slaveholders" as overseers, slave patrollers, and slave hunters.[50] Though white clergy were not in the same social rank as overseers and patrollers, they also served as cogs with their religious justifications for slavery. In 1858, James Henley Thornwell bragged about the dirty work he was doing (although he did not think it was dirty): "Our Theological Professors are preachers upon a large scale—Preachers not only to preachers, but to all the congregations of the land. In their studies they are putting forth an influence, which, like the atmosphere, penetrates to every part of the country."[51] Thornwell exulted in the popular reception of his published sermon on slavery from 1850, which was circulating throughout the nation.

Thornwell connected his defense of slavery to his understandings of biblical interpretation and the church's mission. He proposed a rigid and restrictive literalism when applying scriptural teachings, with a fourfold rubric in which Christians were only permitted to (1) announce what the Bible teaches, (2) enjoin what the Bible commands, (3) prohibit what the Bible condemns, and (4) enforce church discipline through spiritual sanctions. Moreover, the church was compelled to be silent and "put her hand upon her lips" on issues such as slavery about which there was no explicit condemnation in the Bible.[52] Scriptural appeals from Christian abolitionists, including Black and white Presbyterians in the United States, Ireland, and Scotland, uncover one of the obvious challenges to these prescripts. Thornwell was not humbly encouraging Christians to obey God's authority as revealed in the Scriptures. Rather, he was audaciously calling for others to submit to his interpretation of what the Bible teaches, commands, and condemns. Thornwell also set severe restrictions on the very nature of the church itself. The church was not "a moral institute of universal good" and did not have a divine commission to "construct society afresh" or "rearrange the distribution of its classes." Rather, the church, as Thornwell saw it, was a strictly spiritual entity responsible for biblical teaching, administering the sacraments of baptism and Communion, and discipline solely within congregational and denominational confines. Charles Hodge agreed with Thornwell on the point that the Scriptures did not provide direct evidence to support abolition, but even Hodge found Thornwell's position on the church's exclusive identity as a spiritual organization absurd because it denied any opportunity for Christians to mobilize against social evils.[53]

The church has never been, and never will be, a strictly spiritual entity. Congregations and denominations are in fact social as well as spiritual organizations. In the antebellum United States, Presbyterian congregations were often homogenous in the sense that they generally comprised persons of the same race and class. Churches in the southern states were multiracial, but they likely had little class diversity and no free Black worshipers. Between 1840 and 1850, Second Presbyterian Church in Charleston averaged 113 Black and 256 white members.[54] In addition to gathering for worship, churches provided opportunities for members to see good friends, show off their latest clothing purchases (and in some cases, proof of one's generosity in the churchgoing attire of one's enslaved persons), and discuss recent happenings in agriculture, finance, and politics in private conversations before and after worship services. Thornwell, Smyth, and their Presbyterian congregations all existed in a society resting on the foundation of the interconnected power structures of slavery and race.

A century after Thornwell, another white Presbyterian theologian from the southern states, Ernest Trice Thompson, argued in 1961 that the "spirituality of the church" doctrine was a betrayal of the Reformed tradition and "alien to our Calvinistic heritage," because John Calvin and other early modern European Protestant reformers "sought to apply the gospel to the total life of the community."[55] Calvin understood that the church's mission included commitments to education and public health, which are seen in Calvin's meticulous attention to boosting literacy rates and improving sewage systems in Geneva. The condemnable irony in Thornwell's work is his omission, whether conscious or unconscious, of the social realities that motivated his spiritual understanding of the church. In E. Brooks Holifield's history of

Christian theology in the antebellum southern states, Holifield astutely observes, "In fact the Southern churches never truly abstained from social comment; their self-described isolation was merely a protective gesture during the slavery controversy."[56] It was the machinery of slavery, not the inspiration of the Scriptures, that prompted Thornwell to craft his ecclesiology. Yet the influence of the "spirituality of the church" doctrine continues to be felt in some Presbyterian congregations, colleges, and seminaries, as evinced in the selective arbitration of what political issues are deemed permissible for religious engagement.

Many white Presbyterians in the northern states were just as antagonistic toward systemic reforms. Although they did not exhibit racial fragility, white Presbyterians possessed a structural fragility in repelling conversations about the unjust economic and societal foundations of their lives and their nation. In his sermon on Independence Day in 1852, Ruffner encouraged his congregants in Philadelphia to proudly display their patriotism and celebrate the "noble history" of their country's founding. The experiment of American democracy was succeeding, and their young nation, in less than one century, had established itself as the great beacon of freedom throughout the world. But Ruffner criticized the abolitionist movement for inflaming sectional animosities with a "satanic rage" and naive obsession with purity. Although Ruffner advocated for a literalist approach to biblical interpretation, he detested the literalism of the abolitionists in their constitutional and moral appeals.[57]

Ruffner believed that the abolitionists wrongly dealt in abstraction rather than reality in their push for Black liberation based on the founding American ideal of equality. He explained that every principle underwent a process of modification before application and provided the following example: "You may hear another arguing that whilst 'thou shalt not kill' is the true law in morals and religion, yet killing may become a propriety, an imperative duty, in certain circumstances." Ruffner continued with a more specific accusation against the abolitionist movement: "And yet these men seize hold of the abstraction that 'all men being free and equal, and having certain inalienable rights, the holding of a man in bondage is a sin and a shame,' and try to run it like a red-hot ploughshare through society, in utter defiance of all attending and modifying circumstances." Ruffner maligned abolitionists for implying that the United States was evil for allowing slavery to continue as a legal institution after the American Revolution. He opposed the abolitionist movement because it was making white

Americans feel guilty about their patriotism, not their racism. In Ruff-ner's mind, abolitionists were presenting their proud nation as "an old-fashioned, rickety building" that must be "torn down" and replaced with "an entire reconstruction of the edifice" built on "free and social-istic principles." Ruffner wanted no part of a movement that sought to uproot race-based structures and destroy societal foundations. Hence, he urged his congregation to support the colonization movement and patiently work toward the gradual emancipation of enslaved persons and the eventual transportation of the entire Black population in the northern and southern states to Liberia.[58]

In October 1845, two white Presbyterian pastors in Cincinnati held a highly publicized debate on abolition and slavery. Jonathan Blanchard from Sixth Presbyterian Church and Nathan L. Rice from Central Presbyterian Church exchanged addresses over four days to advance their arguments, refute their opponent's reasoning, and ask questions of one another. The pastors themselves were neither abolitionists nor enslavers, but they both desired to engage the ethical and theological questions surrounding Black enslavement. Rice, like many other white Presbyterians in the northern states, argued that he personally hated slavery but willingly defended the institution to explain why the unity of Presbyterians was better than the regional schisms of the Methodists and Baptists. Rice emphasized a literalist interpretation of the Bible, forcefully asking Blanchard on numerous occasions to show him what scriptural verse explicitly denounced slavery as a sin (knowing such a verse does not exist), but he also expressed his resistance to the soci-etal ramifications of abolition. Rice maintained, "Whilst, therefore, I admit that slavery is an evil, I utterly protest against upturning the very foundation of society in order to abolish it." Rice observed that there were "great evils in connection with human society" that could not be immediately removed.[59] He, like other white Presbyterians, accepted that some social injustices were either too big to fix or not within their responsibility to repair.

Some white Presbyterians admitted that their resistance to structural change was arbitrary and motivated by self-interest, especially consid-ering their history of fervent participation in violently overturning an entire system of British colonial rule, but they refused to let the injus-tices of slavery and anti-Black racism trouble their consciences. In 1836, Ethan Allen Andrews encapsulated what the brief rationalization process of white Americans entailed. During a conversation with a companion who bitterly complained about the "shocking separations" of enslaved families in the domestic slave trade, Andrews responded with details from his research showing how this deplorable feature was inevitable in the existing system of Black enslavement and could not be altered apart from abolition. Andrews's friend agreed, and "after a moment's hesitation," simply expressed remorse and moved onto another subject.[60] The most frequent moment of hesitation among white Presbyterians likely occurred on Sunday mornings when someone included a few words about the "poor slaves" in an intercessory prayer.

In the debate between Blanchard and Rice, even Blanchard, in his support of abolition, offered tepid responses to Rice's points about societal upheaval. Blanchard stopped short of advocating for Black citizenship and insisted that he was not in support of equal rights for free Black Americans, such as the right to vote, which was a contentious struggle in Cincinnati and unpopular among most of its white residents. Blanchard was especially on his heels and forced to backtrack when Rice asked him if there was a difference between the abolitionist notion of slavery as unjust because enslavers were purchasing stolen human property, the descendants of abducted Africans, and the blatantly immoral and violent seizure of Indigenous lands across the United States. Rice charged, "Again, he says, my argument fails, because the Africans were all originally stolen; and, if we buy them, we are guilty of the sin of man-stealing. I reply, that if this principle is sound, there is not a man in Ohio who can, honestly and innocently, hold the farm he owns: for the land was, most of it, originally taken by force or fraud from the Indians."[61] Blanchard struggled and ultimately failed to explain why he objected to the stealing of human property in Black enslavement but not the theft of Indigenous land in settler colonialism. What distinguished white enslavers from white settlers? Rice saw Black enslavement and settler colonialism as foundational sins that white Americans inherited from their ancestors. Both injustices had become so deeply embedded in the white-dominant society that they fell outside the realm of potential Christian activism. Blanchard weakly responded that it was too difficult to trace and precisely identify the rightful descendants of the original Indigenous owners of each "piece of land," and therefore the stolen land should remain with the white families that either inherited or purchased it. Rice countered that the process of restoring lands to Indigenous owners would not be arduous because of the presence of extensive documentation, including the claims of some Indigenous nations, such as the Cherokee Nation.[62] Blanchard moved onto another subject.

The Gospel as "Prisoner and Liberator" of American Culture

A third lesson involves the cultural captivity of white Presbyterians. One historian of world Christianity, Andrew F. Walls, identifies the gospel as both "prisoner and liberator of culture." Walls observes that every group of Christians, from the first century to the present, utilizes its own specific cultural idioms and understandings to profess and practice the faith. For example, Hellenistic Christians in the Greco-Roman world constructed a theology of the lordship of Jesus Christ, giving Jesus the title of *Kyrios*, a Greek word that was commonly employed to refer to cult divinities like Osiris and Serapis. Jewish Christians emphasized a theology of Jesus Christ as the *Messiah*, a Hebrew term connecting Old Testament prophecies about the Savior of Israel to the life, death, and resurrection of Jesus, but the addition of Christ as Kyrios developed precisely because it resonated within the cultural context of Hellenistic believers.[63] Thus, the gospel is a prisoner of culture because Christian theology is inherently incarnational, meaning it takes root and grows differently within diverse human cultures. At the same time, the gospel is also the liberator of culture because Christianity challenges every human culture with the universal message of divine love and justice. John Calvin's teachings on the threefold purposes of God's law as a mirror revealing human sinfulness, a curb to restrain evil, and a guide to instruct toward faithful and moral living illustrate the liberating nature of the gospel. Christians, as recipients of divine grace, are inspired to reform the injustices existing in their specific cultures. Walls describes a Christian as a person who expresses gratitude to God for wondrously fashioning the distinctives of every culture but is also necessarily "out of step" with one's own society and perpetually dissatisfied with the status quo.[64]

Christians living in the white-dominant society of the antebellum United States had ample opportunity to apply the liberating promises of the gospel in a culture rampant with barbaric cruelties and terrible racial injustices. David Walker asked white Christians to consider what kind of Christianity could justify their participation in Black enslavement and condone their racism toward Black Americans. He detested the term *nigger*, which he explained was a word "derived from the Latin, which was used by the old Romans, to designate inanimate beings, which were black," such as a pot or soot, or "animals which they considered inferior to the human species," such as a cow or dog. Walker hated how "white Americans have applied this term to Africans, by way of reproach for our colour, to aggravate and heighten our miseries, because they have their feet on our throats."[65] Angelina Emily Grimké deplored slavery because it reduced a Black person to chattel and permitted white Americans "to set our feet upon his neck"—to destroy another person's body, mind, and soul based on skin color.[66] Robert J. Breckinridge, a white Presbyterian pastor and politician from Kentucky, was frustrated with white criticisms of Black criminality. He countered that the criminal justice system was deliberately racist with extreme prejudice against Black Americans: "We have known a slave hanged for what a white man would hardly have been prosecuted for; and we have known free blacks put into the penitentiary for several years, upon evidence that was illegal by statute against a white man." Breckinridge also believed "one of the most abhorrent features of slavery" was that it perpetrated a crime against the unborn fetus inside of an enslaved Black mother. "Men may become slaves, perhaps for life, for crimes lawfully proven," Breckinridge noted. "But no absurdity can be more inconceivably gross than to think of making slaves of the unborn."[67]

However, too many white Presbyterians remained in step, rather than out of step, with their culture. At one level this historical reality is not surprising, because white Presbyterians inhabited a world where anti-Black racism was the norm, inscribed and codified in discriminatory laws. But at another level, the past reveals a legacy of white Presbyterianism as a dishonest faith. All white Presbyterians professed to accept the call to Christian discipleship, but few of them were willing to pay the cost of enacting Christ's teachings. And what made the witness of proslavery Presbyterians so disingenuous was that none were willing to fully admit it. Perhaps Elisha Mitchell, a white pastor and geologist from North Carolina, came the closest when he acknowledged in 1848 that antebellum capitalism ran contrary to scriptural precepts about Christian community in Acts 2, in which all the believers evenly shared their possessions, because of the wealth inequities created by the "unequal division of property." Mitchell believed the eradication of slavery was just as unrealistic as the abolition of private property because "human laws appeal directly and exclusively to the principle of selfishness."[68] Instead of confessing that their support of Black enslavement was selfish, white Presbyterians like Benjamin Morgan Palmer contended that enslavers were among the most selfless and virtuous Christians because they bore the burdens of guardianship over helpless and inferior Black Americans. White Presbyterians like Archibald Alexander pushed to transport Black Americans to Liberia instead of confronting their white congregations about the scourge of anti-Black racism. White Presbyterian leaders refused to concede that they practiced a weak and mediocre kind of Christianity. What especially astonishes and enrages this historian is how some of these leaders demanded that others adhere to their horrible and immoral kind of Christianity because it was the best and most biblical.

White Presbyterians then, just like all Christians now, were not immune to the malicious influences in their culture. But cultural captivity is not an excuse. Harriet Martineau observed that the Presbyterian Church in the antebellum United States comprised the best and worst of humanity, counting in its ranks the most courageous abolitionists and the most nefarious enslavers, which means that white Presbyterian clergy in the southern states were not victims of geographical circumstance and white Presbyterians in the northern states had access to the pathway toward Black liberation that abolitionists within their own denominations helped to forge. American slavery was utterly appalling to foreign observers such as Martineau. Martineau and the Scottish pastor George Lewis were aghast at the sight of enslaved persons at slave auctions and on slave ships in ports heading to the southwestern states. In 1841, the English novelist Charles Dickens was taken aback by the many newspaper advertisements offering rewards for the capture and return of "fugitive slaves." One historian provides a sample of what Dickens read in his New York City hotel room: "Ran away, a negro woman and two children. A few days before she went off, I burnt her with a hot iron, on the left side of her face. I tried to make the letter 'M.'"; "Ran away, a negro named Arthur. Has a considerable scar across his breast and each arm, made by a knife; loves to talk much of the goodness of God."[69] The French pastor Georges Fisch was horrified by Thornwell's declaration that the international slave trade was "the finest of all missionary societies."[70] Fisch also excoriated Alexander H. Stephens's speech defining slavery as the "natural and normal condition of the negro" as an affront against Christianity that defied the fundamental principles of goodness, humanity, and morality: "The whole Christian Church heard this blasphemy, and shuddered. . . . Never was there a more audacious challenge flung down to the civilisation and intellect of our day, or to the spirit of the gospel."[71] My harsh condemnation of white Presbyterianism in the age of Black enslavement is neither a new criticism nor the product of a present perspective aided by the benefit of time. Black and white abolitionists, as well as foreign observers, judged

their white Presbyterian contemporaries with the utmost disdain and
fury for their sins of racism, slavery, and complicity.

I find our memory of the past actively seeks to mute the rage and
dilute the condemnation. Some of us have trouble believing, or do
not want to believe, that most antebellum white Americans held racial
prejudices against Black Americans. It is hard for some to imagine that
white Presbyterians physically abused, psychologically harmed, sexually violated, and spiritually injured enslaved persons. And it is bewil-
dering to behold that many other white Presbyterians did absolutely
nothing about it. These historical facts run counter to our notions of
what it means to be an American and a Presbyterian. It is absurd to us
that a presbytery in Indiana belonging to the Cumberland Presbyterian
Church suspended one of its white ministers, T. B. McCormick, for
his participation in the Underground Railroad. McCormick was found
guilty in 1855 of "Unchristian conduct" for "engaging in the business
of assisting slaves in making their escape."[72] Yet because McCormick
was the one acting in accordance with the Christian faith, then all the
white Presbyterians who voted to censure him were surely not.

Some of us also struggle to wrap our heads around the reality that the
moral compass of the Presbyterian Church was so warped that white
enslavers were welcomed and regarded with great respect, whereas
Black and white abolitionists were maligned and treated with vile
contempt. In 1857, Charles C. Jones was gratified that "the question
of slavery" did not arise for even a moment during the PCUSA (Old
School) General Assembly meeting in Lexington, Kentucky. Wealthy
white residents in the host city paid for all the hotel and dining bills
of the commissioners, and Jones highlighted how the "Northern and
Western commissioners were specially pleased with this trip into a
slave state."[73] In the same year the PCUSA (New School) pastor and
abolitionist Albert Barnes complained, "I am weary—and I am sure
that in this I speak the sentiments of many thousands of others—of
the perpetual deference shown to the holders of slaves in the pulpit
and in the religious literature of the land." Barnes also understood that
white Presbyterian silence on slavery was deliberate and required "all
the power of an efficient and closely-compacted ecclesiastical organization."[74] To remain silent on the most pressing moral conundrum and
human rights violation in their midst was hard work, and it entailed a
lot of maneuvering behind the scenes and within parliamentary proce-
dure. How could these white Presbyterian men, all of them ministers
and ruling elders, so flagrantly betray their ordination vows?

Because some of us cannot imagine that white persons, American citizens, and Presbyterian leaders could have been guilty of such evil, one incorrect contemporary explanation for past crimes and sins is to assert that these white Presbyterian ancestors had a "lack of theological imagination."[75] Princeton Theological Seminary recently concluded that the founding leaders of the institution opposed abolition and supported the American Colonization Society because they could not envision a racially just and integrated society. But Black and white Presbyterian abolitionists, including Theodore S. Wright, a graduate of Princeton Seminary (class of 1828), provided the blueprint for such a society. Wright's vision for Black liberation was in full view of the white leaders at Princeton Seminary, and they intentionally chose to dismiss it.

The seminary where I teach and earn my income, Columbia Theological Seminary, has a staggeringly awful record of anti-Black racism replete with an endowment that includes money from the sale of eighteen enslaved persons in 1834, numerous slave-owning faculty and administrators in its history, and responsibility for the propagation of proslavery literature from Jones, Palmer, Thornwell, and other graduates and professors. In Jennifer Oast's recounting of slave-owning congregations and colleges in Virginia, the historian includes a confession from a white Presbyterian pastor whose salary was paid through his congregation's ownership of enslaved persons. Each year, the congregation's members held an auction to lease the services of their human property to the highest bidders. This pastor therefore surmised his congregation practiced "the worst kind of slavery."[76] Columbia Seminary participated in the worst kind of proslavery advocacy. Other white intellectuals touched on religion, but they primarily justified slavery from their areas of expertise, such as philosophy or sociology. However, the leaders at Columbia Seminary wrested a higher authority from the Bible, the very words of God, and contended that to disagree with them was to quarrel with the Almighty. Slavery was good and Black persons were inferior because the triune God said so. I do not think it is an exaggeration to suggest that Columbia Seminary was among the most wicked places in the nation. But here is the thing—it did not appear that way. It looked and sounded like a church.

Notes

Chapter 1: "What Kind of Christianity?"

1. Katie Geneva Cannon, "A Theological Analysis of Imperialistic Christianity," in *An Ocean with Many Shores: Asian Women Making Connections in Theology and Ministry*, ed. Nantawan Boonprasat Lewis (New York: Asian Women Theologians, Northeast U.S. Group, 1987), 25, as cited in Kwok Pui-lan, *Discovering the Bible in the Non-Biblical World* (Maryknoll, NY: Orbis Books, 1995), 12.

2. *Minutes of the General Assembly of the Presbyterian Church in the United States of America: With an Appendix, A.D. 1836* (Philadelphia: Stated Clerk of the Assembly, 1836), 235. When introducing Presbyterians and most other historical actors throughout the book, I identify their race. The exceptions are well-recognized public persons, such as Harriet Beecher Stowe, William Lloyd Garrison, Harriet Tubman, and George Washington. This is an intentional choice so that the white race is not treated as the assumed default. If persons of color were the only individuals specifically identified, it would contribute to the idea that the white race occupies the normative place in the history of the United States.

3. James Smylie, *A Review of a Letter, from the Presbytery of Chillicothe, to the Presbytery of Mississippi, on the Subject of Slavery* (Woodville, MS: Wm. A. Norris, 1836), 7–8.

4. *Minutes of the General Assembly of the Presbyterian Church in the United States of America from Its Organization, A.D. 1789 to A.D. 1820 Inclusive* (Philadelphia: Presbyterian Board of Publication, 1847), 692–93.

5. *Minutes of the General Assembly of the Presbyterian Church in the United States of America from Its Organization, A.D. 1821 to A.D. 1835 Inclusive* (Philadelphia: Presbyterian Board of Publication, n.d.), 476 and 490.

6. *Minutes of the General Assembly . . . , A.D. 1836*, 247–50.

7. *Minutes of the General Assembly . . . , A.D. 1836*, 269–71.

8. *Minutes of the General Assembly . . . , A.D. 1836*, 272.

9. *Minutes of the General Assembly . . . , A.D. 1836*, 273.

10. William Lloyd Garrison, *Thoughts on African Colonization, with a New Preface by William Loren Katz* (New York: Arno Press, 1969), xix and 54.

11. John Rankin, *Letters on American Slavery, Addressed to Mr. Thomas Rankin, Merchant at Middlebrook, Augusta Co., Virginia* (Boston: Garrison &

Knapp, 1833), 59. Rankin's letters were initially self-published as a book in 1826 and republished by the American Anti-Slavery Society in 1833.

12. "Resolutions Respecting Colonization and Slavery," in *African Repository and Colonial Journal,* July 1836, 218; italics in original.

13. George White, *Historical Collections of Georgia: Containing the Most Interesting Facts, Traditions, Biographical Sketches, Anecdotes, etc. Related to Its History and Antiquities, from Its First Settlement to the Present Time, Compiled from Original Records and Office Documents,* 3rd ed. (New York: Pudney & Russell, 1855), 275. The first edition was published in 1854. Eugenius A. Nisbet's surname had an alternate spelling as "Nesbit," which is the spelling found in both White and the PCUSA General Assembly minutes.

14. Frederick Douglass, *Narrative of the Life of Frederick Douglass, an American Slave* (Boston: Anti-Slavery Office, 1845), 118–19.

15. Douglass, 119.

16. "Scandalous—We Find the Following Notice of a Public Sale, in the Savannah Republican of March 3, 1845," *Evangelical Guardian,* June 1845, 46.

17. Elizabeth Keckley, *Behind the Scenes, or Thirty Years a Slave, and Four Years in the White House* (New York: G. W. Carleton, 1868), 23. In the last moments of Keckley's mother's life, she told Keckley that her real father was her mother's enslaver and not her mother's enslaved spouse. See John E. Washington and Kate Masur, *They Knew Lincoln* (New York: Oxford University Press, 2018), 205–6.

18. *Minutes of the General Assembly . . . , A.D. 1836,* 389.

19. J. W. C. Pennington, *Christian Zeal: A Sermon Preached before the Third Presbytery of New York in Thirteenth-St. Presbyterian Church, July 3, 1853* (New York: Zuille & Leonard, 1854), 13.

20. *The Annual Report of the American and Foreign Anti-Slavery Society Presented at New York, May 6, 1851; with the Addresses and Resolutions* (New York: American and Foreign Anti-Slavery Society, 1851), 56.

21. John Robinson, *The Testimony and Practice of the Presbyterian Church in Reference to American Slavery* (Cincinnati: John D. Thorpe, 1852), 107 and 168.

22. Gary B. Nash and Jean R. Soderlund, *Freedom by Degrees: Emancipation in Pennsylvania and Its Aftermath* (New York: Oxford University Press, 1991), 81 and 88; and Stephanie McCurry, *Masters of Small Worlds: Yeoman Households, Gender Relations, and the Political Culture of the Antebellum South Carolina Low Country* (New York: Oxford University Press, 1995), 165.

23. Smylie, *Review of a Letter, from the Presbytery of Chillicothe,* 13.

24. James O. Farmer Jr., *The Metaphysical Confederacy: James Henley Thornwell and the Synthesis of Southern Values* (Macon, GA: Mercer University Press, 1999), 201.

25. *Minutes of the General Assembly of the Presbyterian Church in the United States of America: With an Appendix, A.D. 1860* (Philadelphia: Presbyterian Board of Publication, 1860), 256–61. Both "members" and "communicants" are employed in the minutes when referring to membership. For example, one summary notes

the number of "members added on certificate" and another summary refers to this same group as "communicants added on certificate." In both summaries, the number of members (or communicants) added on certificate is 11,316.

26. James W. Loewen, *Lies My Teacher Told Me: Everything Your American History Textbook Got Wrong* (New York: Simon & Schuster, 1995), 145–46.

27. Benjamin Morgan Palmer, *Slavery, a Divine Trust: The Duty of the South to Preserve and Perpetuate the Institution as It Now Exists* (New York: Nesbitt, 1861), 7–10.

28. Archibald Alexander, *A History of Colonization on the Western Coast of Africa* (Philadelphia: William S. Martien, 1846), 16–21.

29. Mark Perry, *Lift Up Thy Voice: The Sarah and Angelina Grimké Family's Journey from Slaveholders to Civil Rights Leaders* (New York: Penguin Books, 2001), 38–39.

30. Larry E. Tise, *Proslavery: A History of the Defense of Slavery in America, 1701–1840* (Athens: University of Georgia Press, 1987), 305–6; italics in original.

31. John G. Fee, *Non-Fellowship with Slaveholders: The Duty of Christians* (New York: John A. Gray, 1851), 13–14.

32. *Minutes of the General Assembly . . . , A.D. 1789 to A.D. 1820 Inclusive*, 104–5.

33. James H. Smylie, *A Brief History of the Presbyterians* (Louisville, KY: Geneva Press, 1989), 89–90.

34. D. G. Hart and John R. Muether, *Seeking a Better Country: 300 Years of American Presbyterianism* (Phillipsburg, NJ: P&R Publishing, 2007), 164–65.

35. "General Assembly of the Presbyterian Church in the United States of America, Second Day: Friday, May 20th, 1853," *The Presbyterian*, May 21, 1853, 13–14.

36. Bradley J. Longfield, *Presbyterians and American Culture: A History* (Louisville, KY: Westminster John Knox Press, 2013), 91. The title of Longfield's chapter treating the history of slavery in American Presbyterianism is "Divided Church, Divided Nation."

37. Drick Boyd, *White Allies in the Struggle for Racial Justice* (Maryknoll, NY: Orbis Books, 2015), 31–32.

38. Larry G. Wiley, "John Rankin, Antislavery Prophet, and the Free Presbyterian Church," *American Presbyterians* 72, no. 3 (Fall 1994): 164.

39. Wiley, 166.

40. "Address to Churches," *The Anti-Slavery Reporter under the Sanction of the British and Foreign Anti-Slavery Society*, May 1, 1853, 108–9.

41. Boyd, *White Allies in the Struggle*, 31.

42. Pennington, *Christian Zeal*, 13.

43. Albert Barnes, *An Inquiry into the Scriptural Views of Slavery* (Philadelphia: Perkins & Purves, 1846), 19–20.

44. *Minutes of the General Assembly . . . , A.D. 1789 to A.D. 1820 Inclusive*, 12.

45. Robinson, *Testimony and Practice of the Presbyterian Church*, 171.

46. Robinson, 188–89 and 214.

47. Robinson, 115.

48. William Lloyd Garrison, "To the Public," *The Liberator*, January 1, 1831, 1.

49. "The Charleston Union Presbytery" and "Unchristian Treatment," *The Liberator*, May 11, 1838, 74.

50. C. K. W., "Present Relation of the Presbyterian Church to Slavery," *The Liberator*, November 1, 1861, 174. Although attribution is limited to the author's initials, the author is likely Charles King Whipple.

51. Joseph S. Moore, "Presbyterian Orthodoxies and Slavery," in *Faith and Slavery in the Presbyterian Diaspora*, ed. William Harrison Taylor and Peter C. Messer (Bethlehem, PA: Lehigh University Press, 2016), 260–61.

52. C. K. W., "Present Relation of the Presbyterian Church," 174.

53. Theodore S. Wright, "A Speech to the New York State Anti-Slavery Society, 1837," in *The Presbyterian Experience in the United States: A Sourcebook*, ed. William Yoo (Louisville, KY: Westminster John Knox Press, 2017), 59–62; and Henry Highland Garnet, *A Memorial Discourse* (Philadelphia: Joseph M. Wilson, 1865), 74.

54. *Minutes of the General Assembly . . . , A.D. 1789 to A.D. 1820 Inclusive*, 394, 574–75, and 668; and *Minutes of the General Assembly . . . , A.D. 1836*, 407. The figures are based on self-reporting from presbyteries. In 1807, five presbyteries did not submit reports and seven presbyteries submitted incomplete reports. In 1814, three presbyteries did not submit reports and one presbytery submitted an incomplete report. In 1817, nine presbyteries did not submit reports.

55. Hart and Muether, *Seeking a Better Country*, 128.

56. Palmer, *Slavery*, 5–8.

57. William Wells Brown, "Narrative of William W. Brown, A Fugitive Slave," in *Slave Narratives*, ed. William L. Andrews and Henry Louis Gates Jr. (New York: Library of America, 2000), 387.

58. Shirin Ghaffary and Alex Kantrowitz, "'Don't Be Evil' Isn't a Normal Company Value. But Google Isn't a Normal Company," February 16, 2021, https://www.vox.com/recode/2021/2/16/22280502/google-dont-be-evil-land-of-the-giants-podcast.

59. Fee, *Non-Fellowship with Slaveholders*, 16.

Chapter 2: "Can Christian Americans Deny These Barbarous Cruelties?"

1. David Walker, *Walker's Appeal, in Four Articles; Together with a Preamble, to the Coloured Citizens of the World, but in Particular, and Very Expressly, to Those of the United States of America*, 3rd ed. (Boston: David Walker, 1830), 3, 16, 74, and 83.

2. George D. Armstrong, *The Christian Doctrine of Slavery* (New York: Charles Scribner, 1857), 138–43.

3. Robert H. Bishop, *An Outline of the History of the Church in the State of Kentucky, During a Period of Forty Years: Containing the Memoirs of Rev. David*

Rice, and Sketches of the Origin and Present State of Particular Churches, and of the Lives and Labours of a Number of Men Who Were Eminent and Useful in Their Day (Lexington, KY: Thomas T. Skillman, 1824), 385–90.

4. James W. C. Pennington, *The Fugitive Blacksmith; or, Events in the History of James W. C. Pennington, Pastor of a Presbyterian Church, New York, Formerly a Slave in the State of Maryland, United States*, 2nd ed. (London: Charles Gilpin, 1849), iv.

5. Bishop, *Outline of the History of the Church*, 403.

6. *Minutes of the General Assembly of the Presbyterian Church in the United States of America from Its Organization, A.D. 1789 to A.D. 1820 Inclusive* (Philadelphia: Presbyterian Board of Publication, 1847), 586.

7. Howell Cobb, *A Scriptural Examination of the Institution of Slavery in the United States; with Its Objects and Purposes* (Georgia: Howell Cobb, 1856), 3, 110–15.

8. Jennifer L. Morgan, *Reckoning with Slavery: Gender, Kinship, and Capitalism in the Early Black Atlantic* (Durham, NC: Duke University Press, 2021), 141.

9. Gomes Eannes de Azurura, *The Chronicle of the Discovery and Conquest of Guinea*, vol. 2, trans. Charles Raymond Beazley and Edgar Prestage (London: Hakluyt Society, 1899), 260.

10. Gomes Eannes de Azurura, *The Chronicle of the Discovery and Conquest of Guinea*, vol. 1, trans. Charles Raymond Beazley and Edgar Prestage (London: Hakluyt Society, 1896), 81–82.

11. Herbert S. Klein, *The Atlantic Slave Trade*, 2nd ed. (Cambridge: Cambridge University Press, 2010), 10–11.

12. SlaveVoyages, "Trans-Atlantic Slave Trade Database," accessed on November 4, 2021, https://www.slavevoyages.org/voyage/database.

13. Bartolomé de las Casas, "A Short Account of the Destruction of the Indies," in *Versions of Blackness: Key Texts on Slavery from the Seventeenth Century*, ed. Derek Hughes (Cambridge: Cambridge University Press, 2007), 283.

14. David Brion Davis, *Inhuman Bondage: The Rise and Fall of Slavery in the New World* (Oxford: Oxford University Press, 2006), 98.

15. Las Casas, "Short Account of the Destruction of the Indies," 283.

16. Davis, *Inhuman Bondage*, 99.

17. Thomas Clarkson, *An Essay on the Slavery and Commerce of the Human Species, Particularly the African; Translated from a Latin Dissertation*, 2nd ed. (London: J. Phillips, 1788), 77–78.

18. Alexander Hewat, "An Historical Account of the Rise and Progress of the Colonies of South Carolina and Georgia," in *Historical Collections of South Carolina; Embracing Many Rare and Valuable Pamphlets, and Other Documents, relating to the History of That State*, vol. 1, ed. B. R. Carroll (New York: Harper & Brothers, 1836), 347. Hewat's account was first published in 1779.

19. Clarkson, *Essay on the Slavery and Commerce of the Human Species*, 33–40.

20. Ottobah Cugoano, *Thoughts and Sentiments on the Evil and Wicked Traffic of the Slavery and Commerce of the Human Species, Humbly Submitted to the Inhabitants of Great Britain* (London, 1787), 6.

21. Clarkson, *Essay on the Slavery and Commerce of the Human Species*, 26.

22. SlaveVoyages, "Trans-Atlantic Slave Trade Database"; and Klein, *Atlantic Slave Trade*, 141.

23. Cugoano, *Thoughts and Sentiments on the Evil and Wicked Traffic*, 9.

24. Cugoano, 10.

25. Cugoano, 10.

26. Olaudah Equiano, "The Interesting Narrative of the Life of Olaudah Equiano, or Gustavus Vassa, the African," in *Slave Narratives*, ed. William L. Andrews and Henry Louis Gates Jr. (New York: Library of America, 2000), 50–51.

27. Equiano, "Interesting Narrative of the Life of Olaudah Equiano," 76.

28. Nicholas Radburn and David Eltis, "Visualizing the Middle Passage: The *Brooks* and the Reality of Ship Crowding in the Transatlantic Slave Trade," *Journal of Interdisciplinary History* 49, no. 4 (Spring 2019): 540.

29. SlaveVoyages, "Trans-Atlantic Slave Trade Database"; and Equiano, "Interesting Narrative of the Life of Olaudah Equiano," 76–77.

30. Clarkson, *Essay on the Slavery and Commerce of the Human Species*, 94; Klein, *Atlantic Slave Trade*, 215; and John W. Blassingame, *The Slave Community: Plantation Life in the Antebellum South*, rev. ed. (New York: Oxford University Press, 1979), 10.

31. Equiano, "Interesting Narrative of the Life of Olaudah Equiano," 78.

32. Blassingame, *Slave Community*, 6–7.

33. Equiano, "Interesting Narrative of the Life of Olaudah Equiano," 54 and 56.

34. Clarkson, *Essay on the Slavery and Commerce of the Human Species*, 99–102; and Morgan, *Reckoning with Slavery*, 175.

35. Morgan, *Reckoning with Slavery*, 69.

36. Cugoano, *Thoughts and Sentiments on the Evil and Wicked Traffic*, 24.

37. Equiano, "Interesting Narrative of the Life of Olaudah Equiano," 126.

38. Clarkson, *Essay on the Slavery and Commerce of the Human Species*, 90.

39. Cugoano, *Thoughts and Sentiments on the Evil and Wicked Traffic*, 84.

40. Morgan, *Reckoning with Slavery*, 81.

41. James Ramsay, *An Essay on the Treatment and Conversion of African Slaves in the British Sugar Colonies* (London: James Phillips, 1784), 108–9.

42. George Bourne, *Picture of Slavery in the United States of America* (Middletown, CT: Edwin Hunt, 1834), 171.

43. Morgan, *Reckoning with Slavery*, 1–4.

44. Winthrop D. Jordan, *White over Black: American Attitudes toward the Negro, 1550–1812* (Baltimore: Penguin Books, 1968), 44–48; and Lorenzo Johnston Greene, *The Negro in Colonial New England* (New York: Atheneum, 1968), 16–17.

45. George M. Stroud, *A Sketch of the Laws relating to Slavery in the Several States of the United States of America*, 2nd ed. (Philadelphia: Henry Longstreth, 1856), 34–35. The first edition was published in 1827.

46. Marcus Wilson Jernegan, *Laboring and Dependent Classes in Colonial America, 1607–1783* (New York: Ungar, 1960), 24–27.

47. Stroud, *Sketch of the Laws relating to Slavery*, 13–16.

48. George Lewis, *Impressions of America and the American Churches: From Journal of the Rev. G. Lewis* (Edinburgh: W. P. Kennedy, 1845), 69.

49. Jordan, *White over Black*, 168.

50. Jordan, 168.

51. Daina Ramey Berry, *The Price for Their Pound of Flesh: The Value of the Enslaved, from Womb to Grave, in the Building of a Nation* (Boston: Beacon Press, 2017), 36.

52. Harriet Jacobs, *Incidents in the Life of a Slave Girl* (Boston: Harriet Jacobs, 1861), 11.

53. Jacobs, 45.

54. Here and elsewhere in this book I have used the author's name rather than a pronoun to avoid attributing a gender to the scholar I am referencing. I have chosen this style because I do not know the pronouns that these scholars use (or used) for themselves.

55. Adrienne D. Davis, "'Don't Let Nobody Bother Yo' Principle': The Sexual Economy of American Slavery," in *Black Sexual Economies: Race and Sex in a Culture of Capital*, ed. Adrienne D. Davis and the BSE Collective (Urbana: University of Illinois Press, 2019), 16.

56. Jacobs, *Incidents in the Life of a Slave Girl*, 44–46.

57. Bourne, *Picture of Slavery in the United States of America*, 89.

58. Jacqueline Jones, *Labor of Love, Labor of Sorrow: Black Women, Work, and the Family from Slavery to the Present* (New York: Basic Books, 1985), 25–26.

59. Andrew Delbanco, *The War before the War: Fugitive Slaves and the Struggle for America's Soul from the Revolution to the Civil War* (New York: Penguin Press, 2018), 123.

60. Henry Bibb, "Narrative of the Life and Adventures of Henry Bibb, an American Slave," in Andrews and Gates, *Slave Narratives*, 459.

61. Angela Davis, "Reflections on the Black Woman's Role in the Community of Slaves," *Massachusetts Review* 13, no. 1/2 (Winter–Spring 1972): 97.

62. Bibb, "Narrative of the Life and Adventures of Henry Bibb," 459.

63. Sojourner Truth, "Narrative of Sojourner Truth, a Northern Slave, Emancipated from Bodily Servitude by the State of New York, in 1828, with a Portrait," in Andrews and Gates, *Slave Narratives*, 593.

64. Thomas S. Clay, *Detail of a Plan for the Moral Improvement of Negroes on Plantations, Read before the Georgia Presbytery* (n.p., 1833), 3 and 13.

65. Jordan, *White over Black*, 158.

66. Lucia C. Stanton, *"Those Who Labor for My Happiness": Slavery at Thomas Jefferson's Monticello* (Charlottesville: University of Virginia Press, 2012), 124.

67. Pennington, *Fugitive Blacksmith*, iv–x.

68. Delbanco, *War before the War*, 125.

69. Cugoano, *Thoughts and Sentiments on the Evil and Wicked Traffic*, 143.

70. Stroud, *Sketch of the Laws relating to Slavery*, 48; italics in original.

71. Bourne, *Picture of Slavery in the United States of America*, 88.

72. Jordan, *White over Black*, 161–162.

73. Clay, *Detail of a Plan for the Moral Improvement of Negroes*, 12.

74. Stroud, *Sketch of the Laws relating to Slavery*, 47.

75. Horace Moulton, "Narrative and Testimony of Rev. Horace Moulton," in *American Slavery as It Is: Testimony of a Thousand Witnesses* (New York: American Anti-Slavery Society, 1839), 17–18.

76. Clay, *Detail of a Plan for the Moral Improvement of Negroes*, 12.

77. Eugene D. Genovese, *Roll, Jordan, Roll: The World the Slaves Made* (New York: Pantheon Books, 1972), 546.

78. R. Q. Mallard, *Plantation Life before Emancipation* (Richmond, VA: Whittet & Shepperson, 1892), 18; and Genovese, *Roll, Jordan, Roll*, 541.

79. Frederick Douglass, *Narrative of the Life of Frederick Douglass, an American Slave* (Boston: Anti-Slavery Office, 1845), 27.

80. Blassingame, *Slave Community*, 254.

81. Douglass, *Narrative of the Life of Frederick Douglass*, 57 and 63.

82. Pennington, *Fugitive Blacksmith*, 43.

83. Joseph Ide, "Testimony of Joseph Ide, Esq.," in *American Slavery as It Is*, 101.

84. Herbert Aptheker, *American Negro Slave Revolts*, 50th anniversary ed. (New York: International Publishers, 1993), 82.

85. Cugoano, *Thoughts and Sentiments on the Evil and Wicked Traffic*, 146.

86. Jacobs, *Incidents in the Life of a Slave Girl*, 77.

Chapter 3: "Was There Anything Very Bad in All This?"

1. *Minutes of the General Assembly of the Presbyterian Church in the Confederate States of America: With an Appendix, A.D. 1864* (Columbia, SC: Evans and Cogswell, 1864), 293.

2. John B. Adger, "Northern and Southern Views of the Province of the Church," *Southern Presbyterian Review* 16, no. 4 (March 1866): 390.

3. Benjamin Drew, *The Refugee: Or the Narratives of Fugitive Slaves in Canada, related by Themselves, with an Account of the History and Condition of the Colored Population of Upper Canada* (Boston: John P. Jewett, 1856), 15.

4. Drew, 87–89.

5. Drew, 30.

6. Edward E. Baptist, *The Half Has Never Been Told: Slavery and the Making of American Capitalism* (New York: Basic Books, 2014), 22.

7. Drew, *Refugee*, 30.

8. *A Statement of the Reasons Which Induced the Students of Lane Seminary to Dissolve Their Connection with That Institution* (Cincinnati, 1834), 7.

9. Harriet Beecher Stowe, *The Key to "Uncle Tom's Cabin"; Presenting the Original Facts and Documents Upon Which the Story Is Founded, Together with Corroborative Statement Verifying the Truth of the Work* (London: Clarke, Beeton, 1853), v. This book was also published as *A Key to "Uncle Tom's Cabin"* in some editions.

10. *Minutes of the General Assembly . . . , 1864*, 293.

11. Stowe, *Key to "Uncle Tom's Cabin,"* v.

12. Stowe, 124; italics in original.

13. Stowe, 124.

14. Stowe, 126–27.

15. Christa Dierksheide, *Amelioration and Empire: Progress and Slavery in the Plantation Americas* (Charlottesville: University of Virginia Press, 2014), 17–18.

16. Stowe, *Key to "Uncle Tom's Cabin,"* 131.

17. Charles C. Jones, *The Religious Instruction of the Negroes in the United States* (Savannah, GA: Thomas Purse, 1842), 119.

18. Frederick Law Olmsted, *A Journey in the Back Country* (New York: Mason Brothers, 1863), 82–87.

19. George M. Stroud, *A Sketch of the Laws relating to Slavery in the Several States of the United States of America*, 2nd ed. (Philadelphia: Henry Longstreth, 1856), 41.

20. Stroud, 66.

21. Drew, *Refugee*, 138–42.

22. William T. Allan, "Testimony of William T. Allan, Late of Alabama," in *American Slavery as It Is: Testimony of a Thousand Witnesses* (New York: American Anti-Slavery Society, 1839), 46.

23. Drew, *Refugee*, 105.

24. Bruce Collins, *White Society in the Antebellum South* (London: Longman, 1985), 178.

25. Drew, *Refugee*, 51.

26. Philemon Bliss, "Testimony of Philemon Bliss, Esq.," in *American Slavery as It Is*, 103.

27. Frederick Law Olmsted, *The Cotton Kingdom: A Traveller's Observations on Cotton and Slavery in the American Slave States*, vol. 1 (New York: Mason Brothers, 1862), 128.

28. Drew, *Refugee*, 256.

29. Stowe, *Key to "Uncle Tom's Cabin,"* 133 and 145.

30. Thomas Jefferson, *Notes on the State of Virginia* (Boston: Lilly and Wait, 1832), 169–70. Jefferson's book was first published in Europe in 1785, and multiple editions were published during and after his life.

31. "Rev. Charles Stewart Renshaw, of Quincy, Illinois," in *American Slavery as It Is*, 168.

32. Stephanie E. Jones-Rogers, *They Were Her Property: White Women as Slave Owners in the American South* (New Haven, CT: Yale University Press, 2019), 6.

33. Erskine Clarke, *To Count Our Days: A History of Columbia Theological Seminary* (Columbia: University of South Carolina Press, 2019), 17.

34. Drew, *Refugee*, 29.

35. Drew, 52.

36. David Brion Davis, *Inhuman Bondage: The Rise and Fall of Slavery in the New World* (Oxford: Oxford University Press, 2006), xiii.

37. Paul J. Polgar, *Standard-Bearers of Equality: America's First Abolition Movement* (Chapel Hill: University of North Carolina Press, 2019), 169.

38. Polgar, 170.

39. Dierksheide, *Amelioration and Empire*, 85.

40. Ethan Allen Andrews, *Slavery and the Domestic Slave-Trade in the United States: In a Series of Letters Addressed to the Executive Committee of the American Union for the Relief and Improvement of the Colored Race* (Boston: Light & Stearns, 1836), 49.

41. Andrews, 49.

42. Andrews, 50.

43. Drew, *Refugee*, 30.

44. Charles Ball, *Slavery in the United States: A Narrative of the Life and Adventures of Charles Ball* (New York: John S. Taylor, 1837), 39.

45. Ball, 72.

46. Andrews, *Slavery and the Domestic Slave-Trade*, 123.

47. Ronald Takaki, "The Movement to Reopen the African Slave Trade in South Carolina," *South Carolina Historical Magazine* 66, no. 1 (January 1965): 45.

48. Takaki, 45.

49. John B. Adger, *A Review of Reports to the Legislature of S.C., on the Revival of the Slave Trade* (Columbia, SC: R. W. Gibbes, 1858), 34.

50. Adger, 15.

51. Adger, 4–5.

52. George M. Fredrickson, *The Black Image in the White Mind: The Debate on Afro-American Character and Destiny, 1817–1914* (New York: Harper & Row, 1971), 21.

53. Fredrickson, 23.

54. Davis, *Inhuman Bondage*, 148.

55. Jones-Rogers, *They Were Her Property*, 6.

56. Olmsted, *Journey in the Back Country*, 444–45.

57. George Bourne, *Picture of Slavery in the United States of America* (Middletown, CT: Edwin Hunt, 1834), 80–86.

58. Wm. C. Gildersleeve, "Testimony of Wm. C. Gildersleeve, a Native of Georgia," in *American Slavery as It Is*, 51.

59. John M. Nelson, "Testimony of John M. Nelson, a Native of Virginia," in *American Slavery as It Is*, 51–52.

60. Drew, *Refugee*, 220–21.

61. Drew, 259.

62. Drew, 86.

63. William Wells Brown, "Narrative of William W. Brown, a Fugitive Slave," in *Slave Narratives*, ed. William L. Andrews and Henry Louis Gates Jr. (New York: Library of America, 2000), 419.

64. Brown, 417.

65. Brown, 420–21.

66. Drew, *Refugee*, 381.

67. Eugene D. Genovese, *Roll, Jordan, Roll: The World the Slaves Made* (New York: Pantheon Books, 1972), 446.

68. Genovese, 448.

69. Genovese, 448–49.

70. Leslie M. Harris, *In the Shadow of Slavery: African Americans in New York City, 1626–1863* (Chicago: University of Chicago Press, 2003), 36.

71. Adger, *Review of Reports to the Legislature of S.C.*, 15.

72. Genovese, *Roll, Jordan, Roll*, 449.

73. Harris, *In the Shadow of Slavery*, 36.

74. David W. Blight, *Frederick Douglass: Prophet of Freedom* (New York: Simon & Schuster, 2018), 87–88.

75. Frederick Douglass, *My Bondage and My Freedom* (New York: Miller, Orton & Mulligan, 1855), 343.

76. Steve Luxenberg, *Separate: The Story of Plessy v. Ferguson, and America's Journey from Slavery to Segregation* (New York: W. W. Norton, 2019), 12–13.

77. Frederick Douglass, *Narrative of the Life of Frederick Douglass, an American Slave* (Boston: Anti-Slavery Office, 1845), 122.

78. Stowe, *Key to "Uncle Tom's Cabin,"* 94.

Chapter 4: "Is Jesus Christ in Favor of American Slavery?"

1. Milton C. Sernett, *Abolition's Axe: Beriah Green, Oneida Institute, and the Black Freedom Struggle* (Syracuse, NY: Syracuse University Press, 1986), 18–21.

2. Beriah Green, *Sermons and Other Discourses with Brief Biographical Hints* (New York: S. W. Green, 1860), 29, 50–53.

3. Beriah Green, *The Chattel Principle: The Abhorrence of Jesus Christ and the Apostles; or, No Refuge for American Slavery in the New Testament* (New York: American Anti-Slavery Society, 1839), 3.

4. *Report of the Committee to Whom Was Referred the Subject of the Religious Instruction of the Colored Population of the Synod of South Carolina and Georgia, at Its Late Session in Columbia, South Carolina, December 5th–9th, 1833* (Charleston, SC: Observer Office Press, 1834), 3–4.

5. Charles C. Jones, *The Religious Instruction of the Negroes in the United States* (Savannah, GA: Thomas Purse, 1842), 1–14.

6. Marcus Wilson Jernegan, *Laboring and Dependent Classes in Colonial America, 1607–1783* (New York: Ungar, 1960), 26.

7. Frederick Dalcho, *An Historical Account of the Protestant Episcopal Church in South Carolina* (Charleston, SC: E. Thayer, 1820), 104 and 109.

8. Morgan Godwyn, *The Negro's and Indians Advocate, Suing for Their Admission into the Church: Or a Persuasive to the Instructing and Baptizing of the Negro's and Indians in Our Plantations* (London: J. D., 1680), 2–3, 23, 30, and 101–2; italics in original.

9. Godwyn, 105.

10. "Bristol Parish in the Upper Part of James River," in *Historical Collections relating to the American Colonial Church*, vol. 1, *Virginia*, ed. William Stevens Perry (Hartford, CT: Church Press Company, 1870), 267.

11. "Henrico Parish in the Upper District James River" and "Abingdon Parish in Gloucester County," in Perry, *Historical Collections relating to the American Colonial Church*, 304–5 and 308–9.

12. "Wilmington Parish," in Perry, *Historical Collections relating to the American Colonial Church*, 278.

13. David Humphreys, *An Historical Account of the Incorporated Society for the Propagation of the Gospel in Foreign Parts, Containing Their Foundation, Proceedings, and the Success of Their Missionaries in the British Colonies, to the Year 1728* (London: Joseph Downing, 1730), 234–36.

14. Jones, *Religious Instruction of the Negroes*, 35.

15. Nini Rodgers, "Transatlantic Family Journeys: From Antislavery Ethos to Proslavery Ethic," in *Faith and Slavery in the Presbyterian Diaspora*, ed. William Harrison Taylor and Peter C. Messer (Bethlehem, PA: Lehigh University Press, 2016), 135.

16. Samuel Davies, *The Duty of Christians to Propagate Their Religion among Heathens, Earnestly Recommended to the Masters of Negroe Slaves in Virginia, a Sermon Preached in Hanover, January 8, 1757* (London: J. Oliver, 1758), 8.

17. Davies, 33.

18. Davies, 34.

19. Davies, 27 and 37.

20. Gideon Mailer, "Between Enlightenment and Evangelicalism: Presbyterian Diversity and American Slavery, 1700–1800," in Taylor and Messer, *Faith and Slavery in the Presbyterian Diaspora*, 55.

21. "Extract of a Letter from the Rev. Mr. Sam. Davies to Dr. Doddridge, October 2, 1750," in Perry, *Historical Collections relating to the American Colonial Church*, 368.

22. Davies, *Duty of Christians to Propagate Their Religion among Heathens*, 23.

23. Samuel Davies, *Sermons on Important Subjects, by the Late Reverend and Pious Samuel Davies*, vol. 3, 5th ed. (New York: T. S. Arden, 1802), 252.

24. George William Pilcher, "Samuel Davies and the Instruction of Negroes in Virginia," *Virginia Magazine of History and Biography* 74, no. 3 (July 1966): 296.

25. Pilcher, 296.

26. At the time of Davies's appointment, Princeton University was known as the College of New Jersey. I refer to the current names of higher education institutions here and following.

27. Charles F. Irons, *The Origins of Proslavery Christianity: White and Black Evangelicals in Colonial and Antebellum Virginia* (Chapel Hill: University of North Carolina Press, 2008), 35–39.

28. "Extract of a Letter from the Rev. Mr. Sam. Davies to Dr. Doddridge, October 2, 1750," in Perry, *Historical Collections relating to the American Colonial Church*, 369.

29. Samuel Davies, *Memoir of the Rev. Samuel Davies, Formerly President of the College of New Jersey* (Boston: Massachusetts Sabbath School Union, 1832), 25.

30. Irons, *Origins of Proslavery Christianity*, 37.

31. Forrest G. Wood, *The Arrogance of Faith: Christianity and Race in America from the Colonial Era to the Twentieth Century* (New York: Alfred A. Knopf, 1990), 139.

32. Albert Raboteau, *Slave Religion: The "Invisible Institution" in the Antebellum South* (New York: Oxford University Press, 1978), 318.

33. W. E. B. Du Bois, *The Souls of Black Folk: Essays and Sketches* (Chicago: A. C. McClurg, 1903), 251.

34. Davies, *Duty of Christians to Propagate Their Religion among Heathens*, 8.

35. Alexander Hewat, "An Historical Account of the Rise and Progress of the Colonies of South Carolina and Georgia," in *Historical Collections of South Carolina; Embracing Many Rare and Valuable Pamphlets, and Other Documents, relating to the History of That State*, vol. 1, ed. B. R. Carroll (New York: Harper & Brothers, 1836), 354.

36. Ezra Stiles, *The Literary Diary of Ezra Stiles*, vol. 1, ed. Franklin Bowditch Dexter (New York: Charles Scribner's Sons, 1901), 213–14.

37. Wood, *Arrogance of Faith*, 139.

38. D. G. Hart and John R. Muether, *Seeking a Better Country: 300 Years of American Presbyterianism* (Phillipsburg, NJ: P&R Publishing, 2007), 1.

39. John Witherspoon, "The Dominion of Providence over the Passions of Men," in *Political Sermons of the American Founding Era, 1730–1805*, 2nd ed., ed. Ellis Sandoz (Indianapolis: Liberty Fund, 1998), 549.

40. Lesa Redmond, "John Witherspoon," Princeton and Slavery Project, accessed on August 7, 2021, https://slavery.princeton.edu/stories/john-witherspoon.

41. Jacob Green, *A Sermon Delivered at Hanover (in New-Jersey), April 22d, 1778* (Chatham, NJ: Shepard Kollock, 1779), 12–13.

42. Green, 14.

43. Green, 17–18.

44. Green, 16.

45. James Duncan, *A Treatise on Slavery, in Which Is Shown Forth the Evil of Slaveholding Both from the Light of Nature and Divine Revelation* (Vevay, IN: Indiana Register Office, 1824), ix.

46. Duncan, xi.

47. Beriah Green, *Chattel Principle*, 30–31.

48. Thomas Bacon, *Two Sermons Preached to a Congregation of Black Slaves, at the Parish Church of S. P. in the Province of Maryland* (London: John Oliver, 1749), 11–15; italics in original.

49. Bacon, 71.

50. William Henry Foote, *Sketches of Virginia, Historical and Biographical,* 2nd series (Philadelphia: J. B. Lippincott, 1855), 232–33.

51. Henry Pattillo, *The Plain Planter's Family Assistant; Containing an Address to Husbands and Wives, Children and Servants, with Some Helps for Instructions by Catechisms, and Examples of Devotion for Families, with a Brief Paraphrase on the Lord's Prayer* (Wilmington, DE: James Adams, 1787), 7.

52. Pattillo, 11 and 23.

53. Pattillo, 24–27.

54. *Book of Confessions: Presbyterian Church (U.S.A.), Study Edition* (Louisville, KY: Geneva Press, 1999), 168.

55. Pattillo, *Plain Planter's Family Assistant*, 35.

56. Pattillo, 46–50.

57. Pattillo, 41.

58. Jennifer L. Morgan, *Reckoning with Slavery: Gender, Kinship, and Capitalism in the Early Black Atlantic* (Durham, NC: Duke University Press, 2021), 5.

59. Duncan, *Treatise on Slavery*, xi.

60. *Book of Confessions*, 264 and 273.

61. Harriet Beecher Stowe, *The Key to "Uncle Tom's Cabin," Presenting the Original Facts and Documents upon Which the Story Is Founded, Together with Corroborative Statements Verifying the Truth of the Work* (London: Clarke, Beeton, 1853), 393.

62. George Bourne, *An Address to the Presbyterian Church Enforcing the Duty of Excluding All Slaveholders from the "Communion of Saints"* (New York, 1833), 4.

63. Thomas Clarkson, *An Essay on the Slavery and Commerce of the Human Species, Particularly the African; Translated from a Latin Dissertation*, 2nd ed. (London: J. Phillips, 1788), 73.

64. Jacob Green, *Sermon Delivered at Hanover*, 14.

65. *Minutes of the General Assembly of the Presbyterian Church in the United States of America from Its Organization, A.D. 1789 to A.D. 1820 Inclusive* (Philadelphia: Presbyterian Board of Publication, 1847), 582.

66. George Bourne, *The Book and Slavery Irreconcilable, with Animadversions upon Dr. Smith's Philosophy* (Philadelphia: J. M. Sanderson, 1816), 8 and 53.

67. Bourne, 137.

68. Ryan C. McIlhenny, *To Preach Deliverance to the Captives: Freedom and Slavery in the Protestant Mind of George Bourne, 1780–1845* (Baton Rouge: Louisiana State University Press, 2020), 65.

69. *Minutes of the General Assembly . . . , A.D. 1789 to A.D. 1820 Inclusive*, 645 and 676.

70. McIlhenny, *To Preach Deliverance to the Captives*, 73.

71. *Minutes of the General Assembly . . . , A.D. 1789 to A.D. 1820 Inclusive*, 691.

72. *Minutes of the General Assembly . . . , A.D. 1789 to A.D. 1820 Inclusive*, 692–94.

73. McIlhenny, *To Preach Deliverance to the Captives*, 81–82; and Leonard J. Trinterud, review of *George Bourne and The Book and Slavery Irreconcilable*, ed. John W. Christie and Dwight L. Dumond, *Journal of Presbyterian History* 48, no. 1 (Spring 1970): 71–73.

74. Bourne, *Address to the Presbyterian Church*, 12.

75. Beriah Green, "Letter to a Minister of the Gospel," *Quarterly Anti-Slavery Magazine*, July 1836, 339.

Chapter 5: "But What Do We See When We Look at the American Church?"

1. Paul C. Gutjahr, *Charles Hodge: Guardian of American Orthodoxy* (Oxford: Oxford University Press, 2011), 156. Gutjahr maintains that the inheritance of Lena most likely came from the estate of Charles Hodge's mother, Mary Blanchard Hodge, upon her death.

2. Charles Hodge, "Slavery," *Biblical Repertory*, April 1836, 275–77.

3. Larry E. Tise, *Proslavery: A History of the Defense of Slavery in America, 1701–1840* (Athens: University of Georgia Press, 1987), 278.

4. Gerrit Smith, *Letter of Gerrit Smith to Rev. James Smylie of the State of Mississippi* (New York: R. G. Williams, 1837), 6–9.

5. Beriah Green, *The Chattel Principle: The Abhorrence of Jesus Christ and the Apostles; or, No Refuge for American Slavery in the New Testament* (New York: American Anti-Slavery Society, 1839), 6 and 52.

6. Samuel Crothers, "Slavery, and the Biblical Repertory," *Quarterly Anti-Slavery Magazine*, January 1837, 115.

7. Elizur Wright Jr., "Slavery, and Its Ecclesiastical Defenders," *Quarterly Anti-Slavery Magazine*, July 1836, 355.

8. Wright, 355 and 368–71.

9. *First Annual Report of the American Anti-Slavery Society; with the Speeches Delivered at the Anniversary Meeting, Held at Chatham-Street Chapel, in the City of New York* (New York: Dorr & Butterfield, 1834), 61.

10. *The Seventh Census of the United States: 1850* (Washington, DC: Robert Armstrong, 1853), lvii–lviii. There were also 1,221 Roman Catholic churches

and 1,217 Lutheran churches. The cumulative value of Roman Catholic and Lutheran church property was $9,256,758 and $2,854,286, respectively.

11. *The American Almanac and Repository of Useful Knowledge, for the Year 1850* (Boston: Charles C. Little and James Brown, 1849), 208.

12. Harriet Martineau, *Society in America,* vol. 2 (Paris: Baudry's European Library, 1842), 219–20.

13. George Lewis, *Impressions of America and the American Churches: From Journal of the Rev. G. Lewis* (Edinburgh: W. P. Kennedy, 1845), 100.

14. Georges Fisch, *Nine Months in the United States during the Crisis* (London: James Nisbet, 1863), 27–28.

15. Fisch, 50 and 128.

16. Stephen S. Foster, *The Brotherhood of Thieves, or a True Picture of the American Church and Clergy* (New London, NH: William Bolles, 1843), 41.

17. Albert Raboteau, *Slave Religion: The "Invisible Institution" in the Antebellum South* (New York: Oxford University Press, 1978), 143–44.

18. John H. Wigger, *Taking Heaven by Storm: Methodism and the Rise of Popular Christianity in America* (Urbana: University of Illinois Press, 2001), 150.

19. Charles F. Irons, *The Origins of Proslavery Christianity: White and Black Evangelicals in Colonial and Antebellum Virginia* (Chapel Hill: University of North Carolina Press, 2008), 196–99.

20. Lewis, *Impressions of America and the American Churches*, 296–97.

21. *Minutes of the General Assembly of the Presbyterian Church in the United States of America: With an Appendix, 1844* (Philadelphia: William S. Martien, 1844), 366–67.

22. Lewis, *Impressions of America and the American Churches*, 297–98.

23. *Minutes of the General Assembly of the Presbyterian Church in the United States of America: With an Appendix, 1845* (Philadelphia: William S. Martien, 1845), 16.

24. Benjamin Morgan Palmer, *The Life and Letters of James Henley Thornwell* (Richmond, VA: Whittet & Shepperson, 1875), 286.

25. *Minutes of the General Assembly . . . , 1845*, 16.

26. James Henley Thornwell, "Relation of the Church to Slavery," in *The Collected Writings of James Henley Thornwell*, vol. 4, ed. John B. Adger and John L. Girardeau (Richmond, VA: Presbyterian Committee of Publication, 1873), 385.

27. James Henley Thornwell, *The Rights and the Duties of Masters: A Sermon Preached at the Dedication of a Church, Erected in Charleston, S.C., for the Benefit and Instruction of the Colored Population* (Charleston, SC: Walker & James, 1850), 31 and 45–46.

28. *Minutes of the General Assembly . . . , 1845*, 16.

29. *Minutes of the General Assembly . . . , 1845*, 18.

30. Palmer, *Life and Letters of James Henley Thornwell*, 286.

31. C. Duncan Rice, *The Scots Abolitionists, 1833–1861* (Baton Rouge: Louisiana State University Press, 1981), 23.

32. Thornton Stringfellow, "A Brief Examination of Scripture Testimony on the Institution of Slavery," in *The Ideology of Slavery: Proslavery Thought in the Antebellum South, 1830–1860*, ed. Drew Gilpin Faust (Baton Rouge: Louisiana State University Press, 1981), 139.

33. Gene Dattel, *Cotton and Race in the Making of America: The Human Costs of Economic Power* (Lanham, MD: Ivan R. Dee, 2011), 33–40.

34. Carol Anderson, *White Rage: The Unspoken Truth of Our Racial Divide* (New York: Bloomsbury, 2016), 10–11; and James Oakes, *The Ruling Race: A History of American Slaveholders* (New York: W. W. Norton, 1998), 39.

35. Whitemarsh B. Seabrook, *A Concise View of the Critical Situation and Future Prospects of the Slave-holding States, in Relation to Their Coloured Population*, 2nd ed. (Charleston, SC: A. E. Miller, 1825), 28–29.

36. Rice, *Scots Abolitionists*, 23–24.

37. Samuel J. May, *Some Recollections of Our Antislavery Conflict* (Boston: Fields, Osgood, 1869), 127–28.

38. Charles C. Jones, *Suggestions on the Religious Instruction of the Negroes in the Southern States; Together with an Appendix Containing Forms of Church Registers, Form of a Constitution, and Plans of Different Denominations of Christians* (Philadelphia: Presbyterian Board of Publication, 1847), 31.

39. *An Address to the Presbyterians of Kentucky, Proposing a Plan for the Instruction and Emancipation of Their Slaves, by a Committee of the Synod of Kentucky* (Newburyport, MA: Charles Whipple, 1836), 23–24; italics in original.

40. *Fourth Annual Report of the American Anti-Slavery Society; with the Speeches Delivered at the Anniversary Meeting, Held in the City of New York* (New York: William S. Dorr, 1837), 55.

41. Caitlin Rosenthal, *Accounting for Slavery: Masters and Management* (Cambridge, MA: Harvard University Press, 2018), 121.

42. E. Brooks Holifield, *God's Ambassadors: A History of the Christian Clergy in America* (Grand Rapids, MI: Wm. B. Eerdmans, 2007), 131.

43. *Documents Detailing the Prices of Betts and Gregory Slave Market, Richmond, 1860 to 1861*, Duke University Libraries, https://idn.duke.edu/ark:/87924/r4pr7n94b.

44. Rosenthal, *Accounting for Slavery*, 134.

45. Bonnie Martin, "Neighbor-to-Neighbor Capitalism: Local Credit Networks and the Mortgaging of Slaves," in *Slavery's Capitalism: A New History of American Economic Development*, ed. Sven Beckert and Seth Rockman (Philadelphia: University of Pennsylvania Press, 2016), 117.

46. Peter A. Coclanis, *The Shadow of a Dream: Economic Life and Death in the South Carolina Low Country, 1670–1920* (New York: Oxford University Press, 1989), 127–29.

47. Christa Dierksheide, *Amelioration and Empire: Progress and Slavery in the Plantation Americas* (Charlottesville: University of Virginia Press, 2014), 74.

48. Dierksheide, 69.

49. Oakes, *Ruling Race*, 73.

50. "Rev. C. C. Jones to Mr. Charles C. Jones, Jr., June 7, 1859," in *The Children of Pride: A True Story of Georgia and the Civil War*, ed. Robert Manson Myers (New Haven, CT: Yale University Press, 1972), 487–88.

51. Jennifer R. Loux, "John Hartwell Cocke (1780–1866)," *Dictionary of Virginia Biography*, Library of Virginia, http://www.lva.virginia.gov/public/dvb /bio.asp?b=Cocke_John_Hartwell_1780-1866; and Robert Manson Myers, "Prologue," in Myers, *Children of Pride*, 17.

52. Lewis Tappan, *Address to the Non-Slaveholders of the South on the Social and Political Evils of Slavery* (New York: S. W. Benedict, 1843), 3.

53. Keri Leigh Merritt, *Masterless Men: Poor Whites and Slavery in the Antebellum South* (Cambridge: Cambridge University Press, 2017), 8 and 45. Adjustments to 2021 U.S. dollars here and following come from MeasuringWorth.com, a website founded by Samuel H. Williamson, emeritus professor of economics at Miami University.

54. Charles C. Bolton, *Poor Whites of the Antebellum South: Tenants and Laborers in Central North Carolina and Northeast Mississippi* (Durham, NC: Duke University Press, 1994), 23.

55. Henry Ruffner, *Address to the People of West Virginia; Shewing That Slavery Is Injurious to the Public Welfare, and That It May Be Gradually Abolished, without Detriment to the Rights and Interests of Slaveholders* (Lexington, VA: R. C. Noel, 1847), 17.

56. Ruffner, 35–36.

57. William Gleason Bean, "The Ruffner Pamphlet of 1847: An Antislavery Aspect of Virginia Sectionalism," *Virginia Magazine of History and Biography* 61, no. 3 (July 1953): 277.

58. Merritt, *Masterless Men*, 136–37.

59. M. D. Conway, *Testimonies concerning Slavery*, 2nd ed. (London: Chapman and Hall, 1865), 122.

60. William Yoo, "Cumberland Presbyterian Church," in *Encyclopedia of Christianity in the United States*, ed. George Thomas Kurian and Mark A. Lamport (Lanham, MD: Rowman & Littlefield, 2016), 671.

61. Bruce Collins, *White Society in the Antebellum South* (London: Longman, 1985), 152–54.

62. James Smylie, *A Review of a Letter, from the Presbytery of Chillicothe, to the Presbytery of Mississippi, on the Subject of Slavery* (Woodville, MS: Wm. A. Norris, 1836), 71.

63. "Rev. C. C. Jones to Mrs. Susan M. Cumming, December 7, 1854," in Myers, *Children of Pride*, 113; italics in original.

64. "Rev. C. C. Jones to Mr. Charles C. Jones, Jr., October 2, 1856," in Myers, *Children of Pride*, 244.

65. Daina Ramey Berry, *The Price for Their Pound of Flesh: The Value of the Enslaved, from Womb to Grave, in the Building of a Nation* (Boston: Beacon Press, 2017), 5.

66. Dale Evans Swan, *The Structure and Profitability of the Antebellum Rice Industry, 1859* (New York: Arno Press, 1975), 89.

67. Lorenzo Johnston Greene, *The Negro in Colonial New England* (New York: Atheneum, 1968), 108.

68. Nathaniel B. Shurtleff, *A Topographical and Historical Description of Boston*, 3rd ed. (Boston: Rockwell and Churchill, 1891), 48.

69. Dattel, *Cotton and Race in the Making of America*, 89.

70. Dattel, 89.

71. *Fourth Annual Report of the American Anti-Slavery Society*, 56.

72. *Fourth Annual Report of the American Anti-Slavery Society*, 57–59.

73. Craig Steven Wilder, *Ebony and Ivy: Race, Slavery, and the Troubled History of America's Universities* (New York: Bloomsbury Press, 2013), 105.

74. Allen C. Guelzo, "Charles Hodge's Antislavery Moment," in *Charles Hodge Revisited: A Critical Appraisal of His Life and Work*, ed. John W. Stewart and James H. Moorhead (Grand Rapids, MI: Wm. B. Eerdmans, 2002), 303.

75. *Minutes of the General Assembly of the Presbyterian Church in the United States of America: With an Appendix, A.D. 1836* (Philadelphia: Stated Clerk of the Assembly, 1836), 305–6. The trustees also moved $14,267.25 to a bank in Pittsburgh.

76. William Goodell, *Slavery and Anti-Slavery; A History of the Great Struggle in Both Hemispheres; with a View of the Slavery Question in the United States* (New York: William Harned, 1852), 154; and Victor Howard, "The Anti-Slavery Movement in the Presbyterian Church, 1835–1861," PhD diss. (Ohio State University, 1961), 34.

77. *Minutes of the General Assembly of the Presbyterian Church in the United States of America from Its Organization, A.D. 1789 to A.D. 1820 Inclusive* (Philadelphia: Presbyterian Board of Publication, 1847), 692–694; and *Minutes of the General Assembly . . . , A.D. 1836*, 305–6.

78. Smith, *Letter of Gerrit Smith to Rev. James Smylie*, 62.

79. Oakes, *Ruling Race*, 121; italics in original.

80. Hodge, "Slavery," 278.

81. Kenneth M. Stampp, *The Peculiar Institution: Slavery in the Ante-bellum South* (New York: Alfred A. Knopf, 1956), 417.

82. *Fourth Annual Report of the American Anti-Slavery Society*, 67.

83. Thomas Cary Johnson, *The Life and Letters of Robert Lewis Dabney* (Richmond, VA: Whittet & Shepperson, 1903), 129.

Chapter 6: Anti-Black Racism in a World without White Fragility

1. Matthew Anderson, *Presbyterianism; Its Relation to the Negro* (Philadelphia: John McGill White, 1897), 55–56.

2. Anderson, 28–29, 124, and 236–37.

3. D. G. Hart and John R. Muether, *Seeking a Better Country: 300 Years of American Presbyterianism* (Phillipsburg, NJ: P&R Publishing, 2007), 118.

4. Hart and Muether, 125.

5. Frederick A. Ross, *Slavery Ordained of God* (Philadelphia: J. B. Lippincott, 1857), 49–52 and 67.

6. Michael Burlingame, *The Inner World of Abraham Lincoln* (Urbana: University of Illinois Press, 1994), 32–33.

7. Robin DiAngelo, *White Fragility: Why It's So Hard for White People to Talk about Racism* (Boston: Beacon Press, 2018), 2.

8. "An Address to the Public by the Managers of the Colonization Society," *African Repository and Colonial Journal,* June 1828, 118.

9. Donald G. Mathews, *Religion in the Old South* (Chicago: University of Chicago Press, 1977), 167.

10. David M. Goldenberg, *Black and Slave: The Origins and History of the Curse of Ham* (Berlin: De Gruyter, 2017), 238.

11. John Rankin, *Letters on American Slavery, Addressed to Mr. Thomas Rankin, Merchant at Middlebrook, Augusta Co., Virginia* (Boston: Garrison & Knapp, 1833), 8.

12. James W. C. Pennington, *A Text Book of the Origin and History of the Colored People* (Hartford, CT: L. Skinner, 1841), 7–8.

13. Goldenberg, *Black and Slave,* 5.

14. Goldenberg, 151.

15. Goldenberg, 121–22 and 130.

16. Samuel Sewall, *The Selling of Joseph: A Memorial* (Boston: Green, Allen, 1700), 2.

17. Charles Hodge, "Slavery," *Biblical Repertory,* April 1836, 268.

18. Larry E. Tise, *Proslavery: A History of the Defense of Slavery in America, 1701–1840* (Athens: University of Georgia Press, 1987), 288–89.

19. William W. Freehling, *Prelude to Civil War: The Nullification Controversy in South Carolina, 1816–1836* (New York: Oxford University Press, 1992), 81. This work was first published in 1965.

20. Freehling, 328.

21. John C. Calhoun, *Remarks of Mr. Calhoun, of South Carolina, on the Reception of Abolition Petitions, Delivered in the Senate of the United States, February 1837* (Washington, DC: William W. Moore, 1837), 6.

22. Freehling, *Prelude to Civil War,* 338–39.

23. Ross, *Slavery Ordained of God,* 50.

24. Josiah Priest, *Slavery, as It Relates to the Negro, or African Race, Examined in the Light of Circumstances, History and the Holy Scriptures* (Louisville, KY: W. S. Brown, 1849), 33 and 92; italics in original.

25. Pennington, *Text Book of the Origin and History of the Colored People,* 13; italics in original.

26. Pennington, 17.

27. James A. Sloan, *The Great Question Answered; or, Is Slavery a Sin in Itself (Per Se?) Answered according to the Teaching of the Scriptures* (Memphis, TN: Hutton, Gallaway, 1857), 62–63 and 82.

28. Ross, *Slavery Ordained of God*, 68.

29. Paul DeForest Hicks, *Joseph Henry Lumpkin: Georgia's First Chief Justice* (Athens: University of Georgia Press, 2002), 131–32.

30. Thomas R. R. Cobb, *An Inquiry into the Law of Negro Slavery in the United States of America, to Which Is Prefixed, an Historical Sketch of Slavery* (Philadelphia: T. & J. W. Johnson, 1858), xli.

31. Winthrop D. Jordan, *White over Black: American Attitudes toward the Negro, 1550–1812* (Baltimore: Penguin Books, 1968), 518–19. Rush delivered an oral presentation of his hypothesis to the American Philosophical Society two years before publishing his work in 1799. Rush and his family were engaged in various congregational ministries in Philadelphia. They attended First Presbyterian Church and Second Presbyterian Church in the 1770s and 1780s. After leaving Second Presbyterian, they worshiped at St. Peter's Episcopal Church. Rush also raised funds for the construction of the African Episcopal Church of St. Thomas.

32. Stephen Fried, *Rush: Revolution, Madness, and the Visionary Doctor Who Became a Founding Father* (New York: Crown, 2018), 389.

33. Pennington, *Text Book of the Origin and History of the Colored People*, 94.

34. Samuel Stanhope Smith, *An Essay on the Causes of the Variety of Complexion and Figure in the Human Species*, 2nd ed. (New Brunswick, NJ: J. Simpson, 1810), 5.

35. David N. Livingstone, *Adam's Ancestors: Race, Religion, and the Politics of Human Origins* (Baltimore: Johns Hopkins University Press, 2008), 57–60.

36. Smith, *Essay on the Causes of the Variety of Complexion and Figure*, 9, 71–72, 97, and 195.

37. Priest, *Slavery, as It Relates to the Negro*, 352.

38. Cobb, *Inquiry into the Law of Negro Slavery*, ccxvi.

39. Pennington, *Text Book of the Origin and History of the Colored People*, 95–96; and Smith, *Essay on the Causes of the Variety of Complexion and Figure*, 94–97 and 249–90.

40. Pennington, *Text Book of the Origin and History of the Colored People*, 66.

41. William J. Roulston, "The Reformed Presbyterian Church and Antislavery in Nineteenth-Century America," in *Faith and Slavery in the Presbyterian Diaspora*, ed. William Harrison Taylor and Peter C. Messer (Bethlehem, PA: Lehigh University Press, 2016), 165–70.

42. Alexander McLeod, *Negro Slavery Unjustifiable: A Discourse* (New York: T. & F. Swords, 1802), 41.

43. Samuel Stanhope Smith, *The Lectures, Corrected and Improved, Which Have Been Delivered for a Series of Years in the College of New Jersey; on the Subjects of Moral and Political Philosophy*, vol. 2 (Trenton, NJ: Daniel Fenton, 1812), 169.

44. Smith, 176–77.

45. Isaac V. Brown, *Memoirs of the Rev. Robert Finley, D.D., Late Pastor of the Presbyterian Congregation at Basking Ridge, New Jersey, and President of Franklin College, Located at Athens, in the State of Georgia, with Brief Sketches of Some of His Contemporaries, and Numerous Notes* (New Brunswick, NJ: Terhune & Letson, 1819), 77.

46. Robert Finley, *Thoughts on the Colonization of Free Blacks* (Washington, DC: n.d.), 1, 4–7.

47. Brown, *Memoirs of the Rev. Robert Finley*, 77.

48. Finley, *Thoughts on the Colonization of Free Blacks*, 7–8.

49. Archibald Alexander, *A History of Colonization on the Western Coast of Africa* (Philadelphia: William S. Martien, 1846), 80; and Roulston, "Reformed Presbyterian Church and Antislavery in Nineteenth-Century America," 160.

50. Eric Burin, *Slavery and the Peculiar Solution: A History of the American Colonization Society* (Gainesville: University Press of Florida, 2005), 2, 26, and 34.

51. Samuel E. Cornish and Theodore S. Wright, *The Colonization Scheme Considered, in Its Rejection by the Colored People, in Its Tendency to Uphold Caste, in Its Unfitness for Christianizing and Civilizing the Aborigines of Africa, and for Putting a Stop to the African Slave Trade: In a Letter to the Hon. Theodore Frelinghuysen and the Hon. Benjamin F. Butler* (Newark, NJ: Aaron Guest, 1840), 3–4.

52. Alexander, *History of Colonization on the Western Coast of Africa*, 20.

53. Cornish and Wright, *Colonization Scheme Considered*, 6; italics in original.

54. Samuel E. Cornish, "American Colonization Society," *Colored American*, July 29, 1837.

55. *First Annual Report of the American Anti-Slavery Society; with the Speeches Delivered at the Anniversary Meeting, Held at Chatham-Street Chapel, in the City of New York* (New York: Dorr & Butterfield, 1834), 7.

56. Samuel E. Cornish, "Prejudice in the Church," *Colored American*, March 11, 1837.

57. Samuel E. Cornish, "Prejudice in the Church, No. III," *Colored American*, April 1, 1837.

58. Samuel E. Cornish, "General Assembly of the Presbyterian Church," *Colored American*, June 17, 1837.

59. Cornish, "Prejudice in the Church."

60. Theodore S. Wright, "A Speech to the New York State Anti-Slavery Society, 1837," in *The Presbyterian Experience in the United States: A Sourcebook*, ed. William Yoo (Louisville, KY: Westminster John Knox Press, 2017), 60–61.

61. Lewis Tappan, *The Life of Arthur Tappan* (New York: Hurd and Houghton, 1870), 195.

62. Edwin G. Burrows and Mike Wallace, *Gotham: A History of New York City to 1898* (Oxford: Oxford University Press, 1999), 556.

63. Leslie M. Harris, *In the Shadow of Slavery: African Americans in New York City, 1626–1863* (Chicago: University of Chicago Press, 2003), 197–98.

64. Benjamin Morgan Palmer, *Slavery, a Divine Trust: The Duty of the South to Preserve and Perpetuate the Institution as It Now Exists* (New York: Nesbitt, 1861), 9–10.

65. Richard H. Colfax, *Evidence against the Views of the Abolitionists, Consisting of Physical and Moral Proofs, of the Natural Inferiority of the Negroes* (New York: James T. M. Bleakly, 1833), 31–32.

66. Harriet Beecher Stowe, *Uncle Tom's Cabin: Or, Life Among the Lowly*, vol. 2 (Boston: John P. Jewett, 1852), 300.

67. Stowe, 303; italics in original.

68. Pennington, *Text Book of the Origin and History of the Colored People*, 87.

69. *Sixth Annual Report of the American Anti-Slavery Society; with the Speeches Delivered at the Anniversary Meeting, Held in the City of New York* (New York: William S. Dorr, 1839), 10–11.

70. Harris, *In the Shadow of Slavery*, 228.

71. Harris, 198.

72. Tappan, *Life of Arthur Tappan*, 201–2.

73. Theodore S. Wright, "N.E. Anti-Slavery Convention," *The Liberator*, July 2, 1836, 108.

74. Christopher L. Webber, *American to the Backbone: The Life of James W. C. Pennington, the Fugitive Slave Who Became One of the First Black Abolitionists* (New York: Pegasus Books, 2011), 268.

75. J. W. C. Pennington, "A Lecture Delivered Before the Glasgow Young Men's Christian Association, 1850," in University of Detroit Mercy Black Abolitionist Digital Archive, Doc. No. 10260, https://libraries.udmercy.edu/archives/special-collections/index.php?record_id=941&collectionCode=baa.

76. Samuel E. Cornish, "Title of This Journal," *Colored American*, March 4, 1837.

77. Manisha Sinha, *The Slave's Cause: A History of Abolition* (New Haven, CT: Yale University Press, 2016), 315 and 338.

78. Henry Cleveland, *Alexander H. Stephens, in Public and Private, with Letters and Speeches, before, during, and since the War* (Philadelphia: National Publishing, 1866), 721.

79. Cleveland, 723.

80. R. Q. Mallard, *Plantation Life before Emancipation* (Richmond, VA: Whittet & Shepperson, 1892), 176.

81. *Minutes of the General Assembly of the Presbyterian Church in the Confederate States of America: With an Appendix, A.D. 1861* (Augusta, GA: Steam Power Press Chronicle & Sentinel, 1861), 58.

82. Mallard, *Plantation Life before Emancipation*, 186.

Chapter 7: The American Captivity of the Presbyterian Church

1. Frederick Douglass, "To William Lloyd Garrison, January 1, 1846," in *Frederick Douglass: Selected Speeches and Writings*, ed. Philip S. Foner and Yuval Taylor (Chicago: Chicago Review Press, 2000), 18–19.

2. Patricia J. Ferreira, "Frederick Douglass in Ireland: The Dublin Edition of His *Narrative*," *New Hibernia Review/Iris Éireannach Nua* 5, no. 1 (Spring 2001): 64.

3. Thomas Smyth, *Autobiographical Notes, Letters, and Reflections*, ed. Louisa Cheves Stoney (Charleston, SC: Walker, Evans, and Cogswell, 1914), 365.

4. Smyth, 362.

5. J. F. Maclear, "Thomas Smyth, Frederick Douglass, and the Belfast Antislavery Campaign," *South Carolina Historical Magazine* 80, no. 4 (October 1979): 294.

6. Frederick Douglass, "American Slavery, American Religion, and the Free Church of Scotland," in *The Speeches of Frederick Douglass: A Critical Edition*, ed. John R. McKivigan, Julie Husband, and Heather L. Kaufman (New Haven, CT: Yale University Press, 2018), 36.

7. Maclear, "Thomas Smyth, Frederick Douglass, and the Belfast Antislavery Campaign," 293; and Iain Whyte, *"Send Back the Money": The Free Church of Scotland and American Slavery* (Cambridge: James Clarke, 2012), 115.

8. David W. Blight, *Frederick Douglass: Prophet of Freedom* (New York: Simon & Schuster, 2018), 162.

9. Martin Luther, *Three Treatises* (Minneapolis: Fortress Press, 1970), 152–53.

10. Larry E. Tise, *Proslavery: A History of the Defense of Slavery in America, 1701–1840* (Athens: University of Georgia Press, 1987), xvii and 134–35.

11. J. D. Paxton, *Letters on Slavery; Addressed to the Cumberland Congregation, Virginia* (Lexington, KY: Abraham T. Skillman, 1833), 4–5.

12. William W. Freehling, *Prelude to Civil War: The Nullification Controversy in South Carolina, 1816–1836* (New York: Oxford University Press, 1992), 74–75.

13. George Lewis, *Impressions of America and the American Churches: From Journal of the Rev. G. Lewis* (Edinburgh: W. P. Kennedy, 1845), 131.

14. Robert Manson Myers, "Prologue," in *The Children of Pride: A True Story of Georgia and the Civil War*, ed. Robert Manson Myers (New Haven, CT: Yale University Press, 1972), 12.

15. John Robinson, *The Testimony and Practice of the Presbyterian Church in Reference to American Slavery* (Cincinnati: John D. Thorpe, 1852), 118 and 255.

16. *Proceedings of the Meeting in Charleston, S.C., May 13–15, 1845, on the Religious Instruction of the Negroes, Together with the Report of the Committee, and the Address to the Public* (Charleston, SC: B. Jenkins, 1845), 12.

17. *Proceedings of the Meeting in Charleston*, 34 and 47.

18. *Proceedings of the Meeting in Charleston*, 61.

19. Henry Bibb, "Narrative of the Life and Adventures of Henry Bibb, an American Slave," in *Slave Narratives*, ed. William L. Andrews and Henry Louis Gates Jr. (New York: Library of America, 2000), 497.

20. Jacob D. Green, "Narrative of the Life of J. D. Green, a Runaway Slave, from Kentucky, Containing an Account of His Three Escapes, in 1839, 1846, and 1848," in Andrews and Gates, *Slave Narratives*, 972.

21. *Tenth Annual Report of the Association for the Religious Instruction of the Negroes, in Liberty County, Georgia* (Savannah, GA: P. G. Thomas, 1845), 24.

22. Albert Barnes, *An Inquiry into the Scriptural Views of Slavery* (Philadelphia: Perkins & Purves, 1846), 319.

23. William G. Brownlow and Abram Pryne, *Ought American Slavery to Be Perpetuated?* (Philadelphia: J. B. Lippincott, 1858), 134; italics in original.

24. Barnes, *Inquiry into the Scriptural Views of Slavery*, 381.

25. Joyce Appleby, "The Power of History," *American Historical Review* 103, no. 1 (February 1998): 11–12.

26. E. Brooks Holifield, *God's Ambassadors: A History of Christian Clergy in America* (Grand Rapids, MI: Wm. B. Eerdmans, 2007), 130.

27. "Rev. C. C. Jones to Miss Mary Sharpe Jones, October 22, 1855" and "Rev. John Jones to Mrs. Mary Jones, September 5, 1867," in Myers, *Children of Pride*, 166 and 1394.

28. Harriet Martineau, *Society in America*, vol. 2 (Paris: Baudry's European Library, 1842), 242.

29. "Miss Mary E. Robarts to Mrs. Mary Jones, December 9, 1858," in Myers, *Children of Pride*, 461.

30. Eugene D. Genovese, *The Sweetness of Life: Southern Planters at Home* (Cambridge: Cambridge University Press, 2017), 24.

31. Martineau, *Society in America*, 2:244, 246, and 252.

32. Jack R. Davidson, *American Slavery and the Immediate Duty of Southern Slaveholders: A Transcription of Eli Washington Caruthers's Unpublished Manuscript against Slavery* (Eugene, OR: Pickwick, 2018), vii and 54.

33. Frances Anne Kemble, *Journal of a Residence on a Georgian Plantation in 1838–1839* (New York: Harper & Brothers, 1863), 78.

34. Kemble, 73.

35. Lewis Tappan, *The Life of Arthur Tappan* (New York: Hurd and Houghton, 1870), 192.

36. George Howe, *History of the Presbyterian Church in South Carolina*, vol. 2 (Columbia, SC: W. J. Duffie, 1883), 594–95.

37. Thomas Smyth, *The Sin and the Curse; Or, the Union, the True Source of Disunion, and Our Duty in the Present Crisis: A Discourse Preached on the Occasion of the Day of Humiliation and Prayer Appointed by the Governor of South Carolina, on November 21, 1860, in the Second Presbyterian Church, Charleston, S.C.* (Charleston, SC: Evans and Cogswell, 1860), 12.

38. Richard Nisbet, *Slavery Not Forbidden by Scripture* (Philadelphia: John Sparhawk, 1773), 27–29.

39. Benjamin Rush, *An Address to the Inhabitants of the British Settlements, on the Slavery of the Negroes in America*, 2nd ed. (Philadelphia: John Dunlap, 1773), 26.

40. William Henry Ruffner, *Africa's Redemption: A Discourse on African Colonization in Its Missionary Aspects, and Its Relation to Slavery and Abolition* (Philadelphia: William S. Martien, 1852), 33.

41. *Seventh Annual Report of the American Anti-Slavery Society; with the Speeches Delivered at the Anniversary Meeting, Held in the City of New York* (New York: William S. Dorr, 1840), 9 and 21.

42. *Seventh Annual Report of the American Anti-Slavery Society*, 10 and 55–88.

43. Manisha Sinha, *The Slave's Cause: A History of Abolition* (New Haven, CT: Yale University Press, 2016), 264.

44. Joseph C. Stiles, *Speech on the Slavery Resolutions, Delivered in the General Assembly Which Met in Detroit in May Last* (Washington, DC: Jno. T. Towers, 1850), 25–26.

45. Bruce Collins, *White Society in the Antebellum South* (London: Longman, 1985), 8–13.

46. Jeff Forret, *Race Relations at the Margins: Slaves and Poor Whites in the Antebellum Southern Countryside* (Baton Rouge: Louisiana State University Press, 2006), 116.

47. "From the Lexington (Ky.) Observer and Reporter, Sept. 28, 1838," in *American Slavery as It Is: Testimony of a Thousand Witnesses* (New York: American Anti-Slavery Society, 1839), 166.

48. Paxton, *Letters on Slavery*, 129.

49. Thomas R. R. Cobb, *An Inquiry into the Law of Negro Slavery in the United States of America, to Which Is Prefixed, an Historical Sketch of Slavery* (Philadelphia: T. & J. W. Johnson, 1858), ccxviii–ccxix.

50. Forret, *Race Relations at the Margins*, 25.

51. Elizabeth Fox-Genovese and Eugene D. Genovese, *The Mind of the Master Class: History and Faith in the Southern Slaveholders' Worldview* (Cambridge: Cambridge University Press, 2005), 494.

52. James Henley Thornwell, "Relation of the Church to Slavery," in *The Collected Writings of James Henley Thornwell*, vol. 4, ed. John B. Adger and John L. Girardeau (Richmond, VA: Presbyterian Committee of Publication, 1873), 384.

53. Thornwell, "Relation of the Church to Slavery," 382–383; and Paul C. Gutjahr, *Charles Hodge: Guardian of American Orthodoxy* (Oxford: Oxford University Press, 2011), 312.

54. Howe, *History of the Presbyterian Church in South Carolina*, 2:594.

55. Ernest Trice Thompson, *The Spirituality of the Church: A Distinctive Doctrine of the Presbyterian Church in the United States* (Richmond, VA: John Knox Press, 1961), 24.

56. E. Brooks Holifield, *The Gentlemen Theologians: American Theology in Southern Culture, 1795–1860* (Durham, NC: Duke University Press, 1978), 154.

57. Ruffner, *Africa's Redemption*, 31 and 35–36.

58. Ruffner, 36, 38, and 47–48.

59. Jonathan Blanchard and Nathan L. Rice, *A Debate on Slavery: Held in the City of Cincinnati, on the First, Second, Third, and Sixth Days of October, 1845* (Cincinnati: Wm. H. Moore, 1846), 30.

60. Ethan Allen Andrews, *Slavery and the Domestic Slave-Trade in the United States: In a Series of Letters Addressed to the Executive Committee of the American Union for the Relief and Improvement of the Colored Race* (Boston: Light & Stearns, 1836), 195–96.

61. Blanchard and Rice, *Debate on Slavery*, 342.

62. Blanchard and Rice, 347 and 369.

63. Andrew F. Walls, *The Missionary Movement in Christian History: Studies in the Transmission of Faith* (Maryknoll, NY: Orbis Books, 1996), 3–15 and 34.

64. Walls, 8.

65. David Walker, *Walker's Appeal, in Four Articles; Together with a Preamble, to the Coloured Citizens of the World, but in Particular, and Very Expressly, to Those of the United States of America*, 3rd ed. (Boston: David Walker, 1830), 61.

66. Angelina Emily Grimké, "Appeal to the Christian Women of the South," *Anti-Slavery Examiner*, September 1836, 13.

67. Robert J. Breckinridge, "Hints on Colonization and Abolition," *African Repository and Colonial Journal*, January 1834, 325 and 330.

68. Elisha Mitchell, *The Other Leaf of the Book of Nature and the Word of God* (n.p., 1848), 31, 35, and 69.

69. Andrew Delbanco, *The War before the War: Fugitive Slaves and the Struggle for America's Soul from the Revolution to the Civil War* (New York: Penguin Press, 2018), 23–24.

70. Georges Fisch, *Nine Months in the United States during the Crisis* (London: James Nisbet, 1863), 131.

71. Fisch, 146.

72. "A Presbyterian Clergyman Suspended for Being Connected with the Underground Railroad," *Fayetteville Observer*, November 8, 1855.

73. "Rev. C. C. Jones to Messrs. Charles C. Jones, Jr., and Joseph Jones, June 8, 1857," in Myers, *Children of Pride*, 323–24.

74. Albert Barnes, *The Church and Slavery* (Philadelphia: Parry & McMillan, 1857), 155 and 159.

75. John White, "A Case Study on the Road to Repair: Princeton Theological Seminary," *@ This Point: Theological Investigations in Church and Culture* 14, no. 1 (Spring 2020), https://www.ctsnet.edu/at-this-point/case-study-road-to-repair-princeton-theological-seminary.

76. Jennifer Oast, *Institutional Slavery: Slaveholding Churches, Schools, Colleges, and Businesses in Virginia, 1680–1860* (New York: Cambridge University Press, 2016), 88.

Index

CPSIA information can be obtained
at www.ICGtesting.com
Printed in the USA
BVHW031832190822
645020BV00003B/18